"Carolyn Scott-Hamilton's website, healthyvoyager.com, is truly amazing. It is clear how much she cares for both people and the planet, and is fighting to reconcile the broken relationship between the two. Her site offers ways to be healthy and green in a budget friendly way that doesn't limit your options. She is realistic in her approach, offering alternatives for the well-informed health-nut or greenie, as well as for those just starting out on a path to a healthier lifestyle. I visit her site daily to see what she's got cooking up next."

—KIM BARNOUIN, *New York Times* best-selling co-author of *Skinny Bitch*

"In *The Healthy Voyager's Global Kitchen,* Carolyn Scott-Hamilton takes us on a once-in-a-lifetime culinary journey around the world. Chock full of mouthwatering vegan recipes from countries like Greece (spanakopita!), Thailand (pad thai!), Russia (borscht!), and France (croissants!), Carolyn's passion for great food and travel will make you want to catch the next flight to Bangkok. This cookbook will both inspire and enlighten you, and provide everything you need to create delectable, plant-based meals wherever you are."

—COLLEEN HOLLAND, co-founder/Associate Publisher *VegNews Magazine*

"These recipes marry the health benefits of plant-based eating with tantalizing flavors from around the globe—a dynamite union!"

—JOLIA SIDONA ALLEN, Online Managing Editor, *Vegetarian Times*

THE HEALTHY VOYAGER'S

GLOBAL KITCHEN

150 PLANT-BASED RECIPES FROM AROUND THE WORLD

CAROLYN SCOTT-HAMILTON

First published in the USA in 2012 by
Fair Winds Press, a member of
Quayside Publishing Group
100 Cummings Center
Suite 406-L
Beverly, MA 01915-6101
www.fairwindspress.com

16 15 14 13 12   1 2 3 4 5

ISBN: 978-1-59233-487-2

Digital edition published in 2012
eISBN: 978-1-61058-174-5

Library of Congress Cataloging-in-Publication Data available

Cover design by Carolyn Scott-Hamilton and Dan Hamilton
Book layout by www.meganjonesdesign.com
Artwork by Dan Hamilton
Photography by Celine Steen

Printed and bound in Singapore

CONTENTS

miss you
paris

Constr...
Poid: : 7...
base : 104 m...
pièces de métal...
La 2' à 115...
comportent 1.710...

GRAND

INTRODUCTION

Welcome! *Bienvenidos! Wilkommen! Yokoso!* You are about to embark on a culinary tour of the world. In addition, almost anyone will be able to indulge in these wonderfully ethnic meals without having to leave the comfort of his or her own kitchen. Regardless of your dietary restrictions, this book offers alternatives on how to prepare these popular international meals so that no one is left out of the fun. Whether you are vegan, gluten free, kosher, or just trying to add healthier options to your repertoire, *The Healthy Voyager's Global Kitchen* is your answer to healthier global cooking.

When I first became vegan, there wasn't much out there in the way of convenience vegan products or restaurants. I also traveled extensively, and to my dismay, found that I couldn't partake in many traditional ethnic meals. This made me increasingly interested in "veganizing" some of my favorite dishes, partly for myself and partly to share with my family and friends. I just had to prove that switching to an animal-free or restricted diet didn't mean being forever doomed to a life without traditional global fare. The recipes in this book have been created for folks who may have grown up with these foods and haven't been able to enjoy them since their dietary needs have changed as well as a way for you to experience healthy versions of global cuisine at home when you are unable to travel. With *The Healthy Voyager's Global Kitchen*, you'll be able to bring the world to you, any time you choose!

This book is meant to bring folks into the kitchen, getting them in touch with their food and the process of making it, in addition to learning about other cultures, customs, and techniques. A majority of the recipes in this book follow authentic preparation techniques so that the flavors, textures, and presentations of these dishes will look and taste like the "real deal." This is why it was important to me to provide options to make many of the dishes from scratch when time permits, exactly as people worldwide have been doing for centuries. The dishes in this book are best made with time, fresh ingredients, and traditional technique. And for best results, they are most delicious when enjoyed with family and friends!

WHO IS THIS BOOK FOR?

Over the past few years, the vegan diet has gotten quite a bit of press. We've also seen the gluten-free world gain popularity. And unfortunately, the number of folks who fight obesity, diabetes, heart disease, and other unhealthy diet-related diseases continues to grow.

What *The Healthy Voyager's Global Kitchen* offers is alternatives to dishes that people who need to stick to restrictive diets can enjoy, and the bonus is that they are automatically free of cholesterol and lower in fat. The sugars recommended are natural and because almost everything is made from scratch, the chances of consuming tons of sodium, chemicals, and preservatives are pretty much nil.

Each recipe lists options for special diets so that if the original recipe doesn't work for you, you will still be able to prepare it in a way that will. Even if you don't follow a special diet, these recipes are better for you, are full of flavor, and come without any guilt or negative health effects.

Here is the legend to look for recipes and options that suit your special needs:

Although some of the following recipes may seem more labor-intensive than others, they are most likely the ones that showcase how to make specific ingredients from scratch (such as pita bread, ravioli, marinara sauce, and the like). A lot of these can be store-bought to save time, but if you are looking for the healthiest alternative, you can make it yourself to ensure that you are serving up the most healthful versions of these global dishes.

This book is a great tool for folks who follow special diets as much as it is for those who want to cook for them. Whether you are a grandmother who wants to cook dairy- and gluten-free food for your special-dietary-needs grandchildren, a boyfriend who wants to impress your vegan girlfriend, or a kid who wants to introduce your family to a whole new way of eating, *The Healthy Voyager's Global Kitchen* has something for everyone!

Chapter I

STOCKING A GLOBAL KITCHEN

BEFORE WE GET STARTED, it's important to have a properly stocked kitchen. Be it American food or Thai, there are some staples that you will want to have on hand. You will also want to have some tools and tricks in your arsenal to make life easier in the kitchen. In this section you will find recommendations for ingredients, foods, spices, and products that pop up frequently in this book as well as some base recipes, alternatives to non-vegan ingredients, and some kitchen tips. Welcome to *The Healthy Voyager*'s global cooking school crash course!

FOOD BASICS AND OPTIONS

While I'm certainly not suggesting you go out and buy all the following items, many are good "staples" to have in your pantry, so you can whip up an international meal without a run to the grocery store. Items such as spices, sugars, flours, grains, and oils will be used frequently, so keeping them stocked may be a good idea. I've bolded those items I think are the most important "standbys" to have.

SPICES, HERBS, AND AROMATICS

Allspice
Anise
Asafoetida powder
Basil
Bay leaf
Black pepper (freshly ground)
Capers
Cardamom
Cayenne pepper
Chile peppers and powder
Chives
Cilantro
Cinnamon
Coriander
Creole or Cajun seasoning
Cumin
Dill
Fennel
Fenugreek
Garam masala
Garlic
Ginger
Scallion or scallions
Jalapeño peppers
Lemongrass
Mint
Nutmeg
Onion (white, yellow, and red)
Oregano
Paprika
Parsley
Red pepper flakes
Rosemary
Saffron

Sage
Salt (sea, kosher, and coarse)
Sazón Goya
Shallot
Tarragon
Thyme
Turmeric
White pepper
Zest (lemon, orange, and lime)

SWEETENERS

Agave nectar
Beet sugar
Brown rice syrup
Brown sugar (dark and light)
Cane sugar
Confectioners' sugar
Date sugar
Maple syrup
Stevia (low glycemic)
Sucanat
Turbinado sugar
Xylitol (low glycemic)

FLOUR AND OTHER BAKING PRODUCTS

Active dry yeast
Agar powder
All-purpose flour
Almond flour
Amaranth flour
Arrowroot flour
Baking powder
Baking soda
Buckwheat flour

Cake flour
Chickpea flour
Cocoa powder
Cornmeal
Cornstarch
Egg replacer (powdered)
Masarepa (precooked cornmeal)
Masa harina
Phyllo dough
Potato flour
Potato starch
Quinoa flour
Semolina
Soy flour
Tapioca flour
Teff flour
Vital wheat gluten

MILK AND DAIRY PRODUCT ALTERNATIVES

Almond milk
Cashew milk
Coconut milk
Rice milk
Soy or coconut creamers
Soymilk (liquid and powdered)
Vegan butter
Vegan cream cheese
Vegan heavy cream
Vegan plain yogurt
Vegan sour cream

GRAINS AND GRAIN PRODUCTS

Amaranth

Arborio rice

Basmati rice

Bread crumbs/cracker crumbs

Brown rice

Couscous

Graham crackers

Jasmine rice

Oats

Pasta (lasagne, macaroni, vermicelli, manicotti, ravioli)

Pita bread

Quinoa

Rice paper wrappers

Vegan egg roll, spring roll, and wonton wrappers (for a homemade version, see page 18)

MEAT SUBSTITUTES

Seitan

Tempeh

Textured vegetable protein (TVP)

Tofu (extra firm, firm, and silken)

Vegan beef chunks

Vegan chicken fillets

Vegan sausage

OILS, VINEGARS, CONDIMENTS, FLAVORINGS, AND SAUCES

Almond butter

Almond extract

Apple cider vinegar

Balsamic vinegar

Canola oil

Coconut oil (great for high-heat cooking and rich flavor; lots of health benefits, too!)

Grape leaves

Grapeseed oil

Hoisin sauce

Lemon and lemon juice

Lime and lime juice

Liquid aminos

Liquid smoke

Mirin

Miso paste

Nutritional yeast

Olive oil (great for low-heat sautéing)

Peanut butter

Peanut oil

Pickle relish

Red wine vinegar

Rice vinegar

Safflower oil (another good high-heat oil)

Sauerkraut

Sesame oil (good for flavor and light sautéing at low to medium heat)

Soy sauce or tamari

Sunflower oil (another good high-heat oil)

Tahini

Tamari

Tomato paste

Umeboshi vinegar (sea plum)

Vanilla extract or powder

Vegan beef stock or bouillon

Vegan chicken stock or bouillon

Vegan fish sauce

Vegan mayonnaise

Vegan shortening

Vegan Worcestershire

Vegan yogurt

Vegetable broth or stock

Vegetable bouillon

Vegetable oil

White wine vinegar

NUTS, SEEDS, AND FRUIT

Almonds

Apples

Cashews

Dates

Flax

Kaffir limes

Olives

Peanuts

Pecans

Plantains

Raisins

Walnuts

VEGETABLES

Bok choy

Broccoli

Carrots

Celery

Corn

Kale

Mushrooms (oyster, portobello, button, porcini, cremini, shiitake)

Okra

Peas

Potatoes (russet, red, Yukon Gold)

Seaweed (kombu, nori, arame, hijiki, wakame)

Spinach

Sweet potatoes

Tomatoes

Yams

Yuca (cassava)

BEANS

Black beans

Cannellini beans

Chickpeas

Lentils

Navy beans

Pinto beans

Red beans/kidney beans

BASE INGREDIENT RECIPES

Most of the ingredients in this section, which are referenced in the recipes throughout the book, can be store-bought or homemade. The homemade versions appear here. Note that the egg wash substitute and cashew cream must be homemade.

EGG REPLACERS

Egg Substitute

For 1 egg, use, 1½ teaspoons (4 g) Ener-G powder + 2 tablespoons (30 ml) water, or 2 tablespoons (16 g) cornstarch or potato starch.

Note that in the recipes to come, it will be specified in the ingredients list whether the egg replacer should already be mixed or not. These instructions pertain to Ener-G replacer, because this product must be mixed with water to simulate the egg.

Tofu Egg Substitute for Baking

For 1 egg, use ¼ cup (50 g) puréed silken tofu. For dense baked goods, use ½ cup (100 g) + 1 teaspoon arrowroot or cornstarch to replace 3 eggs to yield lighter, fluffier results.

Egg Yolk Substitute

For 1 egg yolk, use 1 tablespoon (7 g) finely ground flaxseed + 3 tablespoons (45 ml) hot water. Mix it up and let it cool for a minute or two. As it cools it will take on an "eggy" consistency.

Egg White Substitute

For 1 egg white, use 1 tablespoon (8 g) plain agar powder dissolved in 1 tablespoon (15 ml) water, whipped, chilled, and whipped again.

Egg Wash Substitute

For an egg wash, use 1 tablespoon (7 g) ground flaxseed + 3 tablespoons (45 ml) soymilk. After mixing, add ¼ tablespoon (4 ml) more soymilk to thin slightly.

DAIRY PRODUCT ALTERNATIVES

Nut Milk (Any Kind)

1 cup (145 g) raw nuts, soaked and drained (soak for at least 4 hours and up to 24)

3 cups (705 ml) filtered water

2 tablespoons (40 g) agave nectar (or sweetener of choice)

Add all the ingredients to a good blender and liquefy for at least 1 minute. Try to get as much "pulp" as finely chopped as possible to make the most milk. Strain the mixture through a piece of cheesecloth, a nut milk bag, or a fine strainer into a large glass jar or pitcher. The wider mouthed the jar, the better.

For vanilla-flavored milk, add 1 teaspoon (3 g) organic vanilla powder (the next best thing to a vanilla bean, plus it won't break the bank and will last a long time). The powder should ideally contain only ground vanilla beans (no additives).

YIELD: 4 cups (940 ml)

Cashew Cream

You'll need 2 cups (270 g) whole raw cashews, soaked overnight and drained. Place in the blender with enough water to just barely cover the nuts. Blend, strain the pulp, and you've got cashew cream.

YIELD: 2 cups (470 ml)

Vegan Buttermilk

Mix 1 cup (235 ml) plain soymilk with 1 teaspoon (5 ml) apple cider or coconut water vinegar, and set aside to curdle for at least 15 minutes.

YIELD: 1 cup (235 ml)

Vegan Condensed Milk

⅓ cup plus 2 tablespoons (108 ml) boiling water

¼ cup (60 ml) melted vegan butter

1 cup (128 g) powdered soymilk

⅔ cup (132 g) raw sugar or (230 g) agave nectar

⅛ teaspoon vanilla extract

Pour the boiling water and melted butter into a blender first. Add the powdered soymilk, sugar, and vanilla, and blend for 30 seconds. Pour into a glass container and keep covered in your refrigerator until it thickens and cools.

YIELD: 2½ cups (588 ml)

Vegan Evaporated Milk

Allow a large can (14 ounce, or 392 g) of coconut milk to settle for about 30 minutes (or proceed if it hasn't been shaken or jostled at all). The cream will rise to the top and can easily be skimmed off and used in recipes. The liquid below the cream is your evaporated milk substitute.

YIELD: About 1½ cups (353 ml)

Vegan Heavy Cream

Blend 1 package (12 ounces, or 340 g) silken tofu and ½ cup (120 ml) plain soymilk in a blender until thick and creamy and there are no lumps.

YIELD: About 2 cups (470 ml)

STOCK ALTERNATIVES

Seaweed Stock

Soak 8 to 10 kombu slices in 2 quarts (1.8 L) water for 6 hours, then strain out the seaweed.

YIELD: 2 quarts (1.8 L)

Vegetable Broth

3 cups (210 g) sliced mushrooms (any variety)

5 stalks celery, thinly sliced

4 medium to large carrots, thinly sliced

2 large onions, thinly sliced

¼ head green cabbage, thinly sliced

5 leeks, cut in half lengthwise, washed, and thinly sliced

1 small bunch fresh flat-leaf parsley (about 15 sprigs)

1 head garlic, cut in half crosswise to expose the cloves

Salt and pepper, to taste

3 bay leaves

6 to 8 sprigs fresh thyme

Place all the ingredients in a large stockpot. Add cold water to cover. Bring to a boil over high heat. Lower the heat and simmer gently for 45 to 60 minutes. Ladle through a fine strainer, cool, and refrigerate.

YIELD: 3 cups (705 ml)

SPICE MIX AND CONDIMENT ALTERNATIVES

Sazón Goya Spice Alternative for Latin Recipes

Sazon Goya is a very popular type of spice mix used in Latin cooking. If you are unable to find Sazon Goya, use this recipe in its place when called for it in the Latin recipes to come.

> 1 tablespoon (18 g) salt
>
> 1 tablespoon (6 g) ground black pepper
>
> 1 tablespoon (9 g) granulated garlic or garlic powder
>
> 1 tablespoon (5 g) ground coriander
>
> 1 tablespoon (7 g) ground cumin
>
> 1 tablespoon (3 g) dried oregano
>
> 1 tablespoon (7.5 g) ground annatto (achiote chile) seeds
>   (substitute paprika for the achiote, if needed)
>
> 1 teaspoon ground turmeric

Combine all the ingredients in a small bowl and mix well. Store in an airtight container. Use 1½ teaspoons of the mixture for each packet of Sazón Goya called for in a recipe unless a specific amount is called for.

YIELD: Almost ½ cup (58 g)

Sazón Goya with Azafran Spice Alternative for Latin Recipes

Use the Sazón Goya Alternative Spice and add 1 teaspoon ground saffron.

Fish Sauce Alternative

> 1½ cups (75 g) shredded dried seaweed (nori, kombu, wakame, arame, or hijiki)
>
> 6 cups (1,410 ml) water
>
> 4 large cloves garlic, crushed
>
> 1 tablespoons (5 g) black peppercorns
>
> ½ cup (120 ml) soy sauce or tamari
>
> 1 tablespoon (15 ml) umeboshi vinegar or lemon juice

Place the seaweed in a pot and add 4 cups (940 ml) of the water. Bring to a boil, then turn down the heat and simmer for 20 minutes.

Add remaining 2 cups (470 ml) water, and the garlic, peppercorns, soy sauce, and vinegar. Bring back to a boil, then boil fairly high for at least 30 minutes, or until it reduces by about half. It's crazy salty but that means it's perfect.

Strain and let cool.

YIELD: 4 cups (940 ml)

Worcestershire Sauce Alternative

2 cups (470 ml) apple cider vinegar or red wine vinegar

½ cup (120 ml) soy sauce or tamari

¼ cup (60 g) firmly packed light brown sugar

1 teaspoon ground ginger

1 teaspoon mustard powder

1 teaspoon onion powder

1 clove garlic, minced

½ teaspoon ground cinnamon

½ teaspoon black pepper

Combine all the ingredients in a medium-size saucepan. Bring to a boil over medium-high heat; reduce the heat to a simmer and cook until the liquid is reduced by about half, about 20 minutes. Strain and let cool.

YIELD: 1½ cups (353 ml)

OTHER ALTERNATIVES

Wonton, Egg Roll, or Gyoza Wrappers

2 cups (240 g) all-purpose flour

½ to 1 teaspoon salt

1 teaspoon vegetable oil

1 egg replacer, mixed, store-bought or homemade (page 13)

½ cup (120 ml) warm water

Cornstarch

Sift the flour and salt together into a bowl. In a small bowl, beat together the oil and egg replacer and then add to the flour mixture and stir to combine. Slowly stir in the warm water, little by little. The dough will be very stiff. Turn out onto a floured work surface and knead until soft and smooth, 3 to 5 minutes. Cover with a towel and let stand for 20 minutes.

Divide the dough in half and roll out each half as thin as possible, ⅛ to ⅟₁₆ inch (3 to 2 mm) thick. Use the cornstarch to keep it from sticking to your hands and the rolling pin. It is tough to get thin but do the best that you can. To make wonton wrappers, cut into 3-inch (7.5 cm) squares. To make egg roll or spring roll wrappers, cut into 6- to 8-inch (15 to 20 cm) squares. To make gyoza wrappers, cut into 4- to 6-inch (10 to 15 cm) squares.

To store, sprinkle with cornstarch between layers and refrigerate or freeze in an airtight container.

YIELD: 8 to 36 wrappers, depending on size

Basic Seitan Recipe

1 tablespoon vegetable oil

1 large onion, diced

1 to 3 cloves garlic, minced

4 cups (400 g) vital wheat gluten

1 cup (115 g) bread crumbs

1 cup (128 g) nutritional yeast

Herbs of your choice (1 teaspoon of any herb or spice to achieve the flavor you desire)

1 tablespoon (18 g) salt

Pepper, to taste

2 tablespoons (30 ml) vegan Worcestershire sauce, store-bought or homemade (page 18)

½ cup (120 ml) extra-virgin olive oil

4 cups (940 ml) vegetable broth, store-bought or homemade (page 16)
(if making chicken or beef flavored, use vegan chicken or beef bouillon to make broth)

Heat the vegetable oil in a skillet and sauté the onion and garlic over medium heat until golden brown. Transfer to a bowl, add the wheat gluten, bread crumbs, yeast, herbs, salt, and pepper, and stir to combine.

Add the Worcestershire, olive oil, and broth to the dry ingredients and stir until a loose batter forms. Shape the batter into a loaf.

Unroll a large piece of cheesecloth to wrap the loaf. Make sure there's enough cloth so that it can be doubled up and still wrap the loaf completely, with enough to hang over to twist on the sides (like a piece of candy). Tie the sides as well as in the middle to secure the cloth.

Place the loaf into a large pot of boiling water and simmer for at least 2 hours. Remove from the liquid, let cool, and remove the cheesecloth.

At this point you can slice it and fry or roast it. To roast, bake at 350°F (180°C, or gas mark 4) for 20 minutes, or until golden brown. Let rest a few minutes before slicing. You may want to slather it in vegan butter to seal in the moisture as well as add any spice rub you like to get the flavor you desire.

YIELD: 8 servings

SHOPPING AND KITCHEN TIPS

- Make an effort to purchase organic when and where you can. I know it can be pricier; however, think of it as an investment in your health. Also, organically grown produce and food make for better-tasting recipes all around. The less processed or chemically altered your food is, the better it is for you (both health and taste-wise!). Oh, and please, please, avoid GMO (genetically modified) foods!

- When purchasing canned or packaged foods, choose the most natural item. For example, canned tomatoes should really just be canned tomatoes. If it has a bunch of other stuff, or worse, unpronounceable stuff, keep looking; plain canned tomatoes will not only taste better, but they will also be better for you!

- When a recipe calls for vegan meat substitutes, soy or nut milk, or any other store-bought products, buy the plain version. Unless specified, flavored or sweetened items can clash with the flavors of the dish, so always choose plain, regular, original, or unsweetened unless otherwise noted.

- Plan ahead. Planning your meals ahead of time will save you time and money. Try to plan your weekly meals by purchasing ingredients that can be used in various recipes all week. For instance, you may want to cook up a large pot of beans that can be used in salads and main courses and that can later be turned into hummus or another bean dip. Cook once, eat thrice!

- Prepare stocks and broths ahead of time and freeze in ice cube trays. This way, a package doesn't go bad if you don't use it all and you know that the stock is all natural and healthy. In addition, you only use what you need instead of defrosting the whole container.

- A sharp knife is a good knife. Obviously, practice safe chopping, slicing, and dicing, but a dull knife is far more dangerous than a sharp one. Plus, a dull knife can really massacre whatever it is you are slicing, which can ruin your dish.

- Read your recipe well before you start cooking. You may need to do some prep work, such as refrigerating things overnight, so make sure you are fully prepared so you save time and money. It's also smart to read through recipes before you shop, as opposed to when you've returned from the market.

- Always wash your produce thoroughly, even if it says prewashed or is organic. Aim to use fresh produce and herbs unless otherwise noted in the recipe.

- A clean kitchen is an efficient kitchen! Clean as you go to save time later on. This will also help keep you healthy because surfaces will remain clean and sanitary, without foods decomposing or settling into cracks and crevices.

- Your cooking tools should be healthy, too! Do your best to avoid toxic nonstick pans and plastic containers that leach chemicals into your food. I prefer stainless-steel, cast-iron, enameled cast-iron, and glass pots and pans. Wooden spoons and cutting boards are very porous and can harbor bacteria, so switch to silicone where you can. And when storing food, always opt for glass.

- Be mindful not to overcook your food, regardless of how you heat it. Not only will you ruin the texture of a dish, but you will also lose all vital nutrients. Especially when cooking vegetables, steaming, blanching, and lightly sautéing are the best ways to go to seal in as many beneficial vitamins and minerals as possible.

- Be green! Be crafty with what you have in the kitchen. Whether it's leftover red pepper flakes from Thai takeout or the ends of bread loaves, little bits of leftovers add up to great stuff. Better to use them than to throw money into a landfill. Old bread can be cubed and made into croutons or put in a food processor to make bread crumbs. Takeout packets can be saved and used. Should you have any produce that has overripened, composting is better than tossing it. There are so many ways to make use of what you have while being green and saving money, too.

Chapter 2

USA

WELCOME TO THE USA, a nation built by cowboys and crooners, soldiers and shoemakers, all of them at some point dreamers and doers. A veritable melting pot, or tossed salad as some say, the United States is a country full of global contributions that over the last few hundred years have come together to create a culture that is known across the world to be distinctly American. Whether you're in the Deep South or the chilly Northeast, the mountainous terrain of the west or vast valleys of the nation's heartland, American food is incredibly diverse. This young nation has a rich history due to its international citizens, and the cuisine that has come out of this nation of fifty states includes them all.

While in the recent past we have become a nation of foodies, restaurant critics, and home chefs, food has always been a major part of the fabric of our country. Our national celebrations revolve around food. Thanksgiving is one of our most famous food-filled holidays, one that no other country in the world celebrates (at least not for the same historical reasons). Outside of football and family, this last Thursday in November is about the feast. The gathering of friends and family over a smorgasbord of autumnal food is the launching pad for the winter holiday season.

Another uniquely American holiday is the Fourth of July. The national holiday celebrating our independence falls right smack in the middle of summer and has also become a food frenzy. Barbecues are dusted off, ice chests are filled with beer and soft drinks, the men gather around the grill while the gals prepare the sides. Oh yes, and the kids play all day until it's time for fireworks. While the United States has a number of holidays that mark important moments in our nation's history, these are the ones that most Americans participate in and where food is the centerpiece of it all.

What is wildly fun about American cuisine is that it is just as historically interesting as the folks who came up with it and the locations in which they were created. In fact, most of the dishes in this chapter mark specific moments in American history, making them just as important as any American event. As long as these recipes continue to make their way to our tables, we continue to be in touch with our nation's past well into the future.

Let's ring that dinner bell, y'all, 'cause it's chow time!

NO-CRAB CAKES WITH CAJUN CRÈME

*Gluten Free (use gluten-free bread crumbs), **Soy Free (use soy-free vegan mayonnaise),
***Low Fat (use low-fat vegan mayonnaise and bake instead of panfrying)

**These guys go well at everything, from casual parties to lavish dinners.
They're the ultimate crowd-pleaser!**

FOR CAKES:

1½ cups (360 g) chickpeas, drained

⅓ cup (38 g) bread crumbs

1½ cups (240 g) finely chopped onion

2 cloves garlic, crushed

½ cup (75 g) chopped red bell pepper

¼ cup (4 g) chopped fresh cilantro

¼ cup (15 g) chopped fresh parsley

¼ cup (60 g) vegan mayonnaise

½ teaspoon baking powder

Juice of ½ lemon

1 teaspoon Cajun seasoning

½ teaspoon mustard powder

½ teaspoon salt

¼ teaspoon black pepper

½ cup (120 ml) coconut oil (or preferred high-heat oil)

FOR CAJUN CRÈME:

1 cup (240 g) vegan mayonnaise

3 to 4 tablespoons (45 to 60 ml) lemon juice, depending on desired consistency

2 tablespoons (20 g) minced garlic

1 tablespoon (11 g) Dijon mustard

1 scallion, finely chopped

1 teaspoon Cajun or Creole seasoning

To make the cakes: Using a food processor or heavy-duty blender, pulverize the chickpeas, using the pulse function. Pulverize until the beans just form a paste that sticks together when you squeeze it in your hand. Be careful not to overdo it with the chickpeas; do not purée.

Add the bread crumbs, onion, garlic, pepper, cilantro, parsley, mayonnaise, baking powder, lemon juice, Cajun seasoning, mustard, salt, and pepper and combine using the pulse function. After being pulsed approximately 12 times, the batter will look grainy and speckled.

Refrigerate the batter for about 1 hour, until firm. Remove the batter from the fridge and shape into 12 patties, using ⅓-cup (75 g) portions. Be careful not to overhandle the batter or the patties will fall apart (cold batter is easier to handle; once it hits your warm hands, it begins to break apart). Preheat the oven to 350°F (180°C, or gas mark 4).

Place the patties on a plate or baking tray and cover with plastic wrap. Return to the fridge and chill for an additional 10 to 15 minutes.

In a large, shallow skillet, heat ¼ cup (60 ml) of the coconut oil over medium-high heat. Gently place 6 patties into the hot oil (don't crowd the pan) and fry the first side until golden brown, about 3 minutes. Gently turn onto the second side and cook for an additional 3 minutes. Transfer to a baking tray to finish cooking in the oven for 8 minutes. Heat the remaining oil and fry the remaining patties the same way. The patties will have a somewhat dry, crispy appearance on the outside.

To make the Cajun Crème: In a large bowl, combine all the ingredients until well incorporated. For a thicker sauce, use only 3 tablespoons (45 ml) of the lemon juice. Top the cakes with a dollop and enjoy!

YIELD: 12 cakes

fun fact

The first known printed use of the name "Crab Cake" was in the 1939 *New York World's Fair Cookbook*.

CLASSIC COBB SALAD

*Gluten Free (use wheat-free tamari), **Soy Free (use liquid aminos and soy-free meat substitute),
***Low Fat (omit the oil and bake the tofu), ****Low Glycemic (omit the sugar and use date juice or purée)

**The Cobb is an American classic. The original isn't great for those who are watching their waistline,
but you'll get all the taste with none of the guilt in this fully plant-based bowl of yumminess.**

FOR DRESSING:

3 tablespoons (45 ml) olive oil

2 tablespoons (30 ml) red wine vinegar

1 tablespoon (15 ml) lemon juice

1 teaspoon Dijon mustard

1 teaspoon soy sauce

½ teaspoon brown sugar

1 small clove garlic, minced

Salt and pepper, to taste

FOR SALAD:

Sesame oil (or preferred high-heat oil)

8 ounces (225 g) extra-firm tofu,
pressed, drained, and cubed

1 cup (70 g) thinly sliced portobello mushrooms

½ cup (15 g) watercress, stems removed

6 cups (240 g) coarsely chopped romaine lettuce

1½ cups (60 g) arugula or chicory

4 Roma tomatoes, diced

½ large avocado, diced

1 cup (240 g) chickpeas

½ cup (60 g) shredded vegan cheese
(mix of cheddar and mozzarella style is best)

2 tablespoons (6 g) chopped chives

To make the dressing: In a small bowl, whisk together all of the dressing ingredients and set aside.

To make the salad: Add the sesame oil to a pan and preheat over medium-high heat. Sauté the tofu for about 5 minutes, or until lightly grilled, then remove from the heat and set aside. Add the mushrooms to the skillet and sauté, stirring frequently, until lightly grilled, 3 to 5 minutes. Remove from the heat and set aside.

In a large bowl, toss the watercress, romaine, and arugula with two-thirds of the dressing. Put the dressed greens onto a large serving dish. Place the tomatoes on top, forming a row down the middle. In strips/rows on either side of the tomatoes place the avocado, chickpeas, cheese, diced tofu, and grilled mushrooms on top of the greens. Sprinkle with the chives, drizzle with the remaining dressing, and serve.

YIELD: 4 to 6 servings

fun fact

The Cobb salad made its debut in Hollywood at the famed Brown Derby Restaurant. Named after the restaurant's owner, Bob Cobb, it is said that the salad was created during one of his late, hungry nights at the Derby.

NEW NEW ENGLAND CLAM CHOWDER

*Gluten Free (use gluten-free vegan meat substitute and gluten-free flour, use 1 teaspoon liquid smoke if you can't find a suitable vegan bacon or ham option), **Soy Free (use soy-free vegan meat substitute, and replace the heavy cream with cashew cream and soy-free vegan butter, use 1 teaspoon liquid smoke if you can't find a suitable vegan bacon or ham option)

As a child, I lived to crumble little oyster crackers into my clam chowder, a seaside comfort food. I really enjoyed recreating one of my childhood favorites to suit those who can no longer enjoy it at their local seafood joint.

6 slices tempeh bacon, cut into ½-inch (1.3 cm) strips (you can use vegan bacon or vegan ham slices)

¼ cup (55 g) unsalted vegan butter

2 medium-size leeks, white and light green parts only, halved lengthwise and thinly sliced crosswise (2½ to 3 cups [250 to 300 g])

1 cup (160 g) finely chopped onion

1 cup (120 g) finely chopped celery

2 teaspoons minced garlic

6 sprigs fresh thyme

2 bay leaves

2 pounds (910 g) potatoes, peeled and cut into ½-inch (1.3 cm) cubes (about 5 cups [550 g])

¼ cup (28 g) all-purpose flour

2 quarts (1.8 L) seaweed stock, store-bought or homemade (page 16), or vegetable broth, store-bought or homemade (page 16)

2½ cups (175 g) diced oyster mushrooms

2 cups (470 ml) vegan heavy cream, store-bought or homemade (page 15)

½ teaspoon black pepper

1¼ teaspoons salt, or to taste

¼ cup (15 g) finely chopped fresh parsley, for garnish

¼ cup (12 g) finely chopped chives or scallions, for garnish

Cook the bacon or ham in a large, heavy pot over medium heat until crisp. Then add the ¼ cup (55 g) unsalted vegan butter, leeks, onion, and celery and cook until softened, about 5 minutes. Add the garlic, thyme, and bay leaves and cook until the vegetables are translucent, about 3 minutes, being careful not to burn. Add the potatoes, flour, and seaweed stock and bring to a boil. Lower the heat, cover, and simmer until the broth thickens slightly and the potatoes are very tender, about 30 minutes. Remove from the heat, discard the thyme stems and bay leaves, stir in the mushrooms and heavy cream, then season with the pepper and the salt to taste.

Remove from the heat and set aside for 1 hour, covered, to allow the flavors to marry. Place the pot over low heat and slowly reheat, being careful not to let boil. Serve and garnish each bowl with some parsley and chives.

YIELD: 8 servings

Fun Fact

Early English settlers became acquainted with what Native Americans called the *quahog* (clam), which were used for currency, or *wampum*. Clams began to replace fish in their milk stews and hence it became "New" England "Clam" Chowder. Or "chowdah," if you're from Bean Town!

JOE'S UN-CLAMS CASINO

*Gluten Free (use gluten-free bread crumbs, vegan cheese, and bacon), **Soy Free (use soy-free vegan butter and vegan cheese)

A very special friend of the family introduced me to these many years ago. I've never found a non-clam recipe that held a candle to his original appetizer, so I'm very happy to share one that I feel comes closest to his Northeast masterpiece.

2 tablespoons (30 ml) olive oil

2 ounces (55 g) sliced vegan bacon, finely chopped

⅓ cup (53 g) chopped shallot

2 large cloves garlic, minced

½ cup (75 g) finely chopped red bell pepper

¼ teaspoon dried oregano

2 tablespoons (30 ml) lemon juice

3 tablespoons (42 g) vegan butter

2 tablespoons (30 ml) dry white wine

¼ cup (30 g) shredded vegan mozzarella, plus extra for sprinkling

2 tablespoons (14 g) Italian bread crumbs

1 cup (70 g) chopped oyster mushrooms

1 cup (70 g) chopped porcini, cremini, or portobello mushrooms

Salt and pepper, to taste

2 tablespoons (28 g) vegan butter, melted

16 small romaine spears or crackers

Lemon wedges, for serving

Heat the oil in a large, heavy skillet over medium heat. Add the bacon and sauté until crisp and golden, 2 to 3 minutes, then transfer to a plate. Add the shallot, garlic, bell pepper, oregano, lemon juice, and butter to the same skillet and sauté until the shallots are tender and translucent, about 5 minutes. Add the wine and simmer until it is almost evaporated, about 2 minutes. Remove the skillet from the heat and cool completely. Stir in the cooked bacon, vegan cheese, bread crumbs, and mushrooms. Season with salt and pepper to taste. Think of it as stuffing; you don't want it to be too dry. Preheat the oven to 500°F (250°C, or gas mark 10).

Grease a muffin pan and fill each cup halfway with the mixture. Brush the tops with a little of the melted butter. Bake until they are just cooked through and the topping is golden, about 8 minutes. Be sure not to dry them out. If you want to serve these on decorative heatproof spoons, it's best to bake them in the spoons so you don't have to transfer them. They're also nice in soufflé tarts.

Spoon out the mixture into the center of a romaine spear or cracker. Sprinkle with a little vegan mozzarella, and serve as appetizers with a wedge of lemon for extra zest.

YIELD: 16 pieces

Fun Fact

Food lore has it that this appetizer was invented in 1917 at a hotel, the Little Casino, in Rhode Island. A swanky guest, Mrs. Stevens, had requested a fabulous dish be made to impress her friends for an event. The maître d'hôtel whipped up these little critters (real clams, of course), which knocked off Mrs. Stevens' socks and thus she named the fantastic finger food after the hotel.

SUTHUN' BISCUITS AND GRAVY

*Gluten Free (use gluten-free flour and the mushroom option), **Soy Free (use the mushroom option, soy-free vegan butter, and the plain rice/nut milk alternative)

Nothing says Southern breakfast like biscuits and gravy. Although this "healthified" version saves you from the cholesterol and fat found in the traditional dish, I'm sure you will still find that this dish is a decadent treat meant for sharing.

FOR BISCUITS:

2 cups (220 g) all-purpose flour

1 tablespoon (14 g) baking powder

1 teaspoon salt

¼ cup (56 g) vegan shortening or vegan butter

1 cup (235 ml) vegan buttermilk, store-bought or homemade (page 14)

FOR GRAVY:

1 cup (110 g) chopped vegan sausage, tempeh bacon, or vegan ham (about 1 package, 10 to 12 ounces, or 280 to 340 g]) or 1 cup (70 g) chopped portobello mushrooms

3 tablespoons (42 g) vegan shortening

½ cup (55 g) all-purpose flour

Pinch of dried sage, to taste

Pinch of dried thyme, to taste

Salt and pepper, to taste

2½ cups (588 ml) plain soymilk

½ teaspoon liquid smoke if using mushrooms alternative; add it when you add the milk)

To make the biscuits: Preheat the oven to 500°F (250°C, or gas mark 10). In a mixing bowl, combine the flour, baking powder, and salt. Knead the shortening into the mixture with a pastry blender or until it begins to turn into coarse crumbs. Blend in the buttermilk with a fork just until the dough comes together; it will be sticky.

Turn the dough out onto a lightly floured surface (flour your hands as well). Knead gently by folding the dough 8 to 10 times. Press into a large circle 1 inch (2.5 cm) thick.

Cut out biscuits with a 2-inch (5 cm) round cutter, being sure to push straight down through the dough. Place the biscuits on baking sheet so that they barely touch. Gather up the scrap dough, press it into a circle, working it as little as possible, and continue cutting until all the dough has been used; you should get 10 to 12. Bake for 8 to 10 minutes, or until golden brown.

To make the gravy: In a large skillet over medium-high heat, brown the sausage or mushrooms, breaking up the sausage with a spatula. Do not drain.

Add the shortening, flour, sage, thyme, salt, and pepper, stirring constantly until the flour begins to brown. Slowly add the milk (and liquid smoke, if using mushrooms) while continuing to stir. Bring to a boil, reduce the heat to a simmer, and cook for 1 minute, stirring occasionally. As the gravy cools it will thicken, so if you want thinner gravy, add a little more milk. Cut the biscuits in half, place 2 or 3 on a plate per serving, and pour the gravy over the biscuits.

YIELD: 10 to 12 biscuits

COOK'S NOTE

You may also want to try biscuit and gravy breakfast sandwiches! Cut the biscuits in half, pile on the vegan sausage, mushrooms, and even some spinach or tofu scramble, slather on the gravy, and enjoy!

NOT YOUR MOTHER'S MEAT LOAF

*Gluten Free (use gluten-free bread crumbs and vegan cheese), **Soy Free (use soy-free vegan cheese), ***Low Fat (decrease the amount of cheese)

Meat loaf with mashed potatoes, meat loaf sandwich, Italian meat loaf . . . So much fun to be had with this delicious dish. It's so tasty, you'll never know it's not meat!

1 cup (192 g) lentils, rinsed and drained

1 cup (235 ml) vegetable broth, store-bought or homemade (page 16)

½ cup (35 g) minced shiitake or button mushrooms

1 teaspoon olive oil

1 onion, chopped

Salt and pepper, to taste

1 stalk celery, chopped

2 cloves garlic, minced

¼ cup (38 g) chopped green bell pepper

1 tablespoon (15 g) ketchup

1 tablespoon (16 g) tomato paste

1 tablespoon (2 g) dried basil

2 tablespoons (8 g) chopped fresh parsley

1 can (15 ounces, or 420 g) black beans, rinsed and drained

1 cup (115 g) shredded vegan mozzarella cheese

1 cup (115 g) freshly made whole-grain bread crumbs with ground flaxseed (¾ cup [86 g] bread crumbs mixed in with ¼ cup [28 g] ground flaxseed)

Sesame oil, for brushing

Preheat the oven to 350°F (180°C, or gas mark 4). Grease a loaf pan.

Place the lentils in a pan along with the vegetable broth and cook over medium heat until tender, about 5 minutes. Add the mushrooms and cook for another 3 minutes, until the mushrooms are soft. Make sure that this mixture is mushy and does not have excess liquid. Set aside.

In a large skillet, heat the olive oil over medium heat and sauté the onion with a sprinkling of salt until soft, 4 to 5 minutes, then add the celery, garlic, and bell pepper and cook until the vegetables are soft and translucent, 5 to 7 minutes longer. Add the ketchup, tomato paste, basil, and parsley and cook until all the ingredients are well combined, 1 to 2 minutes longer.

Add the vegetable mixture along with the black beans to a food processor and process until pasty. Add to the cooked lentil mixture, then add the cheese and bread crumbs. Stir to combine, then season with salt and pepper.

Transfer to the prepared loaf pan. Level the top and brush with a light coating of sesame oil. Bake for 1 hour, or until the top of the loaf looks crispy.

Cool for a few minutes, remove from the pan, cut into slices, and serve.

YIELD: 4 to 8 servings

COOK'S NOTE

If the inside of the cooked loaf does not firm up enough to slice, place it in the fridge for 1 hour, then cut into slices and reheat.

BIG MOUTH BURGER

*Gluten Free (use gluten-free flour, vegan cheese, and gluten-free buns), **Soy Free (use soy-free vegan cheese and barbecue sauce), ***Low Fat (grill patties without oil and omit the cheese)

Ah yes, the great American burger. Whether it's a fast food version or made over a sizzling barbecue, the burger has permeated our culture for good. Synonymous with carefree days and overall indulgence, the burger has become a pariah to health nuts. However, this non-meat, juicy patty is sure to blow even a carnivore's mind.

¼ cup (64 g) vegan hickory-flavored barbecue sauce

1 tablespoon (20 g) molasses

1 teaspoon plum juice

1 can (15 ounces, or 420 g) black beans, rinsed, drained, and puréed in a blender

2 cups (330 g) cooked brown rice

½ cup (60 g) oat bran or all-purpose flour

2 tablespoons (20 g) finely chopped onion

1 tablespoon (20 g) plum purée

1 tablespoon (10 g) finely chopped beet

1 teaspoon chili powder

1 tablespoon (10 g) minced garlic

½ teaspoon ground cumin

¼ teaspoon cocoa powder

Salt and pepper, to taste

1 tablespoon (15 g) pickle relish

1 vegan egg white, store-bought or homemade (page 13)

1 egg replacer, store-bought or homemade (page 13)

2 teaspoons (10 ml) olive oil

Vegan cheese of your choice (optional)

6 to 8 hamburger buns

Stir together the barbecue sauce, molasses, and plum juice in a medium-size bowl and set aside. In a large bowl, mash the beans (if not already puréed). Stir in 3 tablespoons (48 g) of the barbecue sauce mixture (reserve the remaining for glaze) along with the rice, oat bran, onion, plum purée, beet, chili powder, garlic, cumin, cocoa powder, salt, pepper, relish, egg white, and egg replacer. Form into 6 to 8 patties, wrap each in plastic wrap, and chill for at least 4 hours.

Heat the olive oil in a skillet over medium heat. Grill the patties for about 2 minutes on one side, then turn and brush with the remaining barbecue sauce mixture. Top with the vegan cheese and grill for another 2 minutes, or until the cheese is melted. Serve with the toppings of your choice (these are delicious with grilled onions, mushrooms, and avocado) on a toasty bun.

YIELD: 6 to 8 burgers

COOK'S NOTE

Once you've made the patties, chill for at least 4 hours so that the flavors meld and the patties take shape. Be sure to build this into your prep time! These patties are also not meant to be as uniform as your typical veggie burger patty because they are a little moister.

fun fact

From tales of warriors riding with slabs of beef under their saddles to tenderize the meat to German immigrants bringing over Hamburg-style beef, the origin of the hamburger is a bit hazy. But it was here in the USA that the hamburger became a distinctly American sandwich when the first fast food burger was served at White Castle in 1921.

MOM'S FRIED CHICKEN DINNER WITH GARLIC MASHED POTATOES AND MUSHROOM GRAVY

*Gluten Free (use the tofu steak option and gluten-free flour and cereal), **Soy Free (use soy-free meat substitute, vegan butter, vegan sour cream, cashew cream in place of the heavy cream, and an alternative rice/nut milk)

Is this the ultimate American comfort food? I happen to think it is, but unfortunately it has a dark side. This faux clucker alternative is sure to give you all the comfort with none of the nightmare. My grandmother was the queen of all American meals, and this trio is one that will always remind me of her!

FOR FRIED CHICKEN:

3 recipes vegan egg wash (page 13)

¼ teaspoon salt

Black pepper, to taste

1 teaspoon ground ginger, or to taste

1 clove garlic, crushed

1 teaspoon onion powder

1 teaspoon Dijon mustard

1 teaspoon paprika

½ cup (55 g) all-purpose flour

4 cups (280 g) crushed vegan cornflakes or bran cereal

6 vegan chicken cutlets or tofu steaks

¼ cup (60 ml) vegetable oil, divided

FOR GARLIC MASHED POTATOES:

6 medium-size baking potatoes, peeled and coarsely chopped

2 teaspoons salt

½ cup (112 g) vegan butter, at room temperature

½ cup (115 g) vegan sour cream, at room temperature

2 teaspoons finely minced garlic, or to taste

2 tablespoons (30 ml) plain soymilk, at room temperature or warmed

Salt and black pepper, to taste

To make the chicken: Combine the egg wash, salt, pepper, ginger, garlic, onion powder, mustard, and paprika in a small bowl. Spread the flour and the cornflakes on separate plates.

Working with 1 piece at a time, dredge the chicken cutlets in the flour until the surface is completely dry. Dip in the egg wash mixture to coat, allow the excess to drip off for a few seconds, and then roll quickly in the cornflakes until well coated. Heat 2 tablespoons (30 ml) of the oil in a large skillet over medium heat. Panfry half the cutlets for 2 to 3 minutes on each side, until browned and crisp. Repeat with the remaining 2 tablespoons (30 ml) oil and remaining 3 cutlets.

To make the potatoes: In a large pot, cook the potatoes in water mixed with the 2 teaspoons salt until tender, about 15 minutes. Drain the potatoes and return them to the saucepan.

Add the butter, sour cream, and garlic and mash until the ingredients are blended together. Add the milk, 1 tablespoon (15 ml) at a time, until the potatoes are the desired consistency, then season with salt and pepper.

FOR MUSHROOM GRAVY:

2 tablespoons (28 g) unsalted vegan butter

6 ounces (170 g) shiitake, cremini, or button mushrooms, finely diced

Salt and pepper, to taste

1½ tablespoons (12 g) all-purpose flour

1 tablespoon (15 ml) Marsala or sherry

1 cup (235 ml) vegetable broth, store-bought or homemade (page 16)

¼ cup (60 ml) vegan heavy cream, store-bought or homemade (page 15)

1 teaspoon fresh thyme leaves

To make the gravy: Melt the butter in a skillet over medium-high heat. Add the mushrooms and cook, stirring occasionally, for about 8 minutes, or until tender, then season with salt and pepper. Scatter the flour over the mushrooms and stir until lightly browned, about 1 minute. Add the Marsala and broth and bring to boil, cooking until thickened, about 2 minutes. Add the cream and thyme and stir to combine.

To serve, place 1 cutlet on a plate, spoon on some mashed potatoes, and ladle some gravy over the top.

YIELD: 6 servings

fun fact

Mashed potatoes are said to have originated in 1771, invented by a French man named Antoine Parmentier, who came up with the idea of having a potato cook-off of sorts. He claimed first prize with his creation, and the rest is history!

COOK'S NOTE

If you're not looking for crispy chicken, omit the cornflakes. Instead, dredge the chicken in a mixture of 2 cups (240 g) flour and 2 tablespoons (28 g) baking powder after dipping in the egg wash mixture.

MUSHROOM PO' BOY SANDWICH

*Gluten Free (use gluten-free bread crumbs and bread), **Soy Free (use soy-free butter and mayonnaise)

The po' boy can be found all over Louisiana and each spot will have a different version, from French fries and cheese to crab or shrimp. Tossing local ingredients between two pieces of crusty bread and slathered in sauce , it's the quintessential comfort sandwich.

FOR BATTERED MUSHROOMS:

⅓ cup (47 g) cornmeal

⅓ cup (38 g) dry bread crumbs

½ teaspoon garlic powder

¼ teaspoon salt

¼ teaspoon cayenne

¼ teaspoon black pepper

½ cup (60 g) all-purpose flour

½ cup (112 g) vegan butter, melted

1 cup (70 g) stemmed cremini and oyster mushrooms, mixed

Coconut oil (or high-heat oil of choice), for sautéing

FOR CREOLE MAYONNAISE:

4 tablespoons (55 g) vegan mayonnaise

1 tablespoon (6 g) minced scallion

1 tablespoon (1.3 g) minced fresh parsley

2 teaspoons sweet pickle relish

2 teaspoons Dijon mustard

1 teaspoon capers

½ teaspoon hot sauce (optional)

FOR SANDWICHES:

1 (16-inch, or 40.6 cm) French bread loaf or 4 sub sandwich rolls

2 cups (130 g) shredded lettuce

24 thin slices tomato

To make the mushrooms, combine the cornmeal, bread crumbs, garlic powder, salt, cayenne, and black pepper in a bowl; stir well. Dredge and coat the mushrooms in the flour, shaking off any excess, then dip them into the melted butter, letting the excess drip back into the bowl, and then dredge in the cornmeal mixture again. Make sure the mushrooms are well coated. Coat a large skillet with coconut oil, and place over medium heat until hot. Add the mushrooms, and cook until browned.

To make the Creole mayonnaise: Combine all the ingredients in a bowl; stir well.

Cut the bread loaf in half horizontally, and spread the Creole mayonnaise evenly over the cut sides of the bread. Arrange the lettuce and tomato slices over the bottom half; top with the mushrooms and the top half of the bread. Slice into 4 sandwiches.

YIELD: 4 servings

Fun Fact

The Po' Boy Sandwich is one of Louisiana's most beloved meals. Created by brothers Bennie and Clovis Martin during the Great Depression, this sandwich, hearty with bread and cheap seafood, ham or even French fries, fed many hungry and broke strikers of the New Orleans streetcar unions. The brothers, having worked as streetcar operators before opening their food stand, sympathized with the men and promised to feed any members of their local union division free of charge. "Here comes another poor boy," they would say. In fact, the free po' boy in 1930 was a lettuce and tomato sandwich!

CHICKEN AND DUMPLINGS FOR THE SOUL

*Gluten Free (use gluten-free flour and gluten-free vegan chicken), **Soy Free (use soy-free butter, vegan chicken, alternative rice/nut milk, and cashew cream in place of the heavy cream)

A Southern classic worth all the hype!

FOR CHICKEN:

8 vegan chicken cutlets, cut into chunks or strips

2 sweet onions, coarsely chopped

6 cups (1,410 ml) vegetable broth

2 bay leaves

Salt, to taste

FOR DUMPLINGS:

2 cups (240 g) all-purpose flour

⅓ cup (30 g) minced parsley, tarragon, and scallion

4 teaspoons (56 g) baking powder

1 teaspoon salt

3 tablespoons (42 g) vegan butter

1 cup plus 3 tablespoons (280 ml) plain soymilk

FOR SAUCE:

7 tablespoons (98 g) vegan butter

10 tablespoons (75 g) all-purpose flour

¼ cup (60 ml) dry white wine

2½ tablespoons (18 g) paprika

2 tablespoons (18 g) garlic powder

1 tablespoon (7 g) each onion powder, dried oregano, dried thyme, and black pepper

1 teaspoon fresh thyme leaves

3 stalks celery, chopped

4 carrots, chopped

1 large white onion, chopped

¼ cup (60 ml) vegan heavy cream (page 15)

1 cup (130 g) frozen green peas, thawed

Salt and pepper, to taste

3 tablespoons (12 g) chopped fresh parsley

To make the chicken: Combine the chicken, onions, vegetable broth, bay leaves, and salt to taste in a large pot. Bring to a boil. Reduce the heat to low and simmer, partially covered, for 8 to 10 minutes. Remove the chicken pieces with a slotted spoon and set aside. Reserve the broth.

To make the dumplings: In a medium-size bowl, combine the flour, herbs, baking powder, and salt. In a small saucepan over low heat, bring the butter and milk to a simmer. Add the butter and milk mixture to the dry ingredients, stirring with a fork until the mixture just comes together. Drop the batter by spoonfuls onto a baking sheet and cover with plastic wrap. Refrigerate until ready to use.

To make the sauce: In a Dutch oven or large soup pot, melt the butter over medium heat. Whisk in the flour and cook, stirring, until golden brown, 3 to 4 minutes. Whisk in the wine, reserved broth, paprika, garlic, pepper, onion powder, oregano, and thyme. Cook until the sauce has thickened, about 5 minutes, then add the celery, carrots, and onion. Cook until the vegetables are tender-crisp, about 15 minutes. Add the reserved chicken, heavy cream, and peas and season with salt and pepper. Place the dumplings on top of the sauce. Cover and simmer until the dumplings are cooked through, about 15 to 20 minutes. Serve in large soup bowls, garnished with the parsley.

YIELD: 8 to 10 servings

Fun Fact

Dumplings date back to between 600 to 900 CE. After they made it to the United States, they gained popularity during the Great Depression because they helped thicken soup and increased the amount of people one chicken could feed.

CAJUN VEGGIE GUMBO

*Gluten Free (use gluten-free flour)

Get as spicy as you desire on this culinary trip to the bayou.

FOR BROWN ROUX:

1 cup (235 ml) vegetable oil

1 cup (120 g) all-purpose flour

Salt and pepper, to taste

FOR STEW BASE:

2 tablespoons (30 ml) vegetable oil

1 clove garlic, chopped

¼ cup (33 g) corn kernels

2 bell peppers, one green and one red, cut into a large dice

2 stalks celery, cut into a large dice

1 onion, cut into a large dice

½ cup (60 g) sliced okra

1 gallon (3.8 L) vegetable broth

¼ cup brown roux (above)

1 cup (180 g) whole peeled plum tomatoes

2 tablespoons (6 g) each thyme, sage, rosemary, and Cajun or Creole spice

3 bay leaves

2 tablespoons (4 g) sassafras leaves (gumbo filé)

Lemon juice, to taste

1½ tablespoons (24 g) chile pepper paste

Salt and pepper, to taste

FOR STEW VEGETABLES:

2 tablespoons (30 ml) vegetable oil

2 cups (260 g) mixed peas and corn

2 cups (220 g) peeled and cubed potatoes and yams

1 cup (180 g) skinned, seeded, and diced tomatoes

2 bell peppers, one green and one red, diced

1 cup (40 g) torn collard greens

1 cup (256 g) rinsed and drained kidney beans

2 tablespoons (6 g) each thyme, sage, and rosemary

Salt and pepper, to taste

To make the brown roux: In a large sauté pan, heat the oil over medium heat. When the pan is hot, carefully whisk in the flour and reduce the heat to low, being careful not to burn it. Season with salt and pepper. Stir the mixture constantly for 30 minutes until it becomes a brown, peanut butter color with a nutty aroma. Remove from the heat.

To make the stew base: Heat the oil in a large soup pot over medium-low heat, then sweat the garlic, corn, bell peppers, celery, onion, and okra for 5 to 7 minutes. Add the broth and bring to a simmer. When it begins to boil, remove about ½ cup (120 ml) liquid, place it in a bowl, and slowly stir in the roux, then slowly add that back to the simmering liquid. Let simmer for 15 minutes, then add the tomatoes, thyme, sage, rosemary, Cajun spice, bay leaves, sassafras, lemon juice, and chili paste. Simmer for 10 minutes, then season with salt and pepper. Transfer in batches to a blender and purée.

To make the stew vegetables: In a large pot, heat the oil, then sweat the peas, corn, potatoes, yams, tomatoes, bell peppers, and collards for 2 to 3 minutes. Add the stew base, bring to a simmer, and simmer for 5 minutes. Add the beans, thyme, sage, and rosemary, season with salt and pepper, and simmer for 2 to 3 minutes longer.

You might like to serve over warm rice, or even pasta for a fun twist!

YIELD: 10 to 12 servings

COOK'S NOTE

Gumbo has many incarnations in the Deep South. Feel free to play with the dish by adding your favorite meat substitutes and veggies.

CHICAGO-STYLE DEEP DISH THREE-CHEESE PIZZA

*Gluten Free (use gluten-free flour and vegan cheese), **Soy Free (use soy-free vegan cheese)

Store-bought dough is fine if you're looking to save time. But if you want that super-tasty, real pizzeria taste, plan ahead and make the dough. Nothing makes a Chicago deep dish pie more authentic than homemade dough. Go crazy with your favorite fillings (they're not "toppings," because you're filling a veritable well here) and enjoy!

FOR DOUGH:

1½ packages (2¼ teaspoons, or 9 g each) active dry yeast

1 cup (235 ml) warm water (between 105° and 115°F [40.5° to 46°C]), divided

1 tablespoon (13 g) sugar

3½ cups (420 g) all-purpose flour

1 teaspoon salt

½ tablespoon dried oregano

½ tablespoon dried basil

½ teaspoon garlic powder

½ cup (70 g) yellow cornmeal

¼ cup (60 g) vegetable oil

Olive oil, for brushing

To make the dough: In a small bowl, dissolve the yeast in ½ cup (120 ml) of the warm water. Add the sugar, stir well, and set aside. In a large mixing bowl, combine the flour, salt, oregano, basil, garlic, and cornmeal. Make a well in the center of the flour (like a volcano or mountain with a shallow valley in the middle, but not a hole). Add the yeast mixture, the vegetable oil, and the remaining ½ cup (120 ml) warm water. Stir and mix thoroughly until the dough comes away from the sides of the bowl and a rough mass is formed.

Turn the dough out onto a well-floured work surface. Knead and pound the dough (dust with flour if the dough sticks to your hands) for 5 to 6 minutes, or until it is smooth and soft. Dust the dough and a large mixing bowl lightly with flour. Place the dough in the bowl and cover the bowl with plastic wrap and a kitchen towel. Let rise in a warm place until doubled in size, about 1½ hours.

Preheat the oven to 475°F (240°C, or gas mark 9). Oil the bottom and sides of a 10-inch springform pan or deep-dish pizza pan.

Turn the dough out onto a floured work surface and knead for about 2 minutes. Spread the dough in the pan with your fingers and palms. (It will spread more easily if you let it sit in the pan for about 10 minutes before handling.) Work the dough until it covers the bottom of the pan. Pull the edges of the dough up to form a lip or a pronounced border all around the pan, making sure the dough is touching the walls and corners of the pan. Prick the bottom with a fork at ½-inch (1.3 cm) intervals and prebake the crust on the lowest rack for exactly 4 minutes. Brush the crust lightly with olive oil.

Prebaking the pizza crust ensures a better crust bottom and is necessary to give the dough its initial spring; otherwise, the weight of the cheese, sauce, and toppings will compact the dough and it won't hold up. It's a heavy pie!

FOR PIZZA SAUCE:

2 tablespoons (30 ml) olive oil

1 tablespoon (10 g) chopped garlic

2 teaspoons chopped basil

1 teaspoon chopped oregano

¼ teaspoon fennel seed

½ teaspoon salt

¼ teaspoon black pepper

¼ teaspoon red pepper flakes

3½ cups (630 g) canned or fresh coarsely crushed plum tomatoes

1 tablespoon (15 ml) dry red wine

1 teaspoon sugar

FOR PIZZA FILLINGS:

2 cups (230 g) shredded vegan mozzarella cheese

2 cups (230 g) shredded vegan cheddar cheese

Toppings of choice (chopped veggies, meat substitute, etc.)

2 cups (230 g) shredded vegan Monterey Jack cheese

To make the sauce: In a medium-size saucepan, heat the oil over medium-high heat. Add the garlic and cook, stirring, for 30 seconds. Add the basil, oregano, fennel, salt, black pepper, and red pepper flakes, and cook, stirring, for 30 seconds. Add the tomatoes, wine, and sugar, and bring to a boil. Lower the heat and simmer, stirring occasionally, until thickened, 20 to 30 minutes. Remove from the heat and let cool completely before assembling your pizza.

To assemble the pizza: Preheat the oven to 475°F (240°C, or gas mark 9). Layer the bottom of the crust generously with the mozzarella cheese. Next, add a nice layer of pizza sauce, covering the cheese layer entirely. Next should be a generous layer of cheddar cheese along with any veggies and other toppings you like. Top that layer with more pizza sauce and sprinkle lightly with the Monterey Jack.

Bake until the cheese is golden and bubbly and the crust is golden brown, about 30 minutes. Remove from the oven, place on baking rack to cool for about 5 to 10 minutes, then slice and serve. If it's too hot, the filling of the pizza will ooze out. Waiting until it cools a bit will allow the cheese to harden and keep its form.

YIELD: 8 servings

fun fact

The famous deep-dish pizza popped up in Chicago in the 1940s. A soldier, who had toured Italy during his military service, returned home and began to experiment with a new pie at the restaurant where he worked after the war.

NEW YORK–STYLE CHEESECAKE

*Gluten Free (use gluten-free graham crackers)

OMG! Who can deny that a creamy slice of cheesecake is probably equivalent to a slice of heaven? Cheesecake has many different faces, but the original New York–style cheesecake is the granddaddy version of them all.

FOR CRUST:

6 tablespoons (84 g) unsalted vegan butter, at room temperature, plus more for pans

1 package (9 ounces, or 252 g) vegan graham crackers, finely crushed (about 2 cups [230 g])

3 tablespoons (39 g) sugar or (60 g) agave nectar

Pinch of ginger powder

FOR FILLING:

1 tablespoon egg replacer, not mixed, store-bought or homemade (page 13)

¼ cup (60 ml) water

1 cup (230 g) vegan cream cheese

1 package (12 ounces, or 340 g) silken tofu, pressed and drained

1¾ cups (411 ml) vegan condensed milk, store-bought or homemade (page 15)

3 to 5 tablespoons (45 to 75 ml) lemon juice, to taste

2 teaspoons vanilla extract

½ cup (60 g) all-purpose flour

FOR SERVING:

Fresh strawberries, fresh cherries, or vegan whipped cream, for serving

To make the crust: Preheat the oven to 350°F (180°C, or gas mark 4). Butter the sides of a deep pie tin or a 10-inch (25 cm) springform pan. Wrap the exterior of the pan (including the base) in a double layer of foil.

Melt the butter in a small saucepan over medium heat. Place the crushed graham crackers, sugar, and ginger in a large bowl; stir until well combined. Pour the melted butter over the cracker mixture and mix until evenly moistened. Press the mixture evenly into the bottom of the prepared pan.

Place the pan on a baking sheet. Bake until the crust is set, 10 to 12 minutes. Transfer the pan to a wire rack to cool completely.

To make the filling: Preheat the oven to 350°F (180°C, or gas mark 4). In a small bowl or liquid measuring cup, combine the egg replacer and water, and mix until frothy. Next, in a food processor, by hand, or with an electric mixer in a medium-size bowl, combine the cream cheese, tofu, egg replacer/water mixture, condensed milk, lemon juice, and vanilla. Blend well until very smooth. Slowly fold in the flour and mix until very smooth.

Pour the cream filling into the prepared graham cracker crust. Set the pan inside a large, shallow roasting pan. Carefully ladle boiling water into the roasting pan to reach halfway up the sides of the pan. Bake for 45 minutes; reduce the oven temperature to 325°F (170°C, or gas mark 3). Continue baking until the cake is set but still slightly wobbly in the center, about 15 minutes longer. Turn off the oven and leave the cake in the oven with the door slightly ajar for 1 hour. Transfer the pan to a wire rack and let cool completely. Refrigerate, uncovered, for at least 6 hours or overnight. Before unmolding, run a knife around the edge of the cake.

Serve with fresh strawberries, cherries, or vegan whipped cream.

YIELD: 6 to 8 servings

COOK'S NOTE

This cake is fantastic with a chocolate crust as well! Take vegan chocolate sandwich cookies and unscrew the sides, tossing out the filling. Crush about 2 cups (230 g) and follow the crust recipe. In addition, mixing other ingredients such as chocolate, peanut butter, strawberry jam, pumpkin purée, or even caramel into your filling can really make this a versatile dessert.

MRS. HAMILTON'S RED VELVET CAKE 2.0

*Gluten Free (use gluten-free cake flour), **Soy Free (use soy-free vegan shortening and butter, and alternative rice/nut milk)

I call this Mrs. Hamilton's 2.0 because this is a nondairy, "healthified" version of my mother-in-law's beloved recipe. It is very important for the consistency that you use sifted cake flour. This version features a traditional buttercream, which you may want to double if you like to lay it on thick.

FOR CAKE:

½ cup (112 g) vegan shortening

1½ cups (300 g) sugar

2 egg replacers, mixed, store-bought or homemade (page 13)

2 ounces (60 ml) natural red food coloring or ⅓ cup (40 g) beet powder (if you really want it red, use conventional food coloring)

2 heaping tablespoons (20 g) Dutch-processed cocoa (the lighter, the better)

1 teaspoon salt

2¼ cups (270 g) sifted cake flour

1 cup (235 ml) vegan buttermilk, store-bought or homemade (page 14)

1 teaspoon vanilla extract

1 teaspoon baking soda

1 tablespoon (15 ml) white or apple cider vinegar

FOR FROSTING:

1 cup (225 g) vegan butter

½ cup (112 g) vegan shortening

1 cup (120 g) confectioners' sugar

3 tablespoons (24 g) all-purpose flour

⅔ cup (155 ml) soymilk

1 teaspoon vanilla extract

To make the cake: Preheat the oven to 350°F (180°C, or gas mark 4). Grease and flour two 9-inch (23 cm) cake pans.

Cream together the shortening, sugar, and egg replacer in a large bowl. In a small bowl, stir together the food coloring and cocoa to make a paste, and then add it to the shortening mixture. Add the salt, flour, buttermilk, and vanilla and stir to combine. Add the baking soda and vinegar and blend well without beating. Divide the batter between the two cake pans and bake for 30 minutes, or until a toothpick inserted into the center of the cake comes out clean. Let cool completely on a cooling rack. Place in the refrigerator for at least 1 hour to firm up.

To make the frosting: Cream the butter, shortening, and confectioners' sugar in a large bowl. Add the flour slowly, 1 tablespoon (8 g) at a time, while continuing to mix. Next stir in the soymilk and vanilla. Beat until light and fluffy.

Remove the cakes from the pans and place on a cooling rack with a layer of waxed paper underneath for easier cleanup, allowing the cakes to cool completely. Frost the top of one cake, place the second cake on top, frost the top of that, then frost around the sides.

YIELD: 6 to 8 servings

Fun Fact

The history of the red velvet cake is one of terrific culinary gossip. Some say its roots lie in the Deep South; others claim the recipe came from the Waldorf-Astoria in New York. As the story goes, a customer who fell in love with the decadent dessert requested the recipe from the luxury hotel after she returned home. Although the hotel was more than happy to send it to her, they also sent her a bill for several hundred dollars to pay for their secret recipe. Out of spite, the woman began to circulate the recipe and that is how the cake, and its numerous versions, came to infiltrate American bakeries. Or so "they" say!

Chapter 3
LATIN AMERICA

¡HOLA! YOU WILL FIND THAT this chapter happens to be the largest in the book due to the many countries that make up what we know as the Latin world. The customs and dishes are as diverse as the lands they come from.

In the Americas (North, Central, and South), it was the indigenous peoples, including the Maya, Aztecs, and the Inca, who laid the foundation for modern Latin culture. When the Spaniards settled across their lands, these ancient civilizations began to incorporate into their cuisines new ingredients and spices that came from Europe and beyond. The native peoples were introduced to corn, for instance, which is now a staple in Latin cuisine. To this day, the names of many traditional dishes from Latin America bear the names given to them by the ancient peoples.

Latin American countries span a variety of terrains and locales, which is often reflected in the cuisine. For instance, countries in the Andes Mountains produce dishes that are grain based and hearty. In fact, one of the most used grains in mountainous South American countries is quinoa. Found to be one of the most nutritious foods, quinoa has since gained quite a bit of fame. This grain, along with rice, gave folks sustenance they needed in cold climates, where hunting was difficult due to the terrain.

In warmer climates, you will find a great many seafood dishes from coastal and island nations, one of the most famous being ceviche. Meals from these regions are lighter and incorporate many fruits. And in the Caribbean nations, you will find dishes with a heavy African influence due to the slaves that were brought there by the Spaniards.

Even though Latin cuisine is heavily meat and poultry based, beans are a very important component. Avocados, plantains, lemons, and limes also show up frequently. Many folks associate spicy foods with Latin cooking, and that is true to some degree because Latinos love using cumin, chile peppers, and a variety of aromatics. However, the main ingredients in Latin cooking are family and love!

In this chapter, we will be visiting Argentina, Brazil, El Salvador, Central America, Chile, Colombia, Cuba, Mexico, Peru, Puerto Rico, and Venezuela. So turn on some salsa, put on your sombrero, and hold on to your plantains! *¡Vámonos!* (Let's go!)

CHURRASCO MUSHROOMS AND CHIMICHURRI SAUCE (GRILLED MUSHROOMS)

*Low Fat (decrease the amount of oil in the sauce)

Although churrasco is really a meat-based dish, these mushrooms will give you all the texture and taste you need to feel like you're hangin' out at an Argentinean ranch. This Argentine sauce is incredibly versatile because it can be used as a marinade, dip, or dressing. I'm a sucker for sauces, and chimichurri is one of my all-time favorites!

FOR CHIMICHURRI SAUCE:

½ cup (30 g) fresh flat-leaf parsley

½ cup (8 g) fresh cilantro leaves

1 tablespoon (4 g) dried oregano

Juice of 1 large lime

6 cloves garlic, roughly chopped

¾ cup (180 ml) olive oil

1 tablespoon (7 g) paprika

Salt and pepper, to taste

Red pepper flakes, to taste (optional)

FOR MUSHROOMS:

6 to 8 large portobello mushroom caps

Cooked rice, for serving

To make the sauce: Add all of the ingredients to a food processor and process until the mixture is a creamy, pesto-type consistency, about 2 minutes.

To make the mushrooms: Brush the mushrooms generously with the chimichurri sauce and let marinate for at least 1 hour. Preheat the grill to medium heat. Reduce the heat and grill the mushrooms for 5 minutes on each side. Do not overcook the mushrooms because they will burn easily or become quite tough.

Serve the mushrooms over rice with a side of chimichurri sauce for dipping.

YIELD: 6 to 8 servings

COOK'S NOTE

You may also replace the mushrooms with tofu, seitan, or other meat substitute.

Fun Fact

Even though chimichurri sauce hails from Argentina, it was developed by an Irishman who marched with the troops for Argentine independence in the nineteenth century. Jimmy McCurry was the first to prepare the sauce and became so popular that it has been passed on since he first made it. However, it came to be pronounced "chimichurri" because the Argentineans had trouble pronouncing Jimmy's name!

OUT-OF-THIS-WORLD ALFAJORES
(CARAMEL SANDWICH COOKIES)

*Gluten Free (use gluten-free flour)

Dulce de leche, or caramel, is a popular sweet and dessert in most Latin countries. These sandwich cookies have a rich history but have remained one of Argentina's most beloved treats. If you don't like coconut, roll in chopped nuts instead.

FOR COOKIES:

¾ cup (338 g) vegan butter

1 cup (200 g) granulated sugar (or use 1 cup [120 g] confectioners' sugar for a fluffier cookie)

2 tablespoons (30 ml) soymilk

2 tablespoons (25 g) puréed silken tofu

1 teaspoon vanilla extract

2 tablespoons (30 ml) brandy or cognac

1 teaspoon freshly grated lemon zest

2 cups (240 g) all-purpose flour

1 cup (128 g) cornstarch

⅛ teaspoon salt

½ teaspoon baking soda

1 teaspoon baking powder

FOR DULCE DE LECHE:

1½ cups (390 g) raw, unsalted almond butter

¾ cup (255 g) brown rice syrup

½ cup (170 g) maple syrup or agave nectar or (115 g) light brown sugar

¼ cup (32 g) soymilk powder

1½ teaspoons vanilla powder or extract

1 teaspoon ground cinnamon

FOR SERVING:

¾ cup (60 g) grated coconut (must be grated because shredded is too large)

Confectioners' sugar, for serving

To make the cookies: Beat the butter and sugar until fluffy and creamy. Add the milk and puréed tofu and mix. Add the vanilla, brandy, and lemon zest; mix well and set aside.

In a separate bowl, whisk together the flour, cornstarch, salt, baking soda, and baking powder. Add the dry mixture to the butter mixture and work together with your hands until combined and soft. Do not add any extra flour. Cover and chill in the refrigerator for 2 hours.

Preheat the oven to 325°F (170°C, or gas mark 3). Line baking sheets with parchment paper.

Divide the dough in half and keep half refrigerated. On a floured work surface and using a floured rolling pin, roll out the dough to a thickness of ¼ inch (6 mm). Cut into 2-inch (5 cm) rounds with a cookie cutter and transfer to the prepared baking sheets. Repeat with the remaining half of the cookie dough. Bake for 12 to 15 minutes, or until golden. The cookies should be dry but not brown.

To make the dulce de leche: Mix all the ingredients in a pot and cook over medium heat until it the caramel starts to pull away from the sides of the pot. You may want to prepare this in a double boiler so you lessen the chance of scorching the mixture. Remove from the heat and let cool and thicken before filling the cookie sandwiches.

To assemble the cookies: When the cookies are cool, match them up into pairs of like sizes. Turn one cookie over and spread a dollop of dulce de leche onto the flat part of the cookie (it is much easier to spread when the dulce is warm). Place its partner on top (flat side down) and gently press so that the caramel comes to the edges. Roll the edges in the coconut and place on a rack to set. Repeat with the remaining cookie pairs. When ready to serve, sift a light layer of confectioners' sugar over the tops of the cookies and place them on a platter.

YIELD: 20 to 30 cookie sandwiches

POLENTA BITES WITH CREMA AND AVOCADO SPREAD

*Gluten Free (use wheat-free tamari), **Soy Free (use soy-free vegan cheese and use liquid aminos in place of soy sauce)

**Brazil loves to use polenta in a variety of ways, but nothing says "festa"
like polenta finger food. Cook the polenta according to package instructions
until creamy and thick, or if you buy it loose, cook 1 part polenta to 3 parts liquid.**

FOR POLENTA BITES:

1 cup (225 g) cooked polenta

½ teaspoon salt, or more to taste

½ cup (60 g) shredded vegan mozzarella cheese

¼ cup (25 g) finely chopped scallion

¼ cup (4 g) finely chopped fresh cilantro

½ teaspoon lemon juice

FOR AVOCADO SPREAD:

2 ripe medium-size avocados, peeled and chopped

⅓ cup (80 ml) fresh lime juice

4 large cloves garlic

1 to 2 tablespoons (1 to 2 g) chopped fresh cilantro

Salt and pepper, to taste

FOR CREMA:

½ recipe cashew cream (page 14)

1½ tablespoons (22 ml) rice wine vinegar

1 teaspoon shoyu or tamari

1 tablespoon (15 ml) olive oil

½ teaspoon minced garlic

1 teaspoon mustard powder

1 teaspoon dried dill

FOR FRYING:

Safflower oil (or preferred high-heat oil)

To make the polenta bites: In a saucepan, combine the cooked polenta, salt, and mozzarella cheese. Cook over medium heat, stirring continuously, for about 10 minutes, until thick and well incorporated. Remove from the heat. Stir in the scallion, cilantro, and lemon juice.

Spread the polenta mixture evenly onto a parchment-lined baking sheet, about ¾ to 1 inch (2 to 2.5 cm) thick. Cover with another sheet, pressing to even out, and let cool in the fridge for 1 hour.

To make the avocado spread: Put the avocado in a food processor. Add the lime juice, garlic, and cilantro. Season with salt and pepper. Process until smooth. Transfer to a bowl and cover with plastic wrap until ready to serve.

To make the crema: Blend all the ingredients in a food processor until smooth and creamy. If you find the cream too thick, thin it by adding 1 teaspoon of water at a time.

Once the polenta is solidified, use a 2-inch (5 cm) round cookie cutter to cut out the bites. Fry the bites in a skillet with a little oil over medium heat until golden, turning them frequently to prevent sticking, 1 to 2 minutes per side. Let cool for a few minutes and top generously with avocado spread and a dollop of crema.

If you prefer not to fry the bites, you may bake them as follows: After removing from the heat, spoon 1½ tablespoons (21 g) of the warm polenta mixture into the cups of a greased mini-muffin pan. Using the back of a spoon, pack the polenta firmly into the cups. Chill until set, about 3 hours. (These can be made 1 day ahead. Cover; keep chilled.)

Preheat the oven to 350°F (180°C, or gas mark 4). Line a baking sheet with foil. Using the tip of a knife, lift the polenta bites from the muffin cups. Transfer to the prepared baking sheet and bake for about 5 minutes, or until the bites are warmed through. Remove from the oven, and top with the spread and crema.

YIELD: About 40 bites or 8 appetizer servings

TAMALES DULCES CON UVAS PASAS
(SWEET TAMALES WITH RAISINS)

Sweet or savory, tamales are the quintessential Latin food. Found all over Latin America, they come in all shapes, sizes, colors, fillings, and even names. Some are incredibly labor-intensive while others, like this dulce version, are a bit lighter on the home cook, sacrificing none of the warm and tasty reward!

1 package (8 ounces, or 225 g) dried cornhusks

1 cup (225 g) vegan butter, divided

2½ cups (300 g) masa harina

1½ cups (210 g) yellow cornmeal

¼ cup (50 g) sugar

1 tablespoon (7 g) ground cinnamon

2 teaspoons salt

1½ cups (353 ml) water

1¾ cups (411 ml) vegan condensed milk, store-bought or homemade (page 15)

Dash of vanilla extract

1 cup (145 g) raisins

½ cup (60 g) chopped walnuts

Sort the cornhusks, separating out any that are broken. Soak the intact husks in warm water for at least 1 hour, or until soft and easy to fold. It's best to put something on top of the husks to weight them down in the water to keep them submerged. Once soft, be sure to rinse any residue before filling.

Beat ⅔ cup (150 g) of the butter in a bowl until creamy. In a medium-size bowl combine the masa, cornmeal, sugar, cinnamon, and salt. Alternating mixtures, add the masa mixture, water, and condensed milk to the butter, mixing well after each addition. Melt the remaining ⅓ cup (75 g) butter and add to the dough. Gradually, beat the dough until it forms the consistency of a thick cake batter. Stir in the vanilla, raisins, and nuts.

Spread ¼ cup (60 g) batter in the middle of a cornhusk, using the back of a spoon to form a square-shaped patty. Fold the ends over the batter as though you are wrapping a gift, covering the batter completely. Use strands of cornhusks or kitchen twine to tie them closed. Repeat with the remaining dough and husks.

Place a basket for steaming (such as a vegetable steamer) in a pot with a lid. Pour in water until it just reaches the bottom of the basket. Arrange the tamales upright in the basket. Top them with the remaining unused cornhusks and a damp cloth. Cover with the lid and bring to a boil over high heat. Decrease the heat to low. Simmer, adding more water as necessary, for 1½ to 2 hours, or until the dough begins to loosen the cornhusks. Remove from the steamer with tongs and place on a plate in the husks. Unwrap and enjoy! These are yummy with a little scoop of vanilla ice cream, too!

YIELD: 18 to 20 tamales

COOK'S NOTE

You can get super creative with these! Try filling them with pineapple and drizzling with caramel, or fill with strawberries and drizzle with chocolate. These can also be somewhat savory with sweet potato and rosemary. The possibilities are endless.

MONDONGO
(VEGETABLE AND BEEF STEW)

*Gluten Free (use gluten-free meat alternative), **Soy Free (use soy-free meat alternative),
***Low Glycemic (decrease or omit the yuca, sweet potato, and/or plantain)

**Mondongo is a traditional soup in Latin American and Caribbean countries.
Although the soup usually calls for tripe, I know you won't miss any of the flavor with
this fully plant-based alternative. It's hearty, nutritious, and bursting with flavor!**

4 packages (10 to 12 ounces, or 280 to 340 g each) vegan beef chunks

3 lemons, halved

2 teaspoons salt

2 quarts (1.9 L) water

3 tablespoons (45 ml) vegetable oil

2 onions, chopped

2 green or red bell peppers, chopped

3 or 4 cloves garlic, minced

1 tablespoon (4 g) dried oregano

2½ teaspoons ground cumin

1 teaspoon saffron threads

2 cups (360 g) seeded and chopped tomatoes

1 pound (454 g) yuca or potatoes, peeled and cut into chunks

1 pound (454 g) sweet potatoes, peeled and cut into chunks

3 green plantains, peeled and cut into chunks

1 head cabbage, coarsely chopped

1 large bunch fresh cilantro, chopped

Salt and pepper, to taste

Sliced avocado, for serving (optional)

Cayenne or hot pepper sauce, for serving (optional)

Add the beef, lemons, salt, and water to a large pot and bring to a boil over medium-high heat. Reduce the heat to medium-low and simmer for 1 to 1½ hours, or until the beef is tender.

While the meat is simmering, heat the oil in a skillet over medium heat and add the onions and bell peppers. Sauté for 3 or 4 minutes, or until the onion is translucent. Add the garlic, oregano, cumin, and saffron and sauté for another minute. Add the tomatoes and simmer for 3 or 4 minutes more. Remove from the heat and set aside. When cool, remove saffron threads.

Remove the beef to a cutting board, reserving the broth. Discard the lemon halves. Cut the chinks into bite-size pieces and return them to the broth, along with the sautéed onions, peppers, and tomatoes and the yuca, sweet potatoes, plantains, and cabbage. Bring to a boil again, then reduce the heat to a simmer and cook for another 30 to 40 minutes, or until the vegetables are cooked through and tender. Discard the stringy fiber from the middle of the yuca.

Stir in the chopped cilantro and season with salt and pepper. Top with sliced avocado for added creaminess. If you like a little kick, add some cayenne or hot sauce.

YIELD: 12 to 15 servings

fun fact
Mondongo is, in some Latin countries, also called *Menudo*. No, no, not the Puerto Rican boy band but rather a spicy version of Mondongo!

TIMBAL DE QINUA AND PISTO
(QUINOA AND STEWED VEGETABLE TOWERS)

*Soy Free (use soy-free vegan cheese), **Low Fat (decrease or omit the cheese)

This dish gets its name from its cylindrical shape because a *timbal*, in Spanish, is the name for a particular kind of drum. This is a delicious and healthy meal, and great fun to make as well. For professional-looking results, use a culinary stacking ring.

1 tablespoon (15 ml) olive oil

1 tablespoon (15 ml) water

1 medium-size white or yellow onion, minced

3 or 4 cloves garlic, minced

1 medium-size green bell pepper, finely chopped

1 cup (180 g) finely diced tomatoes

1 medium-size eggplant, finely chopped

1 medium-size zucchini, finely chopped

1 teaspoon dried oregano

½ cup (8 g) chopped cilantro

1 teaspoon ground cumin

1 tablespoon (15 ml) lemon juice

1 cup (173 g) quinoa

2 cups (470 ml) vegetable broth, store-bought or homemade (page 16)

Salt and pepper, to taste

Shredded vegan mozzarella cheese (optional)

In a large saucepan over medium heat, heat the olive oil, then add the water, onions, garlic, bell pepper, tomatoes, eggplant, zucchini, oregano, cilantro, cumin, and lemon juice. Sauté for 10 to 12 minutes, or until the vegetables are tender and "stewy." Set aside.

Bring the quinoa and broth to a boil in a pot, reduce the heat to medium-low, and simmer until all the liquid has been absorbed, about 15 minutes. Season with salt and pepper. Remove from the heat and fluff with a fork.

Place a stacking ring in the center of a plate. The ring should be 2 to 3 inches (5 to 7.5 cm) high and 3 inches (7.5 cm) in diameter. You can also use a can that has both lids removed to make an open-ended cylinder, the squatter the can, the better. Add the first layer of stewed vegetables, filing up the ring about ½ inch (1.3 cm). Then tightly pack about 2 inches (5 cm) of quinoa on top of the veggie layer. Top off with a layer of veggies, lightly sprinkle the vegan cheese on top, and remove the ring carefully, slowly up-ward. Serve hot or warm.

YIELD: 4 to 6 servings

Fun fact

If you haven't heard, quinoa is a magical food. While it is referred to as a grain, it is in fact a seed, which would explain why it is so high in protein and eight essential amino acids, so much so that it rivals the protein found in animal products and is considered a complete protein. In addition, it is rich in calcium, iron, vitamin E, and many B vitamins.

COOK'S NOTE

Get creative with your timbal! If you've got a craving for some crunch, add some chopped or slivered almonds as a layer. Or if you're looking for some protein, add a layer of meat or chicken substitute or tofu. It's also nice to top with a pinwheel of sliced avocado.

RISOTTO DE QINUA, CHAMPIÑONES, Y PIMENTOS AMARILLAS
(QUINOA RISOTTO WITH MUSHROOMS AND YELLOW PEPPERS)

*Soy Free (use soy-free vegan cheese), **Low Fat (decrease or omit the cheese)

Sure, risotto is a traditionally Italian dish. However, many Italians have made South America their home and used the indigenous grain of choice to create this delicious adaptation. It's so creamy and hearty, you'll forget it's good for you.

4 cups (940 ml) vegetable broth, store-bought or homemade (page 16)

2 tablespoons (30 ml) olive oil, divided

1 large shallot, finely chopped

2 cloves garlic, minced

1 (12-ounce, or 340-g) box quinoa

¾ cup (180 ml) white wine

12 ounces (340 g) shiitake or white mushrooms, diced

12 ounces (340 g) trumpet or porcini mushrooms, diced

Salt and pepper, to taste

1 large yellow bell pepper, finely diced

½ tablespoon dried tarragon

2 tablespoons (28 g) vegan butter

½ cup (60 g) shredded vegan mozzarella cheese, plus extra for serving

Toasted pine nuts, for serving

In a medium-size pot, warm the broth over low heat until simmering. The broth should continue bubbling slowly while you prepare the dish.

In another medium-size pot, heat 1 tablespoon (15 ml) of the olive oil over medium heat until shimmering. Add the shallot and garlic and sauté until soft and translucent, stirring often to prevent browning, about 2 to 3 minutes. Add the quinoa and cook until the grains are coated in oil and fragrant, about 3 minutes. Pour in the wine and cook, stirring occasionally, until absorbed.

Ladle ½ cup (120 ml) hot broth into the quinoa and simmer until the liquid is absorbed, about 3 minutes. Continue the process, adding ½ cup (120 ml) broth at a time, until the quinoa is fully cooked and all the broth has been absorbed, about 25 minutes.

While the quinoa is cooking, heat ½ tablespoon (8 ml) of the oil in a small sauté pan until nearly smoking and sauté the diced mushrooms until browned, 1 to 2 minutes. Season to taste with salt and pepper, transfer to a bowl, and set aside.

Stir the cooked mushrooms, bell pepper, tarragon, butter, and cheese into the risotto. Spoon into serving bowls and top with the toasted pine nuts. Sprinkle with a little more cheese and enjoy!

YIELD: 4 to 6 servings

Fun Fact

Quinoa was known as "the mother grain" to the Incas. It served to keep them healthy and strong as well as drunk. What? Yep, not only did they eat quinoa regularly, but they also fermented it to make a type of beer. Additionally, they used it to make detergent and an antiseptic. Told ya quinoa was magic!

GLUTEN FREE* · SOY FREE** · KOSHER

Colombia

YACH AND MARIELLA'S AWESOME AREPAS
(GRILLED CORNMEAL CAKES WITH CHEESE)

*Gluten Free (use gluten-free vegan cheese), **Soy Free (use soy-free vegan cheese)

You'll find these disks of warm deliciousness on many breakfast tables throughout Colombia. While Venezuela has its variations, this traditional Colombian version is my absolute favorite in the morning with some butter and a café con leche. I named these after my mother and her cousin, who perfected these and couldn't get enough of them once they went vegan!

1 cup (120 g) masarepa flour
(or use masa harina if you can't find it)

Salt, to taste

1 cup (235 ml) warm water

2 tablespoons (28 g) vegan butter, plus extra for serving

½ cup (60 g) shredded vegan mozzarella
or Monterey Jack cheese

In a bowl, mix the flour and salt. Add the warm water little by little, kneading as you add, until you've used all the water and the ingredients are well incorporated. Add the butter and mix well until there are no lumps. When the dough has gotten to a firm, moist, and somewhat weighty consistency, add the cheese and mix well into a uniform mass.

Divide the dough into small to medium-size balls, about golf ball size. Flatten the ball between your palms into a flat disk about ¼ to ½ inch (6 mm to 1.3 cm) thick and 5 inches (12.5 cm) wide and set aside on a plate. Repeat with the remaining dough. If you prefer, you may also place the dough between two pieces of plastic wrap and flatten with your hands.

Preheat the griddle or a skillet over medium heat and grill the arepas, with no oil, until they are golden on both sides. Serve warm with vegan butter along with a cup of hot chocolate or coffee at breakfast. These are also great in a bread basket to go with dinner.

YIELD: 5 to 10 arepas

Fun Fact

Corn was introduced to Christopher Columbus by residents of the Americas. South Americans used their grain in a variety of dishes, many of which the explorer was excited to bring back to Europe. The arepa came from the Northern Andes area of South America and variations can be found in Colombia as well as Venezuela.

COOK'S NOTE

Be sure to add the liquid (warm water or warm milk) gradually to the flour as you knead it. You may get the desired consistency before using all of the liquid, so it's best to add it slowly.

GLUTEN FREE* SOY FREE** KOSHER

BELLA'S EMPANADAS

*Gluten Free (use gluten-free vegan ground beef), **Soy Free (use soy-free vegan ground beef)

As a kid, I would grab these fresh out of the fryer as my grandmother, Bella, made them.

FOR DOUGH:

1½ cups (180 g) masarepa flour (precooked cornmeal)

½ tablespoon Sazón Goya, store-bought or homemade (page 17)

½ teaspoon salt

2 cups (470 ml) water

1 tablespoon (15 ml) vegetable oil

FOR FILLING:

2 cups (220 g) peeled and diced white potatoes

1 vegan chicken or vegetable bouillon cube

1 tablespoon (15 ml) olive oil

¼ cup (40 g) chopped white onion

1 cup (165 g) cooked rice

1 cup (180 g) chopped tomato

¼ cup (25 g) chopped scallion

1 clove garlic, chopped

2 tablespoons (2 g) chopped fresh cilantro

½ teaspoon ground cumin

½ teaspoon salt

¼ teaspoon black pepper

1 cup (225 g) vegan ground beef (optional)

Safflower oil, for frying (or preferred high-heat oil)

FOR AJI SAUCE:

2 small green bell peppers or 3 or 4 jalapeños, seeded and chopped, to taste

Salt, to taste

¼ cup (60 ml) white vinegar

⅓ cup (33 g) minced scallion

⅓ cup (55 g) minced white onion

½ cup (8 g) chopped fresh cilantro

¼ to ½ teaspoon lime juice

Lime wedges, for serving

To make the dough: Place the masarepa in a large bowl. Add the sazón and salt and stir to mix well. Add the water and oil and mix to form a dough. Pat the dough into a ball and knead for 2 minutes, or until smooth. Keep your hands moist so that the dough doesn't stick. Cover with plastic and set aside for 20 minutes.

Meanwhile, to make the filling: Cook the potatoes and bouillon in a pot with enough water to cover for 20 to 25 minutes, or until tender. Drain, mash, and set aside.

Heat the olive oil in a large skillet. Add the onion and cook over medium-low heat, stirring frequently, for 5 minutes. Add the rice, tomato, scallion, garlic, cilantro, cumin, salt, and black pepper. Cook for about 15 minutes, then add the ground beef. Cook, breaking up the meat with a spoon, for 10 to 15 minutes, or until the mixture is fairly dry. Add this to the mashed potatoes bowl and mix well.

To make the sauce: Marinate the peppers in a bowl with the salt and vinegar for 30 minutes, then add to a food processor along with remaining ingredients (except lime wedges) and pulse until slightly chunky. Adjust the seasonings to taste. Set aside for at least 30 minutes so that the flavors can marry.

Break off small portions of the dough, about 1½ tablespoons (23 g) for each one, and form each into a ball. Place the balls of dough between two pieces of plastic wrap and roll each out to form a 2½- to 3½-inch (6.4 to 9 cm) circle. Be careful not to make them too thin or they will not hold up and will explode in the fryer. Remove the top plastic and place 1 tablespoon (15 g) of the filling in the center of each. Using the plastic underneath, fold the dough over to enclose the filling, forming a half circle. Tightly seal the edges by crimping with a fork. Repeat with the remaining dough.

Fill a large pot halfway with oil (or use a deep fryer) and heat over medium heat to 360°F (182°C). Carefully place 3 or 4 empanadas at a time in the heated oil and fry for about 2 minutes, or until golden on all sides. Using a slotted spoon, transfer the empanadas to a plate lined with paper towels. Serve with the sauce and lime wedges on the side.

YIELD: About 18 empanadas

◀ CHANGUA DE CARITO
(MILK, EGG, AND CILANTRO STEW)

*Gluten Free (use gluten-free toast), **Soy Free (use alternative rice/nut milk and seitan)

This is a fabulous hot breakfast alternative. I begged my grandmother for this daily!

1 tablespoon (15 ml) sesame oil

1 package (14 ounces, or 395 g) extra-firm tofu, pressed, drained, and cubed

2 cups (470 ml) water

2 cups (470 ml) plain soymilk

Salt and pepper, to taste

6 to 8 teaspoons (2 to 3 g) chopped fresh cilantro

2 scallions, chopped

4 slices toasted bread, cut into small squares

Heat the sesame oil in a skillet over medium heat and sauté the cubed tofu for 5 to 8 minutes, or until golden brown. Set aside.

Place the water and milk in a saucepan, season with salt and pepper, and bring to a boil. Add the tofu, reduce the heat to medium, and simmer for 1 to 2 minutes.

Divide the cilantro and scallions among 4 serving bowls, then ladle the soup into the bowls. Place the squares of toast on top and serve hot.

YIELD: 4 servings

PAN DE BONO PAISA
(CHEESE-FILLED BREAD ROLLS)

*Gluten Free (use gluten-free vegan cheese), **Soy Free (use soy-free vegan cheese), ***Low Fat (reduce the amount of cheese)

Warm, cheesy, and fluffy, these rolls are perfect any time of the day!

1 cup (120 g) yellow masarepa (precooked cornmeal)

½ cup (60 g) tapioca (cassava, yuca) flour

2 teaspoons sugar

2 cups (230 g) shredded vegan mozzarella or Monterey Jack cheese

2 egg replacers, mixed, store-bought or homemade (page 13)

Salt, to taste

Preheat the oven to 400°F (200°C, or gas mark 6). Grease a baking sheet.

Mix the first three ingredients in a bowl. Stir in the cheese and egg replacer. Mix well and add salt to taste.

Knead the dough until smooth. If the dough seems too dry, sprinkle with a little water. Shape dough into balls that are slightly larger than golf balls. Place on the prepared baking sheet and bake for about 20 minutes, or until golden in color and puffed.

YIELD: 15 small rolls

GLUTEN FREE* SOY FREE** KOSHER

Colombia

PATACON PISAO
(SMASHED PLANTAINS)

*Gluten Free (use gluten-free vegan cheese), **Soy Free (use soy-free vegan cheese)

Colombians love this dish so much, they wrote a song about it! It's a funny name, a funny song, and lots of fun to eat! Crispy, crunchy, sweet, and zesty, this dish just might make you sing, too!

½ cup (125 g) dried red beans

1 bay leaf

¼ cup (60 ml) olive oil

1 large white onion, diced

4 cloves garlic, chopped

1½ tablespoons (10 g) ground cumin

4 tablespoons (12 g) dried oregano

¼ cup (65 g) tomato paste

1 tablespoon (15 ml) lemon juice

4 green plantains, blanched until they turn brown-black, then cooled and peeled

About ¼ cup (60 ml) safflower oil (or high-heat oil of choice)

1 cup (115 g) shredded vegan mozzarella or Monterey Jack cheese

Fresh cilantro, for garnish

Lemon wedges, for garnish

Place the beans and bay leaf in a pot with enough water to cover. Bring to a boil, reduce the heat to a simmer, cook until tender, about 1 hour, and then drain.

Heat the olive oil in a skillet and sauté the onion and garlic until translucent, 3 to 5 minutes. Add the cumin and oregano and cook for 2 minutes longer, then add the tomato paste, lemon juice, and cooked beans. Transfer to a food processor and purée. (Be careful when blending hot food. Do it in batches so as not to overflow and hold a towel over the lid.)

Slice the blanched plantains into 1- to 1½-inch (2.5 to 3.8 cm) slices. Heat the safflower oil in a skillet over high heat and fry the plantain slices until tender, about 5 minutes, being careful not to burn. Place between two sheets of plastic wrap and roll to ¼-inch (6 mm) thickness, using a rolling pin to create a round, flattened plantain. You may also use the heel of your hand to mash it down. Return to the pan and cook for 3 minutes on each side, or until the edges are crisp, being careful not to burn or overcook.

Place the plantains on a plate and spread some bean purée over each one. Sprinkle with a little cheese and serve with a sprig of cilantro on each plantain as well as wedges of lemon for a little zing. You may also serve the plantains over a bed of rice, spreading the purée and cheese over the top of the entire plate and serve as a side as opposed to appetizers.

YIELD: About 4 servings

COOK'S NOTE

The plantains on their own are a great base for appetizers. Skip the purée and top with guacamole, salsa, or vegan sour cream, or serve on their own with a squeeze of lime and a dash of salt.

fun fact

Patacon pisao means "stepped on" or "squashed" plantain in Spanish slang.

GLUTEN FREE*   SOY FREE**   LOW FAT   KOSHER

Colombia

CALDO DE SANCOCHO
(VEGETABLE AND CHICKEN SOUP)

*Gluten Free (use gluten-free vegan chicken), **Soy Free (use soy-free vegan chicken)

This hearty soup will feed a family for days. Move over beef stew, this is the Latin soup that eats like a meal! Packed with vegetables, this soup serves up plenty of vitamins, protein, and nutrients in just one steaming bowl!

FOR SEASONING STOCK:

½ medium-size green bell pepper, chopped

½ medium-size red bell pepper, chopped

½ medium-size onion, chopped

4 scallions, chopped

½ teaspoon ground cumin

2 cloves garlic, crushed

1 cup (235 ml) water

½ tablespoon Sazón Goya with azafran, store-bought or homemade (page 17)

FOR CALDO:

6 to 8 vegan chicken cutlets

3 ears fresh corn, each cut into 3 pieces

½ cup (120 g) seasoning stock

2 vegan chicken bouillon cubes

2 green plantains, peeled and cut into 2-inch (5 cm) pieces

Salt and pepper, to taste

3 quarts (2.8 L) water

6 medium-size white potatoes, peeled and cut in half

2 cups (220 g) chopped yuca

¼ cup (4 g) chopped fresh cilantro

FOR SERVING:

Avocado slices, for serving (optional)

White rice, for serving (optional)

Aji Sauce (page 58), for serving (optional)

To make the stock: Place all the ingredients in a food processor or blender and process to make a paste. Store in the refrigerator until ready to use.

To make the caldo: In a large pot, place the chicken, corn, stock, bouillon, and green plantain. Season with salt. Add the water and bring to a boil, then cover and reduce the heat to medium and cook for 30 to 35 minutes.

Add the potatoes and yuca, season with pepper, and continue cooking for 30 more minutes, or until the yuca and potatoes are tender. Discard the stringy fiber from the middle of the yuca. Stir in the cilantro and adjust the seasoning with salt and pepper. Serve in large soup bowls, dividing the chicken and vegetables evenly. Serve with avocado slices on top, and white rice.

YIELD: 8 to 10 servings

fun fact

Sancocho is very much one of the national dishes of Colombia. The broth and veggies are the same; however, depending on where you are in the country, the meat may vary. However it is made, it's basically a lunchtime soup as well as a soup for special occasions.

MARIQUITAS CON MOJO
(PLANTAIN CRISPS WITH GARLIC SAUCE)

**This is the Latin version of potato chips . . . you can't eat just one!
I love drowning these in mojo sauce and chomping away.**

FOR MOJO DRESSING:

1 to 2 heads garlic (yep, heads, not cloves,
depending on how garlicky you can handle it)

1 teaspoon salt

1 teaspoon whole black peppercorns

1 cup (235 ml) orange juice

½ cup (120 ml) lemon juice

½ cup (120 ml) lime juice

1 cup (160 g) minced onion

2 teaspoons dried oregano

1 cup (235 ml) Spanish or other olive oil

FOR PLANTAINS:

2 large green plantains, peeled

Safflower or coconut oil (or preferred high-heat oil)

To make the dressing: Mash the garlic, salt, and peppercorns, using a mortar and pestle, or use food processor on pulse mode so as not to purée. Add the juices, onion, and oregano. Allow to sit for at least 30 minutes at room temperature so that the flavors marry.

In a saucepan, heat the olive oil over medium heat and then remove from the stove. Whisk the oil into the garlic/juice mixture until well blended. This will make a good size batch that will last for at least a week, covered and refrigerated.

To make the plantains: Cut the plantains into thin slices, the thinner the better. You can also slice the plantains diagonally for a larger chip. Soak the chips in ice water for 20 to 30 minutes. Drain the chips and dry them with paper towels.

Pour ¼ inch (6 mm) of the oil into a deep fryer or a frying pan and heat to 350°F (180°C). Fry the chips in small batches, being careful not to crowd the pan or fryer, until crisp and golden, about 5 minutes. Drain on paper towel–lined plates and keep warm in a low oven until it's time to serve. Serve with a small bowl of the dressing for dipping or pour on top of the pile.

YIELD: 2 to 4 servings

COOK'S NOTE

For some, the garlic can be a bit much, so if you're sensitive, start with 1 head of garlic and build up to your perfect taste. Garlic is very detoxifying, can help reduce blood cholesterol levels, and is also a natural antimicrobial.

fun fact

Sometimes these are called *chicharritas*.

PICADILLO AUTENTICO
(AUTHENTIC TOMATOEY GROUND BEEF)

*Gluten Free (use a gluten-free vegan meat), **Soy Free (use a soy-free vegan meat)

Move over, Hamburger Helper—this Cuban meatless dish is sure to spice up your meal! It's so good on its own, with rice, or served as a Cuban Sloppy Joe. You'll love the combination of flavors and textures so much that you won't even notice that it's good for you!

2 to 3 tablespoons (30 to 45 ml) olive oil

2 large onions, diced

1 green bell pepper, diced

1 red bell pepper, diced

3 cloves garlic, minced

1½ teaspoons Sazón Goya, store-bought or homemade (page 17)

4 cups (800 g) vegan ground beef (original, not flavored for tacos or anything else)

1 cup (235 ml) white wine

2 tablespoons (32 g) tomato paste

1 can (15 ounces, or 420 g) diced tomatoes

1 tablespoon (15 ml) apple cider vinegar

1 cup (100 g) chopped green olives

1 cup (145 g) raisins

1 tablespoon (8.6 g) capers

2 bay leaves

1 tablespoon (7 g) ground cumin

1 tablespoon (7 g) paprika

1 tablespoon (3 g) dried oregano

1 teaspoon dried thyme

1 teaspoon sugar

½ teaspoon ground cinnamon

Salt and pepper, to taste

Cooked rice, for serving

Chopped fresh cilantro, for garnish

Heat the olive oil in a large skillet over medium heat. Add the onions, bell peppers, garlic, and sazón seasoning and sauté until soft and tender, 5 to 6 minutes. Add the ground beef and mix well. Add the wine and simmer until it has all been absorbed, 1 to 2 minutes, then add the tomato paste and stir to blend. Add the tomatoes, vinegar, olives, raisins, capers, bay leaves, cumin, paprika, oregano, thyme, sugar, and cinnamon. Cover and simmer over medium-low heat for about 20 minutes. Remove the cover and continue to simmer for another 5 minutes, or until the picadillo begins to thicken. Season with salt and pepper to taste.

Serve over rice and top with chopped cilantro for garnish.

YIELD: 4 to 6 servings

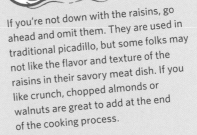

COOK'S NOTE

If you're not down with the raisins, go ahead and omit them. They are used in traditional picadillo, but some folks may not like the flavor and texture of the raisins in their savory meat dish. If you like crunch, chopped almonds or walnuts are great to add at the end of the cooking process.

BETTER THAN THE CLASSIC CUBAN SANDWICH

*Gluten Free (use gluten-free rolls, vegan cheese, and meat), **Soy Free (use soy-free vegan cheese, vegan butter, and meat), ***Low Fat (decrease the amount of ham and cheese)

This sandwich is, hands down, one of my favorite Latin dishes. There's nothing like that hot crusty bread filled with tangy mustard, pickles, and savory pork. This is the closest you'll get to a guilt-free version!

FOR VEGAN ROAST PORK:

2 cans (17 ounces, or 476 g each) "young" or "green" jackfruit, packed in water, not syrup, rinsed well and drained

2 cups (470 ml) water

Juice of ½ lime

Juice of 1 large orange

Juice of ½ lemon

1 teaspoon dried oregano

1½ teaspoons dried thyme

13 cloves garlic, minced, divided

12 black peppercorns

Salt, to taste

2 tablespoons (30 ml) olive oil

1 medium-size white or yellow onion, sliced

Juice of 1 lime

FOR SANDWICH:

1 fresh 16-inch (40.6 cm) loaf Cuban or French bread, cut in half or quarters

½ cup (112 g) vegan butter, softened

Yellow or Dijon mustard

4 to 8 slices dill pickle

2 to 4 thin slices vegan ham

2 to 4 thin slices vegan Swiss cheese or Monterrey Jack

To make the vegan pork: Shred the jackfruit and set aside. In a saucepan over medium heat, combine the water, lime juice, orange juice, lemon juice, oregano, thyme, 10 cloves of the garlic, and peppercorns. Bring to a boil, add the jackfruit, lower the heat to medium-low, and simmer, tightly covered, for about 1 hour, or until almost falling-apart tender. Add salt to taste, then let the meat cool in the broth for at least 3 hours, or overnight in the refrigerator. After refrigeration, remove the meat from the broth.

In a large skillet, heat the olive oil over medium heat, add the shredded meat and sauté until almost crispy, about 5 minutes. Add the onion and remaining 3 cloves garlic and cook another 10 minutes, or until they begin to brown slightly. Add the lime juice and stir to combine thoroughly.

To make the sandwich: Slice the bread horizontally so both halves are still barely connected. Spread the butter on the inside of both halves, spread the mustard on the bottom half; lay 1 or 2 pickles down on top of the mustard. Add 1 or 2 slices of ham, and then spread on some of the roasted pork. Add 1 or 2 slices of cheese, then butter the outsides of the bread with some more softened butter.

Place the sandwich in a sandwich press and press down until the cheese is melted and the bread is slightly hard to the touch. For those of you without a press, you can also place the sandwich in a hot skillet or griddle and press down on it with a sandwich press iron, pot, or pan. The heavier the "pressing" utensil, the better, because you want to get the sandwich down to about one-third of its original size. Grill the sandwich for 2 to 3 minutes, then flip and toast on the other side (those without a press). When the cheese is melted and the bread is golden, the sandwich is done.

When finished, slice the sandwich diagonally across the middle so you have triangle-shaped wedges. Serve hot.

YIELD: 2 or 4 sandwiches

CROQUETTAS DE JAMON
(FRIED HAM ROLLS)

Filled with mashed potatoes and ham, then fried, these are a hit at any party! They're so full of flavor, you'll think you're eating the real thing!

5 cups (1,175 ml) water

2 cloves garlic, minced, divided

1 tablespoon (18 g) salt, plus more to taste

3 large russet potatoes, peeled and cubed

1 tablespoon (14 g) vegan butter

3 tablespoons (30 g) finely chopped onion, divided

2 cups (300 g) shredded vegan ham

2 egg replacers, mixed, store-bought or homemade (page 13)

Lime juice, to taste

2 tablespoons (2 g) minced fresh cilantro

1 cup (115 g) cracker meal (you can make your own by crushing your favorite crackers in a heavy plastic bag with a rolling pin) or bread crumbs

Safflower oil, for frying (or preferred high-heat oil)

Lemon wedges, for serving

In a deep pot, combine the water, 1 minced garlic clove, and the salt. Add the cubed potatoes. Bring to a boil over medium-high heat and cook until fork-tender, 5 to 6 minutes, then drain.

In a small skillet, melt the butter over medium heat. Add 2 tablespoons (20 g) of the chopped onion and the 1 remaining garlic clove. Cook until light golden brown, 2 to 3 minutes.

In a large bowl, mash the potatoes and add the shredded ham. Then add the melted butter and garlic mixture, salt to taste, egg replacers, lime juice to taste, and cilantro and mix well. Refrigerate for about 1 hour.

Sprinkle some of the cracker meal on a cutting board or work surface. Take a generous 1 tablespoon (14 g) of the potato/ham mixture in your hand and form into a ball. Then squeeze and elongate until you have formed a fat little tube, about 2 inches (5 cm) long.

Or if you prefer, you can leave them as small balls. Roll the tube or ball in the cracker meal and repeat with the rest of the mixture.

In a deep skillet or deep fryer, pour in about ½ inch (1.3 cm) safflower oil and heat to 350°F (180°C). Deep-fry the croquettes, turning them to get all sides cooked and golden brown. Remove with a slotted spoon and drain on a paper towel–lined plate. Serve with lemon wedges for extra zing.

YIELD: About 25 croquettas

COOK'S NOTE

If you're serving croquettas as appetizers, you may want to make a batch of Mojo Dressing (page 66) for dipping. Or if you want to add a little kick, serve with hot sauce or Aji Sauce (page 58). Some folks even like dipping these in ketchup!

Fun Fact

Croquettas are hugely popular appetizers on Cuban menus and at parties. However, the croquette is a French invention that spread all over the world. Virtually every country has its own version of the croquette.

NO ES VACA FRITA
(FRIED BEEF AND ONIONS)

*Gluten Free (use jackfruit [see page XX])

In Spanish, *vaca frita* means "fried cow." Talk about straightforward! However, I can assure you that no animals are harmed or used anywhere in this dish (or the entire book, for that matter)! This plant-based version is even better than the original. It's crispy, oniony, garlicky, and all-around delish!

FOR SEITAN FLANK STEAK:

1½ cups (112 g) vital wheat gluten

¼ cup (32 g) nutritional yeast

1 teaspoon garlic powder

2 teaspoons salt

2 teaspoons paprika

1 teaspoon ground cumin

1 teaspoon onion powder

1 teaspoon black pepper

¾ cup (180 ml) cold water

2 tablespoons (30 ml) olive oil

2 tablespoons (30 ml) vegan Worcestershire sauce, store-bought or homemade (page 18)

FOR VACA FRITA:

1 green bell pepper, cored and quartered

2 large onions, thinly sliced, divided

2 bay leaves

2 cloves garlic

Salt and pepper, to taste

6 tablespoons (90 ml) fresh lime juice

3 tablespoons (30 ml) olive oil

FOR SERVING:

Cooked rice, beans, and lime wedges, for serving

To make the seitan steak: Preheat the oven to 325°F (170°C, or gas mark 3). In a large mixing bowl, combine the gluten, yeast, garlic, salt, paprika, cumin, onion powder, and pepper. In a smaller bowl, whisk together the water, oil, and Worcestershire until fully incorporated. Add the liquid ingredients to the dry ingredients, mixing well and kneading for several minutes. Form the dough into a loaf 6 to 8 inches (15.2 to 20.3 cm) long land wrap tightly in foil. Bake for 90 minutes. Let cool completely. Slice to use as desired and wrap to refrigerate the rest.

To make the vaca frita: In a large saucepan, combine the seitan flank steak with the bell pepper, 1 sliced onion, and the bay leaves. Add enough water to cover and bring to a boil. Reduce the heat to medium and simmer for 20 minutes. Transfer the flank steak to a work surface and let the steak cool. Strain the broth and reserve, tightly covered in the refrigerator, for another use. Slice the meat into thin strips and transfer to a bowl.

Using the flat side of a large knife, smash the garlic between the knife and a hard surface, and add ½ teaspoon of salt to make a paste. Stir the garlic/salt paste into the meat, along with the lime juice, olive oil, and remaining sliced onion. Let stand at room temperature for at least 30 minutes or up to 1½ hours.

Heat a large, flat griddle or skillet until very hot. Working in batches, spread the sliced meat mixture on the griddle in a thin layer and season with salt and pepper. Cook over high heat, turning once or twice, until sizzling and crispy in spots, about 6 minutes per batch. Serve with rice, beans, and some lime wedges, or serve on a bun with Mojo Dressing (page 66)!

YIELD: 4 to 6 servings

TANTALIZING TRILOGY: MOROS, PLATANOS, Y YUCA CON MOJO (BLACK BEANS AND RICE, SWEET PLANTAINS, AND GARLIC YUCA)

*Low Fat (skip the plantains)

To vegetarians and vegans, this is the holy trinity of Cuban food. You've got your proteins, grains, and veggies in one hearty and mega-tasty dish. I could live on this platter alone. So much garlicky goodness, I could never be a vampire!

FOR MOROS (BLACK BEANS AND RICE):

¼ cup (60 ml) olive oil

2½ cups (400 g) diced white onion

1 cup (180 g) diced tomatoes

1 cup (150 g) seeded and diced green bell pepper

4 cloves garlic, crushed and chopped

3 tablespoons (48 g) tomato paste

2 cups (312 g) black beans, rinsed and drained

1 teaspoon oregano

1 tablespoon (7 g) ground cumin

1 bay leaf

1 teaspoon dried thyme

3 tablespoons (45 ml) white or apple cider vinegar

4 cups (940 ml) vegetable broth, store-bought or homemade (page 16)

2 cups (370 g) brown rice, rinsed and drained

2 teaspoons salt

½ teaspoon pepper

To make the moros: In a large covered soup or stew pot, heat the oil over medium heat and sauté the onion, tomatoes, and green bell pepper until tender, 5 to 7 minutes. Add the garlic, and sauté for a minute or two longer. Then add the tomato paste, black beans, oregano, cumin, bay leaf, thyme, and vinegar. Cook for about 5 minutes, stirring gently. Add the broth and the rice. Bring to a boil, reduce the heat to low, cover, and cook for 20 to 30 minutes, or until the water has been absorbed and the rice is fully cooked. Remove the bay leaf and season with salt and pepper.

COOK'S NOTE

This essential trilogy of sides goes just as well with any of the meat dishes in this chapter as they do served on their own.

FOR PLATANOS MADUROS (PLANTAINS):

4 very ripe plantains (heavy black spotting to a fully black skin), peeled

½ cup (115 g) packed brown sugar

Coconut oil (or preferred high-heat oil)

FOR BOILED YUCA:

4 cups (440 g) peeled and chopped yuca (2 to 3-inch [5 to 7.5 cm] pieces)

Juice of 2 limes

Salt and pepper, to taste

8 cloves garlic, minced

½ cup (120 ml) olive oil

1 onion, finely chopped

⅓ cup (80 ml) lemon juice

Fun Fact

When the Spanish discovered Cuba, they landed with their African slaves. On the small island, Spanish and African cultures mixed to give us what we now know to be Cuban culture. The name for the rice and beans mixture called *moros* comes from "Moors and Christians," with black beans for the Moors and white rice for the Christians.

To make the plantains: Cut the plantains diagonally into 1-inch (2.5 cm)-thick slices. Lightly roll the plantains in the brown sugar. Heat the oil in a large, deep skillet to 350°F (180°C). Fry the plantains for 1 to 2 minutes per side. Reduce the heat to low and continue cooking, turning occasionally, until brown and caramelized, 1 to 3 minutes longer.

To make the yuca: Place the yuca in a large pot with water to cover by about 1 inch (2.5 cm). Add the lime juice and lightly salt the water. Bring to a boil over medium-high heat. Reduce the heat to medium, cover the pot, and simmer for 20 to 30 minutes, or until the yuca is tender but not falling apart. Remove from the heat and drain, discarding the stringy fiber from the middle of the yuca. Cover and set aside.

Mash the garlic cloves together with about 1 teaspoon salt. In a deep skillet, heat the olive oil over medium-high heat, then add the mashed garlic and salt mixture, chopped onion, and lemon juice. Stir until it starts simmering. Remove from the heat and pour over the cooked yuca. Stir to combine.

Divide the yuca, platains, and moros among 6 to 8 plates and serve.

YIELD: 6 to 8 servings

POSTRE DE TRES LECHES
(THREE MILKS CAKE)

*Gluten Free (use gluten-free cake flour)

This is the ultimate white cake: spongy white cake, sweet white glaze, and luscious white icing . . . looks and tastes like heaven!

FOR CAKE:

2 cups (240 g) sifted cake flour

1 teaspoon baking powder

½ teaspoon salt

½ cup (112 g) vegan butter, at room temperature

1 cup (200 g) sugar

5 egg replacers, mixed, store-bought or homemade (page 13)

1½ teaspoons vanilla extract

FOR GLAZE:

1½ cups (350 g) vegan evaporated milk, store-bought or homemade (page 15)

1¾ cups (411 ml) vegan condensed milk, store-bought or homemade (page 15)

1 cup (235 ml) vegan half-and-half or plain soy creamer

FOR ICING:

2 cups (470 ml) vegan heavy cream, store-bought or homemade (page 15)

1 cup (200 g) sugar

1 teaspoon vanilla extract

To make the cake: Preheat the oven to 350°F (180°C, or gas mark 4). Lightly oil and flour a 13 × 9-inch (33 × 23 cm) metal cake pan and set aside.

Whisk together the cake flour, baking powder, and salt in a medium-size bowl and set aside. Place the butter into the bowl of a mixer (or in a large bowl and use a hand mixer). Using the paddle attachment, beat on medium speed until fluffy, approximately 1 minute. Decrease the speed to low and with the mixer still running, gradually add the sugar for about 1 minute, scraping down the sides of the bowl, if necessary. Add the egg replacers, 1 at a time, and mix to thoroughly combine. Add the vanilla extract and mix to combine. Add the flour mixture in 3 batches and mix until incorporated. Transfer the batter to the prepared pan and spread evenly. (Just a heads-up: it won't look like a lot of batter.)

Bake on the middle rack of the oven for 20 to 25 minutes, or until the cake is a light golden color and a toothpick comes out clean when inserted into the middle of the cake.

Place on a cooling rack and let cool for 30 minutes. Poke the top of the cake all over with a fork. Allow the cake to cool completely and then prepare the glaze.

To make the glaze: Whisk together the evaporated milk, sweetened condensed milk, and half-and-half in a bowl or pitcher (an easily pourable container). Place the cooling rack with the cake on top of a piece of waxed paper for easy cleanup. Pour the glaze over the cake. Cover with plastic wrap or foil so the cake doesn't absorb any fridge odors and refrigerate overnight.

To make the icing: Place the heavy cream, sugar, and vanilla into the bowl of a mixer (or in a medium to large bowl and use a hand mixer). Using the whisk attachment, whisk on low until stiff peaks form. Change to medium speed and whisk until thick. Spread the topping over the cake and allow to chill in the refrigerator until ready to serve.

YIELD: 6 to 8 servings

Fun Fact

The three milks cake gained popularity due to sales promotions in the early 1900s. When canned milk made it to Latin America, it was promoted heavily as a way to preserve milk while saving money because canning kept it from spoiling. So with all of this condensed and evaporated milk on hand, the tres leches cake spread through Latin America like wildfire.

MUSHROOM AND ONION PUPUSAS
(STUFFED CORN TORTILLAS)

*Gluten Free (use gluten-free vegan cheese), **Soy Free (use soy-free vegan cheese), ***Low Fat (limit the amount of cheese)

Depending on where in Central America you find them, pupusas are made with a variety of fillings. Oozing with melty cheese and savory mushrooms, they're like fat little quesadillas!

5 cups (600 g) masa harina flour

4 cups (940 ml) water

2 tablespoons (30 ml) olive oil

1 cup (70 g) finely chopped cremini mushrooms

¼ teaspoon garlic powder

Salt and pepper, to taste

½ cup (50 g) finely chopped scallion

2 cups (490 g) canned vegan refried beans

3 cups (345 g) shredded vegan mozzarella or Monterey Jack cheese

Salsa, guacamole, vegan sour cream, and/or hot sauce, for serving

Place the masa harina in a large mixing bowl and gradually stir in the water until the dough forms a ball that can be handled. Set aside.

Heat the oil in a skillet over medium heat. Add the mushrooms, scallion, and garlic powder and sauté until the onion is soft, about 4 minutes. Season with salt and pepper. Remove from the heat and set aside.

Divide the dough into about 25 pieces. Roll each into a ball and flatten between the palms of your hands to form a 5 × ½-inch-thick (12.7 × 1.3 cm) disk. Then form the disk into a little bowl. Put a spoonful of beans, the mushroom mixture, and a small handful of cheese into the center of each bowl, being careful not to fill it more than halfway. Fold the sides in to form a sealed ball or dumpling and then flatten it between your hands, being careful not to squish out the filling, to form a 4- to 5-inch (10 to 12.7 cm) disk. If you make any tears, just pinch the dough closed and smooth it out.

Heat a heavy, wide-bottomed or flat skillet or griddle until hot, then turn the heat down to medium. Grill the pupusas, with no oil, on each side for 4 to 5 minutes, until a pale golden brown. The outside should be firm.

Serve with salsa, guacamole, vegan sour cream, and/or hot sauce.

YIELD: 25 pupusas

COOK'S NOTE

Mini pupusas are great as appetizers. Just make mini versions, don't overstuff with filling, and top with guacamole and sour cream. Tasty pupusa bites!

Fun Fact

Pupusas have been eaten in El Salvador for almost three thousand years.

TORTA AHOGADA
(SPICY BEEF SANDWICH)

*Soy Free (use the seitan option)

The "drowned sandwich" is a Mexican favorite. I think it's got just the right amount of kick, but feel free to go as spicy as you please. Move over, French dip, you've got competition.

FOR SAUCE:

1 can (10 ounces, or 280 g) chopped tomatoes with diced green chiles

2 cups (490 g) plain tomato sauce

¼ cup (4 g) chopped fresh cilantro

2 or 3 chipotle chiles in adobo, seeded and chopped

2 teaspoons adobo sauce from canned chipotles

Juice of 1 lime

Salt and pepper, to taste

1 cup (235 ml) vegan beef broth (make with vegan beef bouillon)

FOR MEAT:

2 tablespoons (30 ml) vegetable oil

1 large onion, thinly sliced

4 cloves garlic, minced

2 jalapeño chiles, seeded and minced (optional)

1 pound (454 g) plain seitan, store-bought or homemade (page 19), thinly sliced, or vegan roast beef slices, cut into strips

FOR SERVING:

1 medium-size to large avocado, pitted, peeled and smashed

4 crusty sandwich rolls, halved and lightly toasted

To make the sauce: In a large saucepan over medium heat, combine the chopped tomatoes, tomato sauce, cilantro, chipotles, adobo sauce, and lime juice. Add salt and pepper to taste. Simmer for 2 to 3 minutes, stirring, then reduce the heat to medium-low and continue to cook gently for 15 minutes, stirring occasionally. Remove the sauce from the heat and add the broth. Pour the sauce into a blender and purée until smooth (it should be thin). Be very careful when blending hot liquid. Doing it in batches and covering the lid with a towel while keeping your hand on it, pressing it down, is the best way to keep it from spilling out. If you have a stick blender, this is a great time to use it. Keep warm until ready to serve.

To make the meat: Place a large skillet over medium heat and add the oil. When the oil is hot, add the onion. Cook and stir until the onion begins to soften, 2 to 3 minutes, then add the garlic and jalapeños and stir to combine. Cook and stir for 2 to 3 minutes longer, or until the onions are well browned and the garlic and jalapeños have softened. Add the seitan and mix until heated through and well combined, about 2 minutes. Add ¾ cup (185 g) of the tomato sauce, tossing to coat the seitan completely.

Spread the smashed avocado on both sides of each roll. Pile the seitan on the bottom halves of the sandwich buns, close, and cut each sandwich in half. Arrange each sandwich on a plate. Ladle the sauce into 4 bowls for dipping. Make sure the bowls are large enough so the sauce doesn't spill out when the sandwich is dipped. Dip and eat!

YIELD: 4 sandwiches

Fun Fact

The torta was first introduced to Mexico in the city of Puebla, but it is in the region of Guadalajara, Jalisco, where the spicy version, the torta ahogada, came to be.

POTATO FLAUTAS (FRIED TACOS)

*Gluten Free (use gluten-free vegan cheese and corn tortillas)

Crunchy and stuffed with cheese and potatoes, these are hard to resist!

FOR GUACAMOLE:

2 ripe medium-size avocados

1 large tomato, finely diced

¼ cup (4 g) chopped fresh cilantro

2 or 3 scallions, white and green parts, chopped

Juice of 1 lime

Salt and pepper, to taste

1 teaspoon minced garlic

1 jalapeño chile, diced (optional)

FOR FLAUTAS:

1½ tablespoons (23 ml) olive oil, divided

½ cup (80 g) diced yellow onion

1½ cups (225 g) diced red bell pepper, divided

1 serrano chile, finely diced (seeds removed, if desired)

2 tablespoons (20 g) minced garlic

1½ cups (195 g) corn

3 large russet potatoes, peeled, cubed, and boiled

½ cup (115 g) vegan sour cream

¾ cup (173 g) vegan cream cheese, at room temperature

¾ cup (86 g) shredded vegan cheese (cheddar, mozzarella, or both), plus extra for garnish

1 teaspoon ground cumin

Salt and pepper, to taste

1 cup (100 g) sliced scallion, divided

1 can (28 ounces, or 784 g) tomatillos, drained and roughly chopped

2 cups (470 ml) safflower oil (or preferred high-heat oil)

8 (8-inch, or 20.3 cm) flour tortillas

1 can (12 ounces, or 340 g) black beans, rinsed and drained

1 medium-size to large avocado, halved, pitted, and mashed

⅓ cup (5 g) chopped fresh cilantro, for garnish

To make the guacamole: Combine all the ingredients in a bowl by mixing and mashing with a fork. Season to taste.

To make the flautas: In a large skillet over medium-high heat, heat 1 tablespoon (15 ml) of olive oil and sauté the yellow onion, half of the bell peppers, and the serrano pepper for about 3 minutes. Add the garlic and sauté for about 1 minute more. Turn off heat, add the corn, and set aside.

In a medium-size bowl, mash the potatoes with a fork or masher, then fold in the sour cream, cream cheese, cheese, cumin, salt and pepper. Stir in one-third of the sliced scallions and add to the corn/pepper mixture. Season, to taste, with salt and pepper. Keep warm.

In a small pan, over medium heat, add the remaining ½ tablespoon (8 ml) olive oil. Add the remaining half of the red bell peppers and sauté briefly. Stir in one-third more of the scallions, and then the tomatillos. Simmer for 5 to 6 minutes, then purée the sauce in a blender and keep warm.

Preheat the oven to 250°F (120°C, or gas mark ½) and put a cooling rack on a baking sheet. Heat the safflower oil to 350°F (180°C) in a large deep skillet. Be sure to have the tortillas, beans, potato mixture, sliced avocado, and toothpicks ready to go. You will also want to have a plate lined with paper towels for draining.

Put a tortilla on a flat, dry work surface. Lay about 3 tablespoons (45 g) of the black beans along one side. Top with about ⅓ cup (75 g) of the potato mixture and some avocado. Don't overstuff or your flauta will fall apart. Roll tightly, burrito style, and seal length-wise with a toothpick. Set aside and repeat with the remaining ingredients.

When all are assembled, check the oil temperature and gently add them to the pan, maximum 4 at a time. Turn frequently and be careful not to burn because they cook and brown quickly, about a minute or so per side. Drain on the paper towel–lined plate, then keep warm in the oven on the cooling rack.

Put ¼ cup (61 g) of the tomatillo sauce on a plate, then lay flautas on top. Serve with extra cheese, cilantro, remaining scallions, and guacamole.

YIELD: 8 servings

ENTICING SPINACH AND MUSHROOM ENCHILADAS

*Gluten Free (use gluten-free vegan cheese), **Soy Free (use soy-free yogurt and vegan cheese), ***Low Fat (limit the cheese), ****Low Glycemic (limit your portions)

You may be more used to the ranchero sauce version of this dish. Just as delicious, these veggie enchiladas boast a tangy tomatillo sauce that you are sure to love. No restaurant comes close to homemade enchiladas!

2 cloves garlic

½ jalapeño pepper (seeds removed, if desired)

5 medium-size tomatillos, husks removed

Juice of 1½ limes, divided

½ cup (8 g) chopped fresh cilantro

1½ tablespoons (23 ml) olive oil, divided

1 cup (235 ml) vegetable broth, store-bought or homemade (page 16)

1½ tablespoons (23 g) plain vegan yogurt

Salt and pepper, to taste

¾ cup (53 g) thinly sliced button mushrooms

½ red onion, thinly sliced

1 clove garlic, minced

¾ cup (23 g) spinach

1½ teaspoons ground cumin

1 tablespoon (15 g) minced chipotle in adobo (optional)

6 corn tortillas

½ cup (60 g) shredded vegan cheese (cheddar or mozzarella or both)

Cooked rice, beans, guacamole, salsa, and vegan sour cream, for serving

In a blender, combine the whole garlic, jalapeño, tomatillos, juice of ½ lime, and cilantro and blend until smooth. Heat half of the oil over medium-high heat in a small saucepan. Add the blended tomatillo sauce and cook for about 10 minutes, stirring frequently. Add the vegetable broth, reduce the heat to medium, and cook for 10 minutes longer. Add a spoonful of the sauce to the yogurt, and then stir this mixture back into the sauce and season with salt and pepper.

Heat the remaining half of the oil in a large skillet over medium-high heat. Add the mushrooms and cook until they start to turn brown, 3 to 4 minutes, stirring frequently. Add the onion and minced garlic and cook for 3 to 4 minutes longer. Stir in the spinach and cook until it wilts. Add the cumin, chipotle, and remaining juice of 1 lime and mix well. Remove from the heat and season, to taste, with salt and pepper. Let cool slightly. Preheat the oven to 350°F (180°C, or gas mark 4).

Lightly oil the tortillas, lay them out on a baking sheet (it's okay to double them up if they are small or flimsy), and bake for about 3 minutes. Ladle half of the tomatillo sauce into the bottom of a casserole dish. Place about ¼ cup (60 g) of the filling on each tortilla and roll into a cylinder. Place, seam side down, in the dish. Repeat with the remaining tortillas and filling. Top with the remaining sauce. Cover the dish with foil and bake for about 20 minutes. Remove from the oven and top with the shredded cheese. Bake for 10 minutes longer to melt the cheese and make sure the enchiladas are heated through. Serve with rice, beans, guacamole, salsa, and vegan sour cream.

YIELD: 3 or 6 servings

COOK'S NOTE

Feel free to add tofu, tempeh, or meat substitute of choice to give some texture and weight to your enchiladas. Using taco seasoning to prepare your meat can add a little kick as well.

CARAMEL FLAN (CUSTARD)

Think of this as a Latin cheesecake of sorts—a custardy, caramely, crust-free, Latin cheesecake. If you're looking to satisfy a sweet tooth, flan may just be your best friend.

FOR GLAZE:

½ cup (115 g) packed light brown sugar

Pinch of ground cinnamon, ginger, or nutmeg

¼ cup (60 ml) water

FOR CUSTARD:

2 cups (470 ml) plain soy creamer

2 teaspoons agar powder or flakes

½ cup (100 g) silken tofu, pressed and drained

½ cup (115 g) vegan cream cheese

¼ cup (50 g) sugar

1 tablespoon (15 ml) vanilla extract

Pinch of salt

To make the glaze: Place the brown sugar, cinnamon, and water in a small pot over medium heat. Stir until the sugar is dissolved and bring to a rapid boil. Lower the heat and simmer until thickened and coats the back of a spoon. Pour into the bottom of an 8-inch (20.3 cm) cake pan.

To make the custard: While the glaze is cooking, place the creamer in a medium-size pot and stir in the agar. Bring to a boil, and then reduce the heat to low and simmer for about 5 minutes, or until the agar has dissolved, stirring often. If using flakes, it may take a bit longer, so be patient.

Put the tofu, cream cheese, sugar, vanilla, salt, and soy creamer/agar mixture in a blender and blend until very smooth. Be mindful of blending hot liquid because it can spill out and burn you if you overfill the blender. Place a kitchen towel over the lid and press down with your hand to keep it secure. A stick blender is good for this if you have one.

Pour the mixture into the cake pan, on top of the syrup, cover with plastic wrap, and refrigerate for at least 1½ hours. To unmold, slide a knife around the perimeter of the cake pan and lightly shake it from side to side. If the flan doesn't loosen, dip the bottom of the cake pan in hot water for about 15 seconds. When the flan feels loose, turn over onto a plate so the glaze at the bottom of the pan is now the top of the cake.

YIELD: 6 to 8 servings

Fun Fact

Flan dates back to the Roman Empire, where it began as a savory, not a sweet, dish. Traditionally a cream and egg custard, it evolved into a sweet dessert in Spain and took on its Latin name for "flat cake," *flado*, and then *flan*.

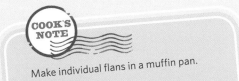

COOK'S NOTE

Make individual flans in a muffin pan.

LAND LOVER'S CEVICHE
(SEAFOOD COCKTAIL)

*Raw (let the mushrooms sit in the salt water for a few hours; do not boil)

Ceviche is traditionally made with raw fish that is cooked by the citrus juice, but this version of the Peruvian favorite might just become one of yours. This former seaside appetizer is full of crunch, creaminess, citrus, and zest, a great way to start a meal or even snack on.

1 quart (946 ml) lightly salted water

½ cup plus 2 tablespoons (150 ml) freshly squeezed lime juice, divided

1 cup (70 g) finely chopped oyster or portobello mushrooms

1 cup (300 g) finely chopped hearts of palm (do your best to find those not canned in salt water)

½ medium red onion, finely chopped

⅓ cup (5 g) chopped fresh cilantro, plus several sprigs for garnish

1 clove garlic, minced

2 tablespoons (30 ml) olive oil

½ cup (60 g) peeled and finely diced cucumber

½ cup (65 g) finely diced jicama

2 Roma tomatoes, finely diced

1 small avocado, peeled, pitted, and cubed

Salt and pepper, to taste

Several lime slices, for garnish

Crackers or tortilla chips, for serving

In a medium-size pot over medium-high heat, bring the salted water to a boil and add 2 tablespoons (30 ml) of the lime juice. Add the mushrooms and hearts of palm, cover, and return to a boil. Immediately remove from the heat and drain. Cover with the lid and set aside, letting the mushrooms and hearts of palm steam in the closed pot for 10 minutes.

Drain the mushrooms and hearts of palm again to remove any remaining liquid and transfer to a large bowl to cool completely. Toss with the remaining ½ cup (120 ml) lime juice, cover, and refrigerate for about 1 hour.

In a small strainer, rinse the chopped onion under cold water, then shake off the excess liquid. Add to the mushrooms along with the cilantro, garlic, olive oil, cucumber, jicama, tomatoes, and avocado. Mix gently and season with salt and pepper. Cover and refrigerate for up to 3 hours. Spoon the ceviche into martini glasses or small bowls. Garnish with sprigs of cilantro and slices of lime. Serve with crackers or tortilla chips.

YIELD: 8 servings

fun fact

In the original dish, the acid in the limes actually "cooks" the raw seafood. In this one, it just makes it taste awesome!

PAPA RELLENA
(FRIED POTATO AND GROUND BEEF BALLS)

*Gluten Free (use gluten-free vegan ground beef or tempeh and gluten-free bread crumbs),
**Soy Free (use soy-free vegan ground beef or chickpeas)

With crispy potatoes and savory ground beef, these are like Tater Tots on steroids! Just sayin'.

3 pounds (1,362 g) yellow potatoes, peeled

Salt and pepper, to taste

2 tablespoons (30 ml) olive oil

½ cup (80 g) chopped onion

2 cloves garlic, minced

1 tablespoon (9 g) minced aji or jalapeño pepper (optional)

1 teaspoon ground cumin

½ teaspoon paprika

2 cups (400 g) taco-flavored vegan ground beef or Picadillo Autentico (page 67)

1 cup (235 ml) vegan beef broth (made from vegan beef bouillon)

1 egg replacer, mixed, store-bought or homemade (page 13)

3 recipes vegan egg wash (page 13)

1 cup (115 g) bread crumbs, cornmeal, or cracker meal

Safflower oil, for frying (or preferred high-heat oil)

Lime wedges, for serving

Hot sauce or ketchup, for serving

Bring a large pot of lightly salted water to a boil and add the potatoes. Cook the potatoes until fork-tender, 5 to 6 minutes. Drain and mash the potatoes thoroughly, and season with salt and pepper to taste. Chill the potatoes for several hours or overnight.

In a saucepan, over medium heat, heat the olive oil and sauté the onion, garlic, and peppers until soft, 3 to 5 minutes. Add the cumin and paprika and cook, stirring, for about 2 minutes longer. Add the ground beef and cook until browned and cooked through, 3 to 5 minutes. Add the broth and simmer for 10 to 15 minutes, until most of the liquid has been absorbed. Season with salt and pepper and remove from the heat.

Once the potatoes are very cold, stir the egg replacer into the mashed potatoes until well combined.

Flour your hands and ball up about ¼ cup (55 g) of mashed potatoes in one hand. Make a well in the center of the ball. Fill the well with 1 to 2 tablespoons (15 to 30 g) of the beef mixture. Mold the potatoes around the beef, adding more potatoes if necessary, and shape the whole thing into a ball or an oblong, tubular shape, about the size of a medium potato. Repeat with the rest of the mashed potatoes and beef mixture.

Pour the egg wash into a bowl and spread the bread crumbs on a shallow plate. Dip each stuffed ball into the egg wash, then roll in the bread crumbs to coat evenly. In a deep skillet or deep fryer, heat 2 inches (5 cm) of safflower oil to 360°F (182°C). Fry the potato balls in batches until they are golden brown, turning to cook evenly, 2 to 3 minutes. Remove with a slotted spoon and drain on a paper towel–lined plate. Keep warm in a low oven until ready to serve. Serve with lime wedges and hot sauce or ketchup.

YIELD: 24 papas

Fun Fact

The potato seems to have its roots (no pun intended) in Peru. The earliest findings of potatoes date back to 400 BCE and were found at an archeological site in Chirpa by Lake Titicaca. You can stop giggling now . . .

GLUTEN FREE* SOY FREE** KOSHER

MOFONGO SIN TOCINO
(PLANTAIN AND BACON HASH)

*Gluten Free (use gluten-free vegan bacon), **Soy Free (use soy-free vegan bacon)

Sure, the name may be chuckle-inducing, but this Caribbean salty, sweet comfort food will be on your mind long after you've taken your last bite.

2 teaspoons salt, divided

4 cups (940 ml) water

3 green plantains, peeled and sliced into 1-inch (2.5 cm) pieces

Coconut oil, for frying (or preferred high-heat oil)

3 cloves garlic

1 tablespoon (15 ml) olive oil

1 cup (80 g) fried, minced tempeh bacon or vegan ham slices

2 cups (470 ml) hot vegetable broth, store-bought or homemade (page 16)

Chopped fresh cilantro, for garnish

Lime wedges, for garnish

Combine 1 teaspoon of the salt and water in a bowl, add the plantain slices, and soak for about 15 minutes, then drain. Pat dry with paper towels. Heat the coconut oil in a deep frying pan or deep fryer to 350°F (180°C), then add the plantain slices and fry for 15 minutes, but do not brown. Drain on a paper towel–lined plate.

Crush the garlic with a mortar and pestle, sprinkle with the remaining 1 teaspoon salt, add the olive oil, and keep pounding to blend and smash.

Crush the fried plantain slices and the bacon. Add the garlic/olive oil mixture and keep pounding. Shape the mixture into eight 2-inch (5 cm) balls. Place the balls in a serving bowl and pour the hot vegetable broth over. Garnish with the chopped cilantro and lime wedges. This is nice with avocado slices, too.

YIELD: 4 servings

COOK'S NOTE

If you're looking for a decadent appetizer, try making these a bit smaller and without the broth, frying them in a good high heat oil, and topping them off with a dollop of the Polenta Bites Crema from page 50!

fun fact

Before making it to the Caribbean, this African dish was called *fufu*.

BESITOS DE COCO
(COCONUT COOKIES)

*Gluten Free (use gluten-free flour), **Soy Free (use soy-free vegan butter)

I can't get enough of these chewy, "coconut kisses" when they're fresh out of the oven and covered in chocolate!

3 cups (255 g) coconut flakes

½ cup (60 g) all-purpose flour

4 vegan egg yolks, store-bought or homemade (page 13)

1 cup (225 g) packed brown sugar

¼ teaspoon salt

½ cup (112 g) vegan butter

2 tablespoons (30 ml) vanilla extract

½ cup (88 g) vegan chocolate chips

Preheat the oven to 350°F (180°C, or gas mark 4) and grease two 13 × 9-inch (33 × 23 cm) cookie sheets.

In a large bowl, thoroughly mix the coconut, flour, egg yolks, brown sugar, salt, butter, and vanilla together into a dough. Divide the dough into 24 uniform balls, place on the greased cookie sheets, and bake for about 35 minutes, or until golden. Remove from the oven and let cool.

Melt the chocolate chips in a double boiler and drizzle on top of the cookies.

YIELD: 24 cookies

COOK'S NOTE

For a little added crunch, feel free to add finely chopped walnuts or pecans to the cookie batter. And for an added sweet treat, drizzle some vegan caramel on top as well!

Fun Fact

Coconut is rich in protein and antimicrobial, which can help soothe sore throats and ulcers, and it prevents goiters!

Chapter 4

CARIBBEAN ISLAND NATIONS

MMMM, THE CARIBBEAN! Crystal-clear water, sandy beaches, palm trees, and fabulous food. Who would skip out on the food of the tropics? It's hard not to feel like you're on a relaxing vacation when enjoying a traditional Caribbean meal.

Although the cuisine of the islands makes use of its local resources, many of its popular dishes are the compilation of all the cultures that have passed through the islands for centuries. The native peoples grew cassava and sweet potatoes and grilled over open fires called *barbacoa*, giving the food a distinctive flavor that was only found in the tropics. The Spanish and Europeans introduced the island cooks to coffee, sugar cane, and new fruits. Rice came by way of Japanese and Chinese workers, who were brought to work on plantations. However, one of the largest influences came with the arrival of African slaves, who brought their own traditional foods and techniques.

Tropical fruit and citrus, global spices, and grilling over open fires make for some divine creations, and fun is a major ingredient. Enjoy it, mon!

GLUTEN FREE*   SOY FREE**   KOSHER

Bahamas

CRISPY CONCH FRITTERS WITH CILANTRO TARTAR SAUCE

*Gluten Free (use gluten-free flour), **Soy Free (use alternative rice/nut milk and soy-free vegan mayonnaise)

These are a sure hit as party appetizers, especially at a Caribbean-themed fete. With just the right crispiness with just the right fluffiness, these fritters will have you thinking you're sitting oceanside in Nassau!

FOR CILANTRO TARTAR SAUCE:

1 cup (225 g) vegan mayonnaise

1 tablespoon (1 g) chopped fresh cilantro

2 tablespoons (30 ml) lime juice

1 tablespoon (10 g) minced garlic

2 tablespoons (20 g) chopped red onion

1 tablespoon (11 g) Dijon mustard

1 tablespoon (15 ml) vodka (optional)

Capers, to taste

Cayenne, to taste

Salt and pepper, to taste

FOR FRITTERS:

2 cups (140 g) chopped oyster mushrooms

½ cup (120 ml) seaweed stock, store-bought or homemade (page 16)

2 medium-size limes

1½ cups (180 g) all-purpose flour

1½ tablespoons (23 g) baking powder

¼ teaspoon salt

⅛ teaspoon cayenne

3 vegan egg yolks, store-bought or homemade (page 13)

½ cup (120 ml) soymilk

½ cup (80 g) minced yellow onion

3 vegan egg whites, store-bought or homemade (page 13)

High-heat oil, for frying

Creole or Cajun seasoning, to taste

Lime wedges, for serving

To make the tartar sauce: Combine all of the ingredients in a blender or food processor and blend for 15 seconds. Keep refrigerated until ready to serve.

To make the fritters: Place the chopped mushrooms in a glass bowl with the seaweed stock and squeeze the limes over them. Allow to sit for 10 minutes, then drain and set aside.

Combine the flour, baking powder, salt, and cayenne in a bowl and whisk to combine. In a separate bowl, whisk together the egg yolks, milk, mushrooms, and onion. Add the dry ingredients to the wet ingredients and stir until just combined. In a third bowl, whip the egg whites until stiff peaks form. Gently fold the egg whites into the mushroom mixture.

Fill a deep fryer with oil or fill a deep saucepan halfway with oil and heat to 330°F (166°C). Drop the batter by tablespoonfuls into the hot oil and cook, stirring occasionally, until golden brown and floating on the surface of the oil, about 4 minutes. Transfer to paper towel–lined plates to drain briefly before serving. Sprinkle lightly with the Creole seasoning and serve with the tartar sauce and lime wedges.

YIELD: 2 servings as a meal, 6 as an appetizer

Fun Fact

Conch was a favorite of the Arawak and Caribe native tribes well before Columbus passed through. It's still a preferred islander shellfish, especially in the Bahamas. Lucky for the queen conch, we can get the same texture from a fungus!

ISLANDER PINEAPPLE UPSIDE-DOWN CAKE

*Gluten Free (use gluten-free flour), **Soy Free (use soy-free vegan butter and alternative rice/nut milk)

Turn that frown upside down with this fruity sweet! Ooey, gooey, warm, and fun to make, you may even be able to get away with serving this cake for breakfast—it's got fruit, right?!

FOR TOPPING:

¼ cup (56 g) vegan butter

½ cup (112 g) packed brown sugar

1 small pineapple, sliced into thin rings, or 1 can (19 ounces, or 532 g) pineapple slices

6 cherries, cut in half

FOR CAKE:

1 cup (120 g) cake flour

1 teaspoons baking powder

¼ teaspoon salt

¼ cup (56 g) vegan butter, softened

½ cup (100 g) sugar

3 egg replacers, mixed, store-bought or homemade (page 13)

1 teaspoon vanilla extract

½ cup (120 ml) soymilk

To make the topping: Gently melt the butter in an ovenproof skillet (9-inch [23 cm] is perfect and cast iron works great) over medium heat. Add the brown sugar and stir to combine. Cook just until a caramel-type sauce begins to form, 2 to 3 minutes. (If you don't have an appropriate skillet, you can melt the butter and brown sugar together in a small saucepan and pour the caramel mixture into a medium-size round or square baking dish.) Remove the skillet from the heat and arrange the pineapple slices over the butter/sugar mixture in a single layer. Place a cherry in the center hole of each pineapple slice, round side down. Set aside.

To make the cake: Preheat the oven to 350°F (180°C, or gas mark 4).

In a bowl, combine the flour, baking powder, and salt with a wire whisk. Cream the butter and sugar until light and fluffy. Beat in the egg replacers, one at a time. Add the vanilla and beat again. Slowly add the flour mixture, alternating with the milk, and beat until smooth. Pour the cake mixture over the pineapple topping in the skillet.

Bake for 30 to 35 minutes, until golden brown and a toothpick inserted into the center comes out clean. Remove from the oven and let cool for 5 minutes on a rack. Run a knife or spatula around the outside edges to loosen and invert the cake onto a serving plate.

YIELD: 6 to 8 servings

Fun Fact

While the practice of putting fruit at the bottom of the baking pan dates back to medieval times, the pineapple upside-down cake became a sensation after the Hawaii-based Dole Food Company ran a recipe contest in 1925 and it won! Besides, canned pineapple didn't become available until 1903.

GLUTEN FREE* SOY FREE** LOW FAT LOW GLYCEMIC KOSHER

Jamaica

JERK UN-CHICKEN

*Gluten Free (use gluten-free vegan chicken), **Soy Free (use soy-free vegan chicken)

Who you callin' jerk? Nobody, but you'll jerk in your chair after a bite of this spicy dish. Consider yourself warned. This is some fiery hot chicken!

FOR JERK SEASONING:

1 red onion, chopped

1½ teaspoons dried thyme

1 teaspoon ground allspice

½ teaspoon ground cinnamon

4 teaspoons white pepper

¼ cup (25 g) chopped scallion tops

2 teaspoons salt

¼ teaspoon ground nutmeg

5 small jalapeño peppers, or to taste

2 tablespoons (30 ml) olive oil

Splash of rum

FOR CHICKEN:

6 vegan chicken cutlets

1 lime, halved

Pinch of salt

4 to 5 tablespoons (24 to 30 g) jerk seasoning

8 to 12 pimiento or allspice leaves

To make the seasoning: Put all the seasoning ingredients into a food processor and pulse 15 times.

To make the chicken: Rub the chicken cutlets with the lime and salt, then rub the seasoning mix over them. Marinate in the refrigerator for 8 hours up to overnight (this yields the best results).

Preheat a grill or grill pan to medium-high heat. Spread the pimiento leaves on the grill and grill over medium-low heat for about 1 minute. Add the chicken and grill for about 10 minutes, turning often to optimize cooking and browning. Let the chicken sit for 10 minutes before serving.

YIELD: 6 servings

Fun Fact

This food is no insult to you, mon! It is the evolution of the Spanish word *charqui*, which means to dry meat, like jerky. This method of cooking, or rather smoking, the meat was a way to preserve it and keep pesky insects away.

COOK'S NOTE

In lieu of grilling, you may bake the chicken in a 375°F (190°C, or gas mark 5) oven until heated through and browned, omitting pimiento leaves, about 20 minutes.

MEATY JAMAICAN PATTIES

*Gluten Free (use gluten-free flour and vegan ground beef or textured vegetable protein [TVP]),
**Soy Free (use soy-free butter, shortening, and vegan ground beef or TVP)

**Many Caribbean countries have versions of patties, so these meat-filled pastries have
all the zing of the tropics. These are fabulous with an ice-cold beer and hot sauce.**

FOR PASTRY DOUGH:

4 cups (480 g) all-purpose flour, plus more for rolling

2 teaspoons ground turmeric or annatto

2 teaspoons salt

½ cup (112 g) vegan shortening, cold

½ cup (112 g) vegan butter, cold

½ cup plus 2 tablespoons (150 ml) cold water,
more as needed

FOR MEAT FILLING:

2 tablespoons (28 g) vegan butter

1 large onion, finely chopped

6 cloves garlic, minced

1 tablespoon (6 g) minced ginger

2 cups (450 g) vegan ground beef

¼ teaspoon ground turmeric or annatto

¾ teaspoon ground cumin

¾ teaspoon ground allspice

½ teaspoon ground cardamom

1 Scotch Bonnet or jalapeño pepper, seeded and minced

2 sprigs thyme, minced

3 scallions, minced

1 tablespoon (4 g) minced fresh parsley

2 cups (360 g) peeled and minced ripe tomatoes

¾ cup (180 ml) vegan beef broth
(make with vegan beef bouillon)

Salt and pepper, to taste

3 tablespoons (45 ml) rum

FOR PATTIES:

2 vegan egg yolks, store-bought or homemade (page 13),
beaten with 1 teaspoon rum

To make the pastry dough: Sift the flour, turmeric, and salt into a large bowl. Add the shortening and butter and crumble with your fingers until the mixture looks and feels like coarse crumbs. Working quickly, add just enough water to form a firm dough, being mindful not to overwork the pastry. Form the dough into a disk, wrap in plastic, and refrigerate for at least 1½ hours or overnight.

To make the filling: In a large skillet, heat the butter over medium-high heat. Add the onion and cook until tender, about 4 minutes. Add the garlic and ginger and cook for 1 minute. Add the ground beef, turmeric, cumin, allspice, cardamom, hot pepper, and thyme and cook until the beef is browned and the spices are fragrant, about 10 minutes. Add the scallions, parsley, tomatoes, and broth and simmer for about 25 minutes, until the flavors have come together and almost all of the liquid has been absorbed. Season to taste with salt and pepper, remove from the heat, and stir in the rum. Set aside to cool before assembling the patties.

Preheat the oven to 400°F (200°C, or gas mark 6). Line 2 baking sheets with parchment paper.

On a lightly floured surface, roll out the pastry to a ¼-inch (6 mm) thickness and cut out circles about 6 to 7 inches (15.2 to 17.8 cm) in diameter. Gather up the scraps, reroll the dough, and continue cutting out circles. You should get about 16 circles. Spoon about ¼ cup (60 g) of the cooled filling onto the center of one side of each circle, and lightly brush the edges of the circle with a little of the beaten egg yolk mixture. Fold the other half of the pastry over so that the edges meet, and use a fork to crimp the edges together. Lightly brush the top of each patty with a little of the beaten egg. Place the patties on the prepared baking sheets and bake until golden brown, about 25 minutes. Serve immediately.

YIELD: 16 patties

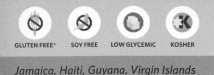

CARIBBEAN CALLALOO
(SPINACH, VEGETABLE AND MEAT BISQUE)

*Gluten Free (omit the seitan)

This African-influenced soup is sure to hit the spot! While callaloo is quite popular on the islands, spinach is a perfect substitute on the mainland. Warming the body as well as the soul, it's delicious and good for you!

2 cups (60 g) callaloo or spinach leaves

2½ cups (588 ml) vegan chicken broth (make with vegan chicken bouillon)

2½ cups (588 ml) vegan beef broth (make with vegan beef bouillon)

1 cup (235 ml) seaweed stock, store-bought or homemade (page 16)

1 onion, chopped

8 ounces (225 g) seitan, store-bought or homemade (page 19), sliced

½ teaspoon black pepper

6 tablespoons (60 g) minced shallot

¼ teaspoon dried thyme

1 green chile pepper, coarsely chopped

1 cup (70 g) chopped oyster mushrooms

1 cup (80 g) sliced okra

Remove the thick stems of the callaloo leaves, roughly chop, and put into a large saucepan. Add all the broths, onion, seitan, black pepper, shallot, thyme, chile pepper, and mushrooms. Cover and simmer until the seitan and mushrooms are tender, about 35 minutes. Add the okra, and cook for 8 minutes.

Carefully remove the chile pepper, then purée the soup in a blender or food processor. Be mindful when blending hot liquids. You should do it in small batches and hold the lid down tightly with a kitchen towel to keep from spilling and burning. Reheat, and adjust the seasonings to taste.

YIELD: 4 to 6 servings

COOK'S NOTE

If you've got a hankering for a chunky soup, skip the step that calls to blend the soup. It's "irie" either way!

fun fact

The Caribbean version of gumbo that has its roots in Africa.

Chapter 5

UNITED KINGDOM

ENGLAND MAY GET A BAD RAP for its cuisine, but I'm here to say that it's quite a bit of fun! Sure, it may seem that traditional English fare is nothing but bready, eggy, sausagey, silly-named stuff, but that has changed a lot in the modern era due to East Indian and American influences. It has also brought about some favorites, such as tea-time, traditional breakfasts, modern curry, and the three-course meal! Either way, the United Kingdom is deep-seated in world history, as is its cuisine.

Much of its classic food was born from its agricultural roots, its geography, and its close proximity to other European nations, from which came a plethora of spices, techniques, and traditions. Being close to the sea, it was hard not to find many cold Atlantic seafood dishes prominent in the coastal regions. With rolling hills and generous farmland, it was virtually a no-brainer to cultivate livestock, mainly sheep, that kept Brits warm in the unforgiving winters. However, one of the largest influences on British food was the country's occupation of India and what they brought back to England and "Britainized." The most popular is what they did for curry. British cooks created shortcuts for what took Indians all day to prepare, whipping up an Indian meal in a fraction of the time.

Britain also learned a lot from its other colonies, such as the tea traditions in China, and contributed ketchup, Worcestershire sauce, scones, puddings, and yes, even the sandwich, to world cuisines.

The two world wars were a detriment to British cuisine due to lack of supplies and energy turned toward the war effort, but in the 1980s, British cooking seemed to return to the scene. Nowadays, UKers have become increasingly aware of organic farming and vegetarianism, so it has become an "island"-wide movement in addition to the increase in the popularity of foodies and chic cuisine. Well mate, let's get to it! Spit spot!

NO TOAD IN THE HOLE ►

*Gluten Free (use gluten-free flour and vegan sausage)

Nope, no toads or frogs anywhere near this dish. Not even in the original version!

½ cup (60 g) all-purpose flour

½ teaspoon salt

¼ cup (50 g) puréed silken tofu

1 cup plus 1 tablespoon (250 ml) soymilk

4 to 6 vegan sausages or 8 to 12 vegan breakfast sausages

Mushroom Gravy, for serving (page 35)

Preheat the oven to 400°F (200°C, or gas mark 6) and grease a 9 × 6-inch (23 × 15 cm) casserole or baking dish.

Place the flour, salt, tofu, and milk in a large mixing bowl and whisk until smooth and free and lumps. Place the sausages in the greased dish in a single layer, then pour the batter over. Bake in the oven for 40 to 45 minutes, or until well risen and golden, without opening the oven door. Serve immediately with the gravy.

YIELD: 4 to 6 servings

SCRUMPTIOUS SCONES

*Gluten Free (use gluten-free flour), **Soy Free (use soy-free vegan butter, shortening, and creamer)

As I always say, good scones can put a muffin to shame!

2 cups (240 g) all-purpose flour, plus more for rolling

4 teaspoons (18 g) baking powder

¾ teaspoon salt

⅓ cup (67 g) sugar

¼ cup (56 g) vegan butter

2 tablespoons (28 g) vegan shortening

¾ cup soy creamer

1 egg replacer, mixed, store-bought or homemade (page 13)

¼ to ½ cup (30 to 60 g) dried cranberries, blueberries, or strawberries

Preheat the oven to 375°F (190°C, or gas mark 5). Grease 2 baking sheets.

In a large bowl, combine the flour, baking powder, salt, and sugar, mixing well. Add the butter and shortening, and blend with your fingers until a coarse crumb forms. In a separate bowl, combine the creamer and egg replacer, then add to the flour mixture. Stir in the cranberries.

Turn the dough out onto a clean, floured surface. Roll out the dough to ½-inch (1.3 cm) thickness, and cut out rounds with a 2- to 3-inch (5 to 7.5 cm) biscuit cutter or glass. Gather up the scraps, reroll the dough, and continue cutting out rounds. You should get about 16 scones, depending on size. Place on the greased baking sheets, and bake for 15 minutes, or until golden brown.

YIELD: 16 scones

YUMMY YORKSHIRE PUDDING
(BEEF-FLAVORED BREAD ROLLS)

*Gluten Free (use gluten-free flour)

This bread, not pudding, is traditionally served with roast beef but here at the Healthy Voyager Kitchen, it goes great with soup, mashed potatoes and gravy, or even a delicious portobello steak!

¾ cup (90 g) self-rising flour (or use ¾ cup [90 g] all-purpose flour mixed with 1 teaspoon baking powder)

½ teaspoon salt

½ cup (100 g) silken tofu, blended with 1 teaspoon arrowroot or cornstarch

¾ cup (180 ml) soymilk

¼ cup (60 ml) vegan beef broth (make with vegan beef bouillon) blended with ¼ cup (56 g) vegan shortening

Preheat the oven to 450°F (230°C, or gas mark 8). Grease a 6-cup muffin pan (or use a nonstick one).

Sift the flour and salt together into a bowl. In another bowl, beat together the tofu and milk until light and foamy. Stir in the dry ingredients just until combined.

Pour the broth/shortening evenly into the cup of the muffin pan (about 1 teaspoon in each cup). Put the pan in the oven and get the broth hot. Carefully take the pan out of the oven and pour the batter into the wells, filling about one-third full. Put the pan back in the oven and cook until puffed and dry, 25 to 30 minutes.

YIELD: 6 puddings

fun fact

Originally Yorkshire puddings were square shaped, in the shape of the dish they were cooked in. They were cut into smaller portions and served as an appetizer. If food was scarce, it was served with gravy. And nope, there is no evidence that this meaty-flavored bread originated in Yorkshire. So if not there, then where?

SHEPHERD'S DAY OFF PIE

*Gluten Free (use gluten-free flour and vegan ground beef or [TVP])

Creamy mashed potatoes with veggies and vegan meat all in one heaping spoonful, this is like your meat and two veg all in one dish! This meatless concoction will put the shepherd out of business!

FOR POTATOES:

3 pounds (1,362 g) russet potatoes, peeled and diced into ½-inch (1.3 cm) cubes

½ cup (120 ml) soy creamer

½ cup (112 g) vegan butter

Salt and pepper, to taste

FOR FILLING:

2 tablespoons (30 ml) olive oil

1 cup (160 g) chopped onion

2 carrots, peeled and finely diced

2 cloves garlic, minced

1½ cups (338 g) vegan ground beef

Salt and pepper, to taste

2 tablespoons (15 g) all-purpose flour

2 teaspoons (32 g) tomato paste

1 cup (235 ml) vegan chicken broth (make with vegan chicken bouillon)

1 teaspoon vegan Worcestershire sauce, store-bought or homemade (page 18)

2 teaspoons chopped fresh rosemary

1 teaspoon chopped fresh thyme

½ cup (65 g) corn kernels

½ cup (65 g) peas

To make the potatoes: Place the potatoes in a medium-size saucepan and cover with cold water. Set over high heat, cover, and bring to a boil. Once boiling, uncover, decrease the heat to maintain a simmer, and cook until tender and easily crushed with a fork, 10 to 15 minutes.

Place the creamer and butter in a saucepan and warm over medium heat, about a minute or so. Drain the potatoes, then return to the saucepan. Mash the potatoes and then add the creamer and butter, and salt and pepper to taste, and continue to mash until smooth.

Preheat the oven to 400°F (200°C, or gas mark 6).

To make the filling: Pour the olive oil into a 12-inch (30.5 cm) sauté pan and set over medium-high heat. Once the oil shimmers, add the onion and carrots and sauté just until they begin to color, 3 to 4 minutes. Add the garlic and stir to combine. Add the ground beef, and salt and pepper to taste, and cook until browned and cooked through, approximately 3 minutes. Sprinkle the meat with the flour and toss to coat, continuing to cook for another minute. Add the tomato paste, broth, Worcestershire, rosemary, and thyme, and stir to combine. Bring to a boil, reduce the heat to low, cover, and simmer for 10 to 12 minutes, or until the sauce is thickened slightly. Add the corn and peas and stir to combine.

Spread the mixture evenly into a glass lasagna or baking dish. Top with the mashed potatoes, starting around the edges to create a seal to prevent the mixture from bubbling up, and smooth with a rubber spatula. Place on a parchment-lined half sheet pan on the middle rack of the oven and bake for 25 minutes, or just until the potatoes begin to brown. Remove from the oven and place on a cooling rack for at least 15 minutes before serving.

YIELD: 8 to 10 servings

fun fact

Yet another peasant dish made of leftovers—but a dang good one!

PUB-STYLE FISH AND CHIPS WITH TARTAR SAUCE

*Gluten Free (use gluten-free flour)

**As a child, a basket of fish and chips by the water was such a simple pleasure.
I am very excited to be able to rekindle that memory with this dish.**

FOR FISH:

1 package (14 ounces, or 392 g) extra-firm tofu, drained and pressed, or 1 pound (454 g) tempeh, cut into strips

1 bottle (12 ounces, or 355 ml) malt vinegar

2 sheets (6 inches, or 15 cm square) seaweed (kombu or nori works best)

1 cup (120 g) all-purpose flour

1 tablespoon (15 g) baking powder

½ teaspoon garlic powder

1 teaspoon paprika

Salt and pepper, to taste

1 cup (235 ml) full-bodied beer

Cornstarch, for dredging

6 cups (1,410 ml) safflower oil, for frying (or preferred high-heat oil)

FOR CHIPS:

3 large russet potatoes, peeled, cut into strips, blanched (about 4 minutes, until soft), and drained

Salt, for sprinkling

FOR VEGAN TARTAR SAUCE:

1 cup (225 g) vegan mayonnaise

¼ cup (60 g) pickle relish

2 tablespoons (30 ml) lemon juice

1 tablespoon (11 g) mustard

1 tablespoon (15 ml) vodka (optional)

Capers, to taste

Cayenne, to taste

Salt and pepper, to taste

To make fish: In a baking dish, marinate the tofu, submerging it entirely, in the vinegar and sandwiched between the 2 sheets of seaweed for 2 hours or overnight.

Combine the flour, baking powder, garlic, paprika, salt, and pepper in a large bowl and whisk together. Add the beer slowly and mix gently. Keep refrigerated until ready to use.

Remove the tofu from the marinade, drain and pat dry, then slice into ¼-inch (6 mm) strips. Spread the cornstarch on a shallow plate. Heat the oil in a large pot or deep fryer to 350°F (180°C). Dip the tofu slices into cornstarch, shaking off any excess, and then into the batter, coating them well. Place them in the hot oil, cooking in batches to avoid overcrowding and turning once to fry on all sides, and fry until golden brown, 2 to 3 minutes. Remove with tongs and drain on a paper towel–lined plate. Keep warm in a low oven until ready to serve.

To make the chips: Reheat the oil to 350°F (180°C). Add the potato strips in and fry until golden brown, 2 to 3 minutes. Remove with a slotted spoon and drain on a paper towel–lined plate. Sprinkle with salt. Keep warm in a low oven until ready to serve.

To make the tartar sauce: Combine all the ingredients in a bowl, mixing well. Keep refrigerated until ready to serve.

Divide the tofu between 2 plates, place half of the fries alongside. Serve with tartar for dipping.

YIELD: 2 servings

Fun Fact

This English fast food gained popularity among the seaside working class. It was brought to London by a Jewish restaurateur who began to fry the fish in the Jewish fashion along with chips, better known as French fries.

GLUTEN FREE*   KOSHER

WASTE NOT, WANT PLENTY BREAD PUDDING

*Gluten Free (use gluten-free bread)

Talk about an eco-friendly dessert! Don't toss out your old, stale bread. Sweeten it up and go to town with this warm and gooey confection!

FOR PUDDING:

2 cups (400 g) granulated sugar

¾ cup (150 g) silken tofu blended with 1½ teaspoons arrowroot powder

2 cups (470 ml) soymilk

2 teaspoons vanilla extract

3 cups (150 g) cubed crusty bread (French or Italian), allowed to stale overnight in a bowl

1 cup (225 g) packed light brown sugar

1 to 2 teaspoons ground cinnamon

¼ cup (56 g) vegan butter, softened

1 cup (145 g) raisins or chopped pecans (optional)

FOR SAUCE:

1 cup (200 g) sugar

½ cup (112 g) vegan butter, melted

¼ cup (50 g) puréed silken tofu

2 teaspoons vanilla extract

¼ cup (60 ml) brandy or rum

To make the pudding: Preheat the oven to 350°F (180°C, or gas mark 4) and grease a square baking pan.

Mix together the granulated sugar, tofu, and milk in a bowl; add the vanilla. Pour over the cubed bread and let sit for 10 minutes.

In another bowl, crumble together the brown sugar, cinnamon, butter, and raisins. Pour the bread mixture into the prepared pan. Sprinkle the brown sugar mixture over the top and bake for 35 to 45 minutes, or until springy and set. Remove from the oven and let cool.

To make the sauce: Mix together the sugar, butter, tofu, and vanilla in a saucepan over medium heat. Stir together until the sugar is melted. Add the brandy, stirring well. Pour the sauce over the bread pudding, cut into squares, and serve warm.

YIELD: 6 servings

fun fact

Wild guess? Yes, this was a poor folks' dessert. See how creative we can get, regardless of funds?

COOK'S NOTE

Step up the indulgence factor and top your pudding off with some vegan white chocolate shavings. Mmm!

SINFUL STICKY TOFFEE PUDDING

*Gluten Free (use gluten-free flour)

This dessert showcases dates so well you'll want them to sweeten everything you ever eat! This rich dessert will put a smile on anyone's face.

FOR PUDDING:

1 cup plus 1 tablespoon (128 g) all-purpose flour

1 teaspoon baking powder

¾ cup (134 g) finely chopped pitted dates

1¼ cups (295 ml) boiling water

1 teaspoon baking soda

¼ cup (56 g) vegan butter, softened

¾ cup (150 g) sugar

1 egg replacer, mixed, store-bought or homemade (page 13)

1 teaspoon vanilla extract

FOR TOFFEE SAUCE:

½ cup (112 g) vegan butter

½ cup (120 ml) vegan heavy cream, store-bought or homemade (page 15)

1 cup (225 g) packed light brown sugar

To make the pudding: Preheat the oven to 350°F (180°C, or gas mark 4). Grease a 10-inch (25 cm) soufflé dish or square baking dish.

Sift the flour and baking powder onto a sheet of waxed paper. Place the dates in a small bowl and add the boiling water and baking soda; stir and set aside.

In another bowl, beat the butter and sugar until light and fluffy. Add the egg replacer and vanilla; beat until blended. Gradually beat in the flour mixture. Fold in the date mixture until well blended. Pour into the greased baking dish and bake until the pudding is set and firm on top, about 35 minutes. Remove and place on a cooling rack.

To make the toffee sauce: Combine the butter, heavy cream, and brown sugar in a small saucepan; bring to a boil, stirring constantly. Boil gently over medium-low heat until the mixture is thickened, about 8 minutes.

Preheat the broiler. Spoon about ⅓ cup (80 ml) of the sauce over the pudding. Spread evenly on top. Place the pudding under the broiler until the topping is bubbly, about 1 minute. Serve immediately in dessert bowls and drizzle with the remaining toffee sauce. If you've got vegan whipped cream, top it off with a little!

YIELD: 8 to 10 servings

Fun Fact

Much like the stories behind Red Velvet Cake and Clams Casino in the USA chapter, the true origins of sticky toffee pudding seem to come from chefs who created this scrumptious dessert for a lavish hotel and its guests.

Chapter 6

SPAIN

SPAIN IS THE BIRTHPLACE of Latin culture. Influenced by many different cultures, Spanish food differs from region to region. As the third largest country in Europe, Spain has a landscape that ranges from mountainous to arid, seaside to countryside. This gives way to a wide variety of fantastic foods and local ingredients.

Spain's history includes conquests by the Phoenicians, Greeks, Moors, and Romans, and each people brought their own culinary styles to the nation; imports from the New World added other goodies to the mix. Spanish cuisine features quite a bit of garlic, saffron, and peppers, as well as tomatoes, zucchini, potato, sweet potato, vanilla, chocolate, and all sorts of beans (favas, chickpeas, and lentils are popular). Although these ingredients are fairly national, cuisine in Spain is quite regional.

Food in the Iberian Peninsula, for example, is much like that of the Middle East. Family cooking is very much central to Iberian cuisine, as is using a variety of fresh ingredients. There are a great many dishes featuring beans, rice, eggs, and vegetables, and savory pies, meat, poultry, game, and fish are standard main courses. Tapas, or small plates eaten throughout the day, are very popular in this region.

In the northwestern, known as Galicia, you'll find culinary roots that echo ancient Celtic heritage, with lots of meat and fish. In the Asturias, along the eastern coast, fabada is a popular bean dish. The Basque region is quite heavily into seafood. Valencia is a region where rice is creatively prepared on a daily basis. Paella is the region's most famous dish. Andalucia to the south is a parched and arid region, best suited to grape vines and olive trees. Gazpacho is native to this area.

The Spanish love their dining schedules, much more so than any other country. A typical day of dining involves a light breakfast at 8 a.m.; a mid-morning breakfast at 11 a.m.; tapas at 1 p.m.; a three-course lunch around 2 or 3 p.m.; a merienda for tea and pastries or a snack at 5 or 6 p.m.; evening tapas at 8 p.m. or later; and a three-course supper at 10 p.m. The two main meals of the day—*la comida*, or lunch, and *la cena*, or dinner—aren't skimpy despite the all-day snacking. With all that food, everyone takes a siesta, or nap, in the middle of the day. Schools and businesses all close for the folks of Spain to get their shut-eye. But that doesn't mean it's time for you to nap! Get cooking and *buen provecho* (eat well)!

ARROZ CON POLLO
(CHICKEN AND RICE)

*Gluten Free (use gluten-free vegan chicken and beer), **Soy Free (use soy-free vegan chicken)

This is quintessential Spanish comfort food. While each country does it differently, this is a dish that all Latin kids grow up with. I did, and I am happy to share this delicious one-pot meal with you!

FOR CHICKEN:

1 teaspoon dried oregano

1 teaspoon ground cumin

½ teaspoon freshly ground white pepper

1 tablespoon (15 ml) red wine vinegar

8 vegan chicken cutlets, cut into strips

2 tablespoons (30 ml) annatto oil or olive oil

FOR SOFRITO AND BROTH:

1 medium-size white onion, finely chopped

1 small red bell pepper, cored, seeded, and finely chopped

3 cloves garlic, minced

1 tomato, seeded and diced

3 cups (705 ml) vegetable broth, store-bought or homemade (page 16)

1 cup (235 ml) dry white wine

1½ cups (353 ml) light-colored beer

1 tablespoon (16 g) tomato paste

½ teaspoon ground cumin

Salt and black pepper, to taste

½ teaspoon annatto seeds or ¼ teaspoon saffron threads

2 cups (390 g) Valencia or Arborio rice (or preferred rice)

½ cup (8 g) chopped fresh cilantro

½ cup (50 g) sliced red pimientos

1¼ cups (225 g) green peas

To make the chicken: Mix the oregano, cumin, white pepper, and vinegar in a large bowl. Add the chicken, turning the pieces to cover with the mixture, and let marinate for at least 15 minutes. Heat the oil over medium heat in a large pan and brown the chicken pieces all over, about 2 minutes per side. Transfer the chicken to a platter and set aside.

To make the sofrito and broth: Add the onion, bell pepper, and garlic to the oil in the pan that cooked the chicken, and cook over medium heat until soft but do not brown, 1 or 2 minutes. Add the tomato and cook for 1 more minute. Return the chicken to the pan with the sofrito and cook for 1 or 2 more minutes. Add the broth, wine, beer, tomato paste, cumin, and salt and pepper to taste. Bring to a boil, reduce the heat, cover, and simmer for about 30 minutes.

While the chicken is cooking, place the annato seeds in a small saucepan with ¼ cup (60 ml) of the chicken/sofrito liquid. Simmer for about 5 minutes. Strain this mixture back into the chicken. Bring the chicken mixture to a boil, stir in the rice, reduce the heat, cover, and simmer until the rice is tender, 20 to 25 minutes. If it starts to dry out and the rice is still al dente, add more liquid. If it gets too soupy, uncover during the last 10–15 minutes of cooking. About 5 minutes before done, stir in half the cilantro, half the pimientos, and half the peas. Serve and garnish with the remaining halves.

YIELD: 6 to 8 servings

COOK'S NOTE

Be sure to make a lot, as the leftovers get even better with time. You might also want to try a portion for breakfast. Yum!

PLENTIFUL PAELLA

*Gluten Free (use gluten-free vegan chicken and sausage), **Soy Free (use soy-free vegan chicken and sausage)

Paella is normally quite costly to make and therefore reserved for special occasions. Lucky for you, this one is chock-full of herbs and veggies and texture, so you won't miss the seafood or your empty wallet! You may want to halve this recipe if you're just making this for a regular dinner because this yields quite a large amount. It's a hit for a potluck!

FOR SPICE RUB:

1 tablespoon (8 g) paprika

2 teaspoons dried oregano

Salt and pepper, to taste

FOR CHICKEN:

8 vegan chicken cutlets, cut into chunks, or 4 cups (800 g) sliced plain seitan, store-bought or homemade (page 19)

¼ cup (60 ml) olive oil

2 large vegan sausages, thickly sliced

Salt and pepper, to taste

1 large sweet onion, diced

4 cloves garlic, crushed

½ cup (30 g) chopped fresh parsley, plus some for garnish

1 can (15 ounces, or 420 g) whole tomatoes, drained and hand crushed

3 cups (570 g) short-grain rice

4½ cups (1,058 ml) warm vegan chicken broth or vegetable broth, store-bought or homemade (page 16)

1 red bell pepper, diced

1 green bell pepper, diced

2 teaspoons turmeric

Generous pinch of saffron threads

2 cups (140 g) chopped portobello mushrooms

2 cups (600 g) chopped artichoke hearts

½ cup (65 g) peas

Lemon wedges, for serving

To make the spice rub: Combine all the ingredients in a small bowl.

To make the chicken: Place the chicken in a baking dish, rub the spice mix all over, cover, and marinate for 1 hour in the refrigerator.

Heat the oil in a paella pan or large cast-iron skillet over medium-high heat. Sauté the sausage until browned, then remove from the pan and set aside. Add the chicken and brown on all sides, turning with tongs and seasoning with salt and pepper. Remove from the pan and set aside.

In the same pan, make a sofrito by sautéing the onion, garlic, and parsley for 2 or 3 minutes over medium heat. Add the tomatoes and cook until the mixture caramelizes a bit and the flavors marry well, 2 to 3 minutes. Fold in the rice and stir-fry to coat the grains. Pour in the broth and simmer for 10 minutes, gently moving the pan around so the rice cooks evenly and absorbs the liquid. Add the chicken, sausage, bell peppers, turmeric, and saffron and stir to combine. Add the mushrooms and artichokes, mixing them well into the rice. Cook until tender, 3 to 5 minutes. Shake the pot once or twice (be careful to not spill; you may want to cover it for this step) and let it simmer, without stirring, until the rice is al dente, about 15 minutes. When the paella is cooked and the rice looks fluffy and moist, turn up the heat and cook for 40 seconds, until you can smell the rice toasting on the bottom (called *socarrat*), but don't let it burn. Remove from the heat and let rest for 5 minutes. Garnish with the peas, parsley, and lemon wedges.

YIELD: 8 servings

fun fact

The name *Paella* from the Latin word patella, meaning pan.

TORTILLA DE PATATAS CON SALSA FRESCA (POTATO AND EGG FRITTATA WITH FRESH SALSA)

I call it tortilla. You call it frittata. Tortilla, frittata, let's call the whole thing brunch!

FOR OMELET BATTER:

2 packages (12 ounces, or 340 g each) silken tofu

¼ cup (60 ml) plain soymilk

¼ cup (32 g) nutritional yeast

¼ cup (32 g) potato starch or cornstarch

2 teaspoons soy sauce, tamari, or liquid aminos

¼ teaspoon lemon pepper seasoning

¼ teaspoon ground turmeric

Salt and pepper, to taste

FOR TORTILLA:

1 to 2 tablespoons (15 to 30 ml) olive oil

3 cloves garlic, peeled and lightly crushed

2 large potatoes, washed, peeled, and sliced

2 scallions, white and green parts, chopped, plus some for garnish

1 medium-size tomato, diced

Salt and pepper, to taste

FOR SALSA FRESCA:

4 medium-size tomatoes

½ cup (8 g) chopped fresh cilantro

2 or 3 scallions, white and green parts, chopped

Juice of 1 small to medium-size lime

Salt and pepper, to taste

1 small jalapeño pepper, diced (optional)

To make the omelet batter: Blend all the ingredients together until smooth.

To make the tortilla: In a large frying pan, heat the oil over medium heat. Add the garlic, crushing with a large wooden spoon or the side of a large knife. When the garlic is very lightly browned, remove and discard, leaving garlic-infused oil in the pan. Add the potatoes and cook, stirring frequently, until soft and thoroughly cooked, 5 to 7 minutes. Remove the potatoes from the pan and pour out the oil.

Coat the pan with olive oil spray. Add the cooked potatoes, scallions, tomato, and omelet batter to the pan and cook over medium heat for 10 to 15 minutes, or until fluffed up. Using a plate or wide spatula, flip the tortilla and cook on the other side, 2 to 4 minutes longer. When thoroughly cooked, flip again; both sides should be well browned. Remove from the pan by flipping onto a plate and season with salt and pepper. Garnish with scallions.

To make the salsa: Combine all the ingredients in a blender and pulse until chunky (do not purée). Make sure that any big chunks are gone but the mixture is not soupy. Season to taste.

Cut the tortilla into wedges and serve the salsa alongside.

YIELD: 6 to 8 servings

COOK'S NOTE

Adding tempeh, seitan, or other meat substitute, as well as mushrooms and other veggies, can really give this dish a whole slew of variations. Have fun with your Spanish omelet!

ARROZ CON LECHE
(RICE PUDDING)

*Low Fat (use low-fat soymilk)

Rice pudding—it's like dinner and dessert all in one. Just the right sweetness and just the right spice, it makes for a dessert that is very nice!

1 cup (190 g) long-grain rice

1½ cups (353 ml) water

1 or 2 cinnamon sticks

1 cup (235 ml) vegan condensed milk, store-bought or homemade (page 15)

1 cup (225 g) vegan evaporated milk, store-bought or homemade (page 15)

1 cup (235 ml) soymilk

½ cup (73 g) raisins

1 teaspoon lemon zest (optional)

Ground cinnamon

In a medium-size pot, combine the rice, water, and cinnamon sticks and cook, covered, over medium heat. When most of the water has been absorbed, add the condensed, evaporated, and regular milk and stir gently, being careful not to let burn or spill over. Do not let a "skin" form on top. Cook for about 20 minutes, or until the rice is tender. Remove the cinnamon sticks and stir in the raisins and lemon zest. Serve in small bowls, sprinkled with ground cinnamon on top.

YIELD: 6 to 8 servings

fun fact

Brought to Spain by Moorish travelers, this dessert was a great way to keep from wasting precious food while also extending the life of a batch of rice.

Chapter 7
FRANCE

I BET YOU'RE THINKING CREAMY, cheesy, and rich sauces right about now! Or Julia Child, perhaps? Either way, you'd be right! The most lavish and famed of all the food in the world, French cuisine and techniques have influenced multitudes of worldwide chefs and home cooks alike and is the pride and joy of France and its people.

In medieval times, French cuisine involved painstaking preparation and artful presentation, with thick and heavily seasoned sauces. The sauces became the foundation of French cooking and were often made in large quantities. Later on, the French developed the "brigade system" of cooking. Professional kitchens assigned cooks to one of five separate stations so they could focus on one item well, as opposed to one chef handling the whole meal (or feast!). This led to chefs' specializing in something particular, such as vegetables, pastry, and so on.

As with other European countries, regional cooking is quite diverse in France and certain regions are famous for their specialties. For example, impressive fruit preserves come from Lorraine, Normandy, boasts great cider due to its lush orchards, and I'm pretty sure you know what the main export is from Champagne!

Contrary to popular belief, the French love their vegetables. Creative salads have been perfected in France, including salade aveyronnaise and salade niçoise from the Côte d'Azur. The French also make good use of a variety of locally grown vegetables in their recipes. Carrots, potatoes, French green beans, leeks, eggplant, truffles, shallots, turnips, and many different kinds of mushrooms, such as porcini and oyster, are common selections. Additionally, they have a beautiful array of regional spices and herbs, including marjoram, lavender, fennel, sage, and tarragon, not to mention as the many desserts and pastries that are loved the world over: chocolate mousse, tarts, choux à la crème, crepes, croque en bouche, croissants, and petits fours. Yum!

On that note, enjoy your haute cuisine and *bon appetit*!

C'EST MAGNIFIQUE BUTTERY CROISSANTS

*Gluten Free (use gluten-free flour)

I doubt whether anything comes closer to a fabulous breakfast companion than these flaky, buttery morsels! I remember discovering croissants for the first time as a child while on vacation with my parents in New York City. I thought they were heaven-sent and to this day, I still do!

4 cups plus 2 tablespoons (495 g) all-purpose flour, divided

1½ cups (338 g) vegan butter, at room temperature, plus ¼ cup (56 g), melted, for brushing the croissants

½ teaspoon salt

3 tablespoons (38 g) sugar

2 packages (2¼ teaspoons or 9 g each) active dry yeast

¼ cup (60 ml) lukewarm water

1 cup (235 ml) soymilk

½ cup (120 ml) vegan heavy cream, store-bought or homemade (page 15)

Sprinkle 2 tablespoons (15 g) of the flour over the softened butter and mix it together with your hands in a mixing bowl or on a work surface. Transfer the butter to a length of foil or parchment paper and pat it into a 6-inch (15 cm) square. Fold up the foil to make a packet and refrigerate until chilled, about 2 hours.

Combine 2 cups (240 g) of the flour with the salt and sugar in a mixing bowl. Dissolve the yeast in the lukewarm water and set aside until frothy, about 10 minutes. Meanwhile, warm the milk and heavy cream in a saucepan over low heat until lukewarm. Add the yeast mixture and milk and cream mixture to the flour mixture and stir well. The dough will have a batterlike consistency. Stir in the remaining 2 cups (240 g) flour, ¼ cup (30 g) at a time, to form a soft dough (you may not need it all to get the right consistency). It should no longer be sticky. Turn the dough out onto a lightly floured work surface and knead until smooth, about 5 minutes. Place the dough in a mixing bowl and cover with plastic wrap. Refrigerate for 1 hour.

To begin the rolling and folding process, both the butter and the dough should be at a cool room temperature (the butter should be taken out of the fridge about 1 hour before this step). The butter should be bendable but not greasy or too hard. Place the dough on a floured surface and roll it into a 10-inch (25.4 cm) square. Set the block of butter diagonally on the square dough. Bring each point of dough to the center of the butter square; the edges of the dough should overlap. Pinch the edges together to seal. Starting from the center of the square and working outward, use a rolling pin to roll the dough into a rectangle. The butter should be pliable enough to roll smoothly with the dough; if it's too soft and starts to ooze out the corners, wrap the dough in plastic and refrigerate before going any further. Roll the dough into a long rectangle, about 8 × 18 inches (20.3 to 45.7 cm). Fold the length of dough into thirds, like a business letter.

If the dough is still cool, you can continue with the next fold. Otherwise, wrap it in plastic and refrigerate for 45 minutes to 1 hour. Remove the dough from the refrigerator and let it warm up for about 10 minutes before you begin rolling it out again. Position the dough so that the open ends are at 12 and 6 o'clock (vertically laid out in front of you). Roll the dough into a rectangle, working from the center of the dough and pressing outward. Reposition the dough as necessary to fit your workspace. You should have a long rectangle to make a book fold. Fold both ends of the dough into the middle; the ends don't have to be touching, but should be close. Fold the already folded dough in half; it will look like a thick book. Wrap the dough well with plastic and refrigerate for 1 to 2 hours.

Remove the dough from the refrigerator and let it rest at room temperature for about 20 minutes. Roll the dough into a rectangle again and fold it into thirds, like a business letter. Wrap it in plastic and refrigerate for 4 to 6 hours or overnight.

To shape the croissants, roll the dough into a 10 × 38-inch (25.4 × 96.5 cm) rectangle (or as close as you can) on a lightly floured, flat, and dry work surface. It should be about ¼ inch (6 mm) thick. Use a pizza wheel or sharp paring knife to trim the edges of the dough. Divide the rectangle in half so that you have two strips of dough 5 inches (12.7 cm) wide. Use a clean ruler to mark each strip into triangles that are 5 inches (12.7 cm) wide at their bases. Cut the triangles and place them on parchment-lined baking sheets. Chill for 15 to 20 minutes, if necessary.

Starting at the base of the triangle, roll the dough up into a log; the tip of the triangle should be under the body of the croissant to prevent it from unraveling. Bend in the corners to form the traditional crescent shape. Repeat with the remaining dough. Arrange the croissants on the parchment-lined baking sheets and allow to rise until doubled in size, 1 to 2 hours.

Preheat the oven to 425°F (220°C, or gas mark 7). Brush the croissants with the remaining ¼ cup (56 g) melted butter and bake until deep brown, 22 to 25 minutes. Cool on a rack before serving.

YIELD: 12 to 16 croissants

fun fact

The croissant dates back to 1683. It just so happened that Austria was under siege by the Turkish Empire. Viennese bakers, who were working underground, heard noises of Turks digging an underground tunnel to the city and called in the army. The bakers were honored for their great help and created the crescent moon–shaped bread, the symbol of the Turkish flag, for their celebration. One hundred years later, Austrian-born Marie Antoinette brought the croissant to France.

SWEET OR SAVORY CREPES

*Gluten Free (use gluten-free flour), **Soy Free (use soy-free vegan butter and alternative rice/nut milk)

Prepared either way, these should be renamed "Gone in 60 Seconds" because they will disappear from the plate super fast! Be they sweet or savory, these will be a hit at any breakfast or dinner table.

FOR CREPES:

½ cup (60 g) all-purpose flour

½ cup (60 g) buckwheat, soy, or chickpea flour

½ teaspoon salt

¼ cup (56 g) vegan butter, melted

1 cup (235 ml) soymilk, plus more as needed

1 to 2 teaspoons vanilla extract, for sweet crepes

¼ cup (50 g) sugar or (85 g) agave nectar, for sweet crepes

SWEET FILLING IDEAS:

Strawberries or blueberries (or both) with vegan whipped cream

Sliced bananas with vegan whipped cream or maple syrup

Fruit jelly

Vegan chocolate chips and vegan whipped cream

Peanut butter and jelly

SAVORY FILLING IDEAS:

Sautéed mushrooms and grilled onions

Sautéed spinach, garlic, and mushrooms

Vegan mozzarella and tomato sauce

To make the crepes: In a large mixing bowl, blend (with a stick blender, hand mixer, or whisk) together the flours, salt, butter, and soymilk. If you are making sweet crepes, add the vanilla and sugar and blend well. Cover and chill the mixture for 2 hours.

Spray a crepe pan, round griddle pan, or skillet with nonstick spray or lightly grease with vegan butter. Heat the pan over medium heat. Pour about 3 tablespoons (45 ml) to ¼ cup (60 ml) batter into the skillet. Swirl and tilt the pan to make the batter cover the skillet's bottom (you may also use the back of a spoon to spread, but be careful not to "tear" the batter). Cook until the crepe is golden and starts to pull away from the edge of the pan, 1 to 2 minutes, then flip and cook on the other side, 1 to 2 minutes, being careful not to burn. Slide from the pan, fold in half, place on a plate, and cover with a clean dish towel to keep warm.

Fill with the desired filling, then roll into cigar shapes or fold into triangles. Top with the appropriate garnish for sweet or savory crepes. If you don't feel like filling them, serve them warm with butter or syrup and enjoy!

YIELD: About 18 crepes

Fun Fact

Crepes originated in Bretagne (Brittany), in northwestern France, and were eaten while drinking cider. Traditionally, they were eaten on February 2 to celebrate the coming of spring.

TRÈS BIEN SALADE NIÇOISE

*Soy Free (omit the tofu or use soy-free vegan meat), **Low Fat (limit the dressing)

This yummy salad comes from Nice, France. How nice! This salad is quite flavorful and light, kind of like a warm and breezy day on the French Riviera.

FOR MARINATED TOFU:

2 tablespoons (40 g) molasses

1 teaspoon agave nectar

1 teaspoon soy sauce or tamari

1 tablespoon (15 ml) olive oil

¼ teaspoon dried thyme

¼ teaspoon dried tarragon

¼ cup (60 ml) water

2 tablespoons (30 ml) apple cider vinegar

2 cloves garlic, minced

1 package (14 ounces, or 392 g) extra-firm tofu, pressed, drained and cubed

FOR DRESSING:

3 tablespoons (45 ml) red wine vinegar

1 tablespoon (20 g) minced shallot

2 cloves garlic, minced

Juice of ½ lemon

1 teaspoon Dijon mustard

2 tablespoons (8 g) chopped fresh tarragon

½ teaspoon agave nectar

3 tablespoons (45 ml) olive oil

Salt and pepper, to taste

FOR SALAD:

1 pound (454 g) small red potatoes, cubed

1 cup (100 g) green beans, trimmed

6 cups (180 g) mixed baby greens

1 cup (150 g) cherry or grape tomatoes, halved

1 cup (100 g) pitted Niçoise or kalamata olives

2 teaspoons capers, drained

½ cup (24 g) chopped fresh chives

To make the tofu: Combine the molasses, agave, soy sauce, oil, thyme, tarragon, water, vinegar, and garlic in a large bowl. Add the tofu cubes and marinate for at least 1 hour. Preheat the broiler to high. Transfer the tofu to a baking sheet and broil the tofu for 10 to 12 minutes, basting periodically with the marinade.

To make the vinaigrette: Combine all the ingredients in a glass jar with a tight-fitting lid. Screw the cap on the jar and shake the vinaigrette vigorously to emulsify. Set the dressing aside while preparing the salad so the flavors can marry.

To make the salad: Place the potatoes in a medium-size pot, add salted water to cover, and bring to a boil. Reduce the heat to medium-low and simmer until tender, 12 to 15 minutes; drain and set aside to cool. Bring a large pot of salted water to a boil, add the green beans and cook until just tender, 3 to 4 minutes; rinse under cold water and drain well. Set aside.

Evenly divide the mixed salad greens among 4 to 6 plates. Compose small piles of potatoes, green beans, tomatoes, olives, and tofu on top of each bed of greens. Sprinkle with the capers, drizzle with the dressing, and garnish with the chives.

YIELD: 4 to 6 servings

TEATIME TARTINES

*Gluten Free (use gluten-free bread), **Soy Free (omit the cream cheese or substitute with soy-free spread)

These open-faced sandwiches are a fabulous appetizer for any gathering!

4 thick slices crusty bread

½ cup (115 g) vegan cream cheese, softened

1 teaspoon dried basil

½ cup (112 g) thinly sliced beets

2 heaping cups (70 g) mixed salad greens

1 medium-size avocado, peeled, pitted, and sliced

1 tablespoon (11 g) Dijon mustard

2 tablespoons (30 ml) balsamic vinegar

Salt and pepper, to taste

¼ cup (60 ml) olive oil

¼ cup (30 g) coarsely chopped toasted pecans or walnuts

Lightly toast the bread for about 3 minutes, then set aside.

Mix the cream cheese and basil, then spread evenly on the bread. Top with a few beet slices, a small handful of greens, and a few slices of avocado.

Whisk together the mustard and vinegar in a small bowl until blended; season with salt and pepper. Slowly pour in the olive oil while continually whisking until the dressing is smooth. Drizzle the vinaigrette over the top, sprinkle with the nuts, and serve.

YIELD: 4 servings

COOK'S NOTE

For easier, more bite-sized, one-handed eats, slice the bread into triangle-shaped wedges. This way you can have your tartine in one hand and your champagne in the other—tres chic!

SANS COQ AU VIN
(NOT CHICKEN IN WINE)

*Gluten Free (use gluten-free vegan chicken and bacon), **Soy Free (use soy-free vegan chicken, bacon, and butter)

**That's right, Julia Child, this version is sans *coq*! Julia was a master
of French cooking, but you don't have to be to master this classic dish.
The rich flavors of wine and herbs go incredibly well with plant-based bird.**

1 package (5 ounces, or 140 g) tempeh bacon
or vegan bacon slices, cut into 1-inch (2.5 cm)
cubes or pieces (about 1½ cups [120 g])

20 pearl onions, peeled

12 vegan chicken cutlets

6 cloves garlic, peeled

Salt and pepper, to taste

2 cups (470 ml) vegan chicken stock
(make with vegan chicken bouillon)

2 cups (470 ml) dry red wine

2 tablespoons (32 g) tomato paste

2 bay leaves

6 fresh thyme sprigs

6 fresh parsley sprigs

1 cup (70 g) trimmed and roughly
chopped button mushrooms

2 tablespoons (28 g) vegan butter

1 tablespoon (30 g) all-purpose flour (optional)

Chopped fresh parsley, for garnish

Cooked rice, potatoes, or noodles, for serving

Brown the bacon over medium-high heat in a Dutch oven or stew pot, about 5 minutes. Remove from the pot and set aside. To the same pot, add the onions and chicken. Brown the chicken well, on all sides, about 5 minutes (you may have to do this in batches, depending on the size of your pan). Halfway through the browning, add the garlic and sprinkle the chicken with salt and pepper.

Add the stock, wine, tomato paste, bay leaves, thyme, parsley, and cooked bacon. Lower the heat to a simmer. Cover and cook for 20 minutes, or until the chicken is tender and cooked through. Transfer the chicken and onions to a separate platter. Remove the bay leaves, herb sprigs, and garlic and discard.

Add the mushrooms to the remaining liquid and turn the heat to high. Boil quickly and reduce the liquid by about three-fourths, or until it becomes thick and saucy, 8 to 10 minutes. Lower the heat and stir in the butter; add the flour if you need to thicken the sauce more. Return the chicken and onions to the pot to reheat and coat with the sauce. Season with salt and pepper to taste, garnish with parsley, and serve hot with rice, potatoes, or noodles.

YIELD: 8 servings

Fun Fact

Rumor has it that Julius Caesar's cook prepared the first coq au vin, meaning "rooster in wine" in French, for a victory dinner. The history is a bit spotty on this famous French dish; however, methinks the Julius story is a good one to take a stab at! (Yes, pun intended.)

RAT-A-TAT RATATOUILLE

There are no rodents needed in the preparation of this dish, just a lot of savory veggies and herbs, resulting in a happy tummy.

1½ to 2 tablespoons (23 to 30 ml) olive oil

1½ large white onions, sliced

4 or 5 cloves garlic, minced

3 small green bell peppers, seeded and chopped into ½-inch (1.3 cm) squares

1 medium-size red bell pepper, seeded and chopped into ½-inch (1.3 cm) squares

2 large eggplants, cut into small cubes

4 large zucchini, cut into small cubes

4 large tomatoes, chopped

½ cup (30 g) chopped flat-leaf parsley, plus some for garnish

¼ to ½ cup (10 to 20 g) chopped fresh basil

⅓ cup (80 ml) dry white wine

Salt and pepper, to taste

In a frying pan, heat the oil over medium-high heat and sauté the onion, garlic, and bell peppers, stirring frequently. When the peppers are almost cooked but still crunchy, about 10 minutes, remove the peppers from the pan, set aside, and keep warm.

Add the eggplant to the pan and sauté until cooked through, 8 to 10 minutes, and then set aside. Add the zucchini to the pan, sauté until they start to turn golden, 2 to 3 minutes, then add the tomatoes and parsley and cook for 2 to 3 minutes longer. Return the peppers and eggplant to the pan, mix all the vegetables thoroughly, add the basil, and stew for about 30 minutes, making sure the vegetables don't get mushy. In the last 5 minutes of cooking, add the white wine and season with salt and pepper. Transfer to a serving dish and garnish with more parsley.

YIELD: 6 servings

COOK'S NOTE

For some added weight and a smidge of protein, you might like to add in some grilled tofu, tempeh, or even white beans or lentils.

Fun Fact

This vegetable stew was predominantly made with summer vegetables by poor farmers; it has since grown to be both a French and a global favorite.

POPEYE'S SPINACH SOUFFLÉ

*Gluten Free (use gluten-free flour)

**This soufflé is so fluffy and cheesy, even if you're not
a spinach lover like Popeye, you'll love this dish!**

5½ tablespoons (77 g) vegan butter, softened, divided

3 tablespoons (24 g) nutritional yeast

2 cups (60 g) stemmed and chopped spinach

2 tablespoons (15 g) all-purpose flour

Salt and pepper, to taste

1 cup (235 ml) soymilk

⅓ cup (38 g) shredded vegan mozzarella cheese

2 or 3 cloves garlic, minced

1 cup Omelet Batter (page 111)

Brush the inside of a soufflé or casserole dish with 1½ table-spoons (21 g) of the softened butter. Sprinkle the buttered surface evenly with the nutritional yeast and set aside.

In a large saucepan, sauté the spinach until it wilts and the juices have evaporated, 2 to 3 minutes.

Preheat the oven to 375°F (190°C, or gas mark 5).

In a separate medium saucepan, melt the remaining 4 tablespoons (56 g) butter over medium heat and stir in the flour and salt to taste, whisking constantly, and cook for 30 seconds. Add the milk, still whisking constantly, and cook for about 4 minutes, until the mixture thickens. Add the mozzarella and garlic and stir to combine. Add the spinach and continue cooking over medium heat for 1 minute, and then season with pepper. Whisk in the omelet batter and stir to combine.

Pour the mixture into the prepared dish and bake for 30 minutes, or until the soufflé is puffed up and cooked through.

YIELD: 6 to 8 servings

Fun Fact

Souffle means "puffed up" in French, and the technique was made popular in eighteenth-century France.

CRÈME DE LA CRÈME BRÛLÉE

This has got to be one of the world's most decadent desserts. Make it all for yourself or impress your dinner guests with the rich flavors and your terrific technique. Enjoy!

2 cups (470 ml) vegan heavy cream, store-bought or homemade (page 15)

1 vanilla bean, split lengthwise

6 tablespoons (48 g) vegan vanilla custard powder

¼ cup plus 1 tablespoon (95 g) agave nectar

Pinch of salt

⅓ to ½ cup (75 to 112 g) packed light brown sugar

Fresh berries, vegan whipped cream, fruit compote, or orange or lemon zest and sprig of mint, for serving

In a medium-size saucepan, heat the cream and vanilla bean over medium-low heat for 15 minutes, stirring to ensure it does not burn; do not let it boil. Remove from the heat and let steep for 15 minutes. Remove and discard the vanilla bean and strain the cream through a fine-mesh strainer or sieve.

Pour the heavy cream back into the pot (or a blender) and add the custard powder, agave, and salt. Blend with a stick blender or carefully blend in a blender until creamy. Be very careful when blending hot liquids in a blender. Cover the lid with a dish towel and hold the lid on securely while you blend.

Preheat the broiler and pour the mixture back into the pot (if you blended in a blender) and heat over medium heat, stirring until thickened and coats the back of a spoon. Pour the mixture into 2 individual ceramic, metal, or glass baking dishes, ramekins, or custard cups. Sprinkle generously with the brown sugar. Place the dishes under the broiler until the sugar begins to brown and crisp up, being careful not to burn. Remove from the broiler and let cool. Serve on its own or top with fresh berries and vegan whipped cream, fruit compote, or simple orange and lemon zest with a sprig of mint.

YIELD: 2 servings

Fun Fact

Custard has been around for centuries. In the Middle Ages, the Romans created many egg-based dishes and custard fillings. The Spanish have a similar dessert; however, it was when the French coined the name crème brûlée (meaning "burnt cream" in French) that the dessert gained worldwide popularity as being of French origin.

Chapter 8

SWITZERLAND, THE NETHERLANDS, AND DENMARK

WE'RE BOUNCING AROUND EUROPE in this chapter, but these countries' cuisines are not to be missed. Let's hop to it!

Switzerland is more then just delicious cheese and chocolate. Stuffed between Germany, France, Italy, and Austria, this mountainous European nation is the amalgamation of all of their neighbors and more. Swiss food reflects all these cuisines, as does the nation's multilingual culture. Although dairy is still a staple for the Swiss, in recent years healthy eating habits and a taste for ethnic fare are growing.

If you're looking for windmills, tulips, and clogs, visit The Netherlands! During the nation's era as a major colonial and trading power, Dutch voyagers brought back many culinary influences from the Caribbean, Africa, and Indonesia. As of late, both Turkish and Moroccan cuisines have influenced traditional Dutch cooking. One of this nation's biggest culinary contributions to the world is the cookie, or *koekje*.

Food is definitely not rotten in the state of Denmark. In fact, it's most likely preserved, smoked, or pickled. Still using old-world nonrefrigeration techniques, the Danes eat quite a bit of seafood and pork, keeping their history and heritage very much alive and well. Danish folks are very eco-minded and health conscious and even consider fresh tap water a beverage, called *postevand*. Popular Danish exports include rye bread and the smorgasbord.

I bet you're hungry after all of that hopping around Europe, so I won't keep you. *Spaß haben, have det sjovt,* and *veel plezier* (have fun)!

ZÜRCHER GESCHNETZELTES WITH BASLER RÖSTI (BEEF AND MUSHROOM STEW WITH POTATO FRITTERS)

*Soy Free (use soy-free vegan butter and cheese)

It's not just about the cheese, chocolate, and fondue, folks! This is THE Swiss dish. Meat and mushrooms with creamy sauce and crispy, cheesy potatoes. Seconds, anyone?

FOR ZÜRCHER GESCHNETZELTES (STEW):

2 tablespoons (28 g) vegan butter, divided

12 ounces (340 g) seitan, store-bought or homemade (page 19), sliced into strips

2 or 3 shallots, minced

2 cups (140 g) sliced mushrooms

1 tablespoon (8 g) all-purpose flour

1 cup (235 ml) dry white wine

1 cup (235 ml) vegan beef broth (make with vegan beef bouillon)

¼ cup (60 ml) vegan heavy cream, store-bought or homemade (page 15)

1 teaspoon lemon zest

Salt and pepper, to taste

2 tablespoons (8 g) chopped fresh parsley, for serving

FOR RÖSTI (POTATO FRITTERS):

6 large baking potatoes, peeled

1 tablespoon (18 g) salt

1 tablespoon (15 ml) olive oil

½ cup (80 g) diced onion

½ teaspoon dried thyme

½ cup (35 g) diced mushrooms

2 tablespoons (30 ml) safflower oil (or preferred high-heat oil)

¼ cup (56 g) vegan butter

½ cup (60 g) shredded vegan mozzarella or cheddar cheese

To make the zürcher geschnetzeltes: Melt 1 tablespoon (14 g) of the butter in a skillet over high heat, add the seitan strips, and brown quickly, about 2 minutes. Remove from the pan and keep warm. Add the remaining 1 tablespoon (14 g) butter, if necessary, to the pan, add the shallots, and cook, stirring, for 2 minutes, then add the mushrooms and cook until soft and brown, 2 to 3 minutes. Sprinkle the mushrooms with the flour and stir to coat. Cook for 1 minute. Slowly add the wine and broth to the mixture, stirring. Bring to a boil and cook until the sauce is reduced by half, 10 to 20 minutes. Stir in the cream, lemon zest, and salt and pepper to taste. Add the seitan back to the pan and warm, but do not cook the sauce any longer.

To make the rösti: Boil the potatoes for 10 to 15 minutes in salted water, being careful not to overcook, then drain and cool. Grate them into a large bowl and sprinkle with salt.

In a medium-size pan, heat the olive oil, add the onion, and sauté over medium heat until transclucent, 2 to 3 minutes. Add the thyme and then the mushrooms and cook for about 5 minutes, or until soft. Combine with the potatoes and mix gently, being careful not to mash them too much.

Heat the safflower oil in a frying pan and add 3 or 4 spoonfuls of the mixture. Pat them down to flatten and brown over high heat. When the bottom side is cooked, flip them over and cook on the other side, about 2 minutes on each side. Repeat with the remaining potato mixture to make 8 rösti. Drain on a paper towel–lined plate.

Preheat the broiler. Grease a baking sheet. Put ½ tablespoon (7 g) of the butter on each cake and sprinkle with 1 tablespoon (8 g) of the cheese. Place on the prepared baking sheet and melt under the hot broiler for 2 to 3 minutes. Place 2 rösti on each of 4 plates, spoon a portion of stew next to them, sprinkle with parsley, and enjoy!

YIELD: 4 servings

Switzerland

QUINTESSENTIAL QUICHE

*Gluten Free (use gluten-free flour)

Okay, so you may think this is traditionally French and you'd be right! But the Swiss love their cheese and adopted this versatile dish as a national favorite. This is a flavorful brunch dish that can just as easily fit into any dinner menu.

FOR PIE CRUST:

1¼ cups (150 g) all-purpose flour

½ tablespoon sugar

½ teaspoon salt

¼ cup (56 g) cold vegan butter, cut into pieces

⅓ cup (75 g) frozen vegan shortening, cut into pieces

2 to 4 tablespoons (30 to 60 ml) ice water

1 teaspoon apple cider vinegar

FOR FILLING:

¼ cup plus 1 tablespoon (70 g) vegan butter, softened, divided

½ cup plus 1 tablespoon (112 g) silken tofu blended with 1⅛ teaspoons arrowroot powder

2 cups (470 ml) vegan heavy cream, store-bought or homemade (page 15)

¾ teaspoon salt, divided

¼ teaspoon ground turmeric

½ cup (60 g) shredded vegan mozzarella cheese

½ to ¾ cup (35 to 53 g) sliced mushrooms

2 tablespoons (12 g) minced scallion

2 cloves garlic, minced

1 cup (70 g) stemmed and chopped broccoli

Pinch of ground pepper

To make the crust: Combine the flour, sugar, and salt in a food processor; pulse to blend. Add the butter and shortening and cut into the flour mixture. When the mixture resembles coarse meal, transfer to a large bowl.

Combine 2 tablespoons (30 ml) of the ice water and the cider vinegar in a small bowl; pour over the flour mixture. Stir with a fork until moist clumps form, adding the remaining 2 tablespoons (30 ml) ice water if necessary. Gather the dough into a ball and flatten into a disk. Wrap in plastic and chill for 30 minutes or up to 4 days. Well-wrapped dough can be frozen for up to 2 weeks. Allow the dough to soften slightly at room temperature before rolling out.

To make the filling: Preheat the oven to 425°F (220°C, or gas mark 7). Spread the pie crust evenly into a pie plate or round baking dish. Carefully spread ¼ cup (56 g) of the butter onto it, then chill in the refrigerator.

In a medium-size bowl, with a wire whisk, beat the tofu mixture, heavy cream, ½ teaspoon of the salt, and turmeric. Stir in the shredded cheese.

Melt the remaining 1 tablespoon (14 g) butter in a skillet over medium-high heat. Add the sliced mushrooms, remaining ¼ teaspoon salt, scallion, garlic, broccoli, and pepper. Cook for 5 minutes, or until the vegetables are tender, stirring frequently. Add to the cream mixture and stir to combine. Pour into the pie crust and bake for 15 minutes. Reduce the heat to 325°F (170°C, or gas mark 3) and bake for 25 minutes longer, until golden brown. Cover the edges with foil if they begin to brown too much.

Remove from the oven and allow to stand for 10 to 15 minutes before serving warm.

YIELD: 6 to 8 servings

fun fact

Most folks think that quiche was developed by the French, but in actuality it came from Germany, and the Swiss have embraced it as a national dish with their beloved Gruyere.

SAVORY ASPARAGUS HOLLANDAISE

**Hollandaise is simple to make and yet the epitome of rich sauces.
No one will miss the dairy version when you serve this up!**

1 cup (225 g) vegan butter

½ cup (100 g) puréed silken tofu

1 tablespoon (15 ml) lemon juice

1 tablespoon (15 ml) water

⅛ teaspoon ground turmeric

¼ teaspoon salt

⅛ teaspoon white pepper

1 pound (454 g) asparagus, trimmed

Olive oil, for brushing

Lemon wedges, for serving

Melt the butter in a saucepan over medium heat. Remove from the heat and let stand for 3 minutes.

Whisk together the tofu, lemon juice, and water in another 1-quart (1 L) saucepan until frothy. Set the pan over low heat and whisk vigorously until the mixture is slightly thickened, 3 to 4 minutes. Remove from the heat and gradually whisk in the melted butter, then whisk in the turmeric, salt, and white pepper.

Preheat the grill or a grill pan. Brush the asparagus with olive oil and grill over high heat for 5 minutes, until lightly browned and tender. Transfer to a serving bowl and pour the sauce over. Serve with the lemon wedges.

YIELD: 4 servings

fun fact

This was originally called *Sauce Isigny* after a town in Normandy that was known for its high quality and tasty butter, a key ingredient in Hollandaise sauce.

MOUTHWATERING WATERZOOI
(CHICKEN SOUP)

*Gluten Free (use gluten-free vegan chicken)

Cute name, delicious soup! I much prefer this to a traditional vegan chicken noodle soup because it's creamy and chunky. Under the weather or not, you'll find this soup hits the spot every time!

2 tablespoons (28 g) vegan butter

2 carrots, peeled and diced

2 leeks, chopped, rinsed, and dried

2 large potatoes, peeled and diced

Salt and white pepper, to taste

1 fresh bay leaf

4 sprigs fresh parsley, plus a handful chopped for garnish

4 sprigs fresh thyme

6 cups (1,410 ml) vegan chicken broth
(make with vegan chicken bouillon)

4 vegan chicken cutlets

1 cup (235 ml) vegan heavy cream,
store-bought or homemade (page 15)

1 vegan egg yolk, store-bought or homemade (page 13)

In a deep pot over medium heat, melt the butter, add the carrots, leeks, and potatoes, and sauté for 5 minutes, or until soft. Season with salt and white pepper. Tie the bay leaf, parsley, and thyme into a bundle and add to the pot along with the broth. Cover the pot, increase the heat to high, to bring to a boil. Add the chicken to the pot, cover, reduce the heat to medium-low, and cook for about 10 minutes. Uncover the pot, remove the chicken, and slice.

Whisk the cream and egg yolk together in a small bowl. Add a ladle of the cooking broth to the cream and egg to temper it. Add this mixture to the pot and stir constantly for 2 to 3 minutes to thicken.

Add the chicken back to the pot along with the chopped parsley, remove and discard the herb bundle, and season to taste. Serve with crusty bread and enjoy!

YIELD: 6 to 8 servings

fun fact
Zooien means "to boil"
in Dutch.

OH-SO-CUTE EBELSKIVERS
(FILLED PANCAKE PUFFS)

*Gluten Free (use gluten-free flour)

These bite-size pancakes have a surprise in the middle. I love eating these fresh out of the pan. You will need an ebelskiver iron or a pancake puff pan to make these.

½ cup (100 g) silken tofu blended with 1 teaspoon arrowroot powder

2 to 3 teaspoons sugar

½ teaspoon salt

2 cups (470 ml) vegan buttermilk, store-bought or homemade (page 14)

2 cups (240 g) all-purpose flour

1 teaspoon baking powder

1 teaspoon baking soda

⅝ cup (140 g) applesauce or filling of choice

In a medium-size mixing bowl, beat the tofu, sugar, salt, and buttermilk. Combine the flour, baking soda, and baking powder in a bowl, then slowly fold into the tofu mixture.

Grease the cups of the pan and fill each one-third full (about 1 teaspoon), then add ½ teaspoon applesauce and cover with a little more batter (about 1 teaspoon). You don't want them more then three-fourths full. Place the iron on the stove top over medium heat. Cook until the bottoms and sides turn golden brown, 1 to 3 minutes, and then carefully flip them over within the cups, cooking 1 to 2 minutes more, until golden brown and cooked through. You may want to use wooden skewers or a small silicone spatula to flip them as quickly as possible without losing too much batter. Flip them onto a plate to cool, then repeat with the remaining batter and applesauce to make 3 more batches.

YIELD: 28 ebelskivers

fun fact

Lacking space and just being dudes, Vikings used their helmets and shields as cooking devices. After battle, their gear was dented, so when cooking pancakes over the campfire, the ones in the wells became the first ebelskivers!

COOK'S NOTE

Some filling options besides applesauce are strawberry jam, chocolate chips, custard, or even vegan nutella!

FRICKIN' AWESOME FRIKADELLER
(MEATBALLS IN CREAM SAUCE)

*Soy Free (use soy-free vegan ground beef or TVP, alternative rice/nut milk, and soy-free butter),
**Low Fat (omit the sauce or substitute Mushroom Gravy [pages 34–35])

Danish meatballs, anyone? These have all the heartiness and flavor of meatballs, plus the richness of a delicious cream sauce.

FOR FRIKADELLER:

1 cup (225 g) vegan ground beef

1 cup (200 g) sliced plain seitan, store-bought or homemade (page 19)

1 cup (115 g) bread crumbs

2 cups (470 ml) soymilk

1 egg replacer, mixed, store-bought or homemade (page 13)

1 tablespoon (10 g) diced onion

½ teaspoon dried sage

Salt and pepper, to taste

Vegan butter, for frying

FOR SAUCE:

2 tablespoons (15 g) all-purpose flour

1 cup (235 ml) vegan chicken broth (make with vegan chicken bouillon)

1 cup (230 g) vegan sour cream

To make the frikadeller: Put the ground beef and seitan together in a food processor and pulse until combined and ground together. In a bowl, combine the beef mixture, bread crumbs, milk, egg replacer, onion, sage, salt, and pepper, mixing thoroughly. You may make roll into meatballs or drop large spoonfuls of the mixture onto a buttered frying pan. Fry over medium-low heat until browned and crisp on the outside, 2 to 3 minutes, using a slotted spoon to turn and brown the meatballs evenly.

To make the sauce: Stir the flour into the pan in which the meatballs were cooked, add the broth, and cook until thick, 3 to 5 minutes. Stir in the sour cream and heat gently. Pour over the frikadellers and serve.

YIELD: 6 to 8 servings

COOK'S NOTE

For added oomph, serve over noodles or rice!

Chapter 9

ITALY

HANDS DOWN, ITALIAN IS ONE of the most popular cuisines in the world. From pizza, to pasta, to risotto, Italian food definitely holds a top spot on the "what are you in the mood to eat?" list. Full of flavor, history, and even romance (aren't most dinner dates at Italian restaurants?), Italian food is loved worldwide.

Although many of us enjoy Italian food, most may not know that the dishes we love are from all different regions of the boot-shaped country. Ingredients are seasonal, and fresh local produce is a priority in Italian cooking. Southern Italy is where we get the bulk of the popular tomato sauce–based dishes. As we move up the boot, the dishes get heavier, due to the colder climate. Additionally, the influences of bordering countries are illustrated in their dishes. You will see many Austrian, Greek, French, and Hungarian staples bleed into more inland Italian foods. Central Italy is where we get Bolognese sauce, lasagne, tortellini, and Parmigiano cheese. Northern Italian cuisine is almost void of tomato sauce dishes and is much more hearty. You find quite a bit of potato, rice, corn, heavy meats, and fish. Basil is heavily used here, making pesto is a northern Italian favorite. Venice is known for its risotto and polenta, Liguria for its gnocchi, and Tuscany for its minestrone. And the most popular dish, pizza, comes from Naples. The list goes on and on, so when visiting Italy, you can literally eat your way through it without having the same thing twice!

However, the one important dish that we've all come to know well is Italian pasta. Italy is incredibly diverse in its pasta styles. With virtually hundreds of shapes and dozens of thicknesses, pasta is internationally recognized. It is made either fresh or dried. Fresh pasta is made with eggs and is found mainly in northern Italy; dried pasta, made with durum wheat or semolina flour, is more commonly used in southern Italy.

Finally, the time it takes to enjoy an Italian meal (or feast) can last hours. The Italians love to socialize and enjoy their food so much that a meal can have up to nine courses, from the aperitivo liqueur that is enjoyed before the antipasto (appetizer) all the way to the digestivo liqueur that comes after the dolce and caffe. Italians live to eat and make eating lively!

It's time to join in the fun, and the following dishes are *molto buono* (delicious). *Hanno un buon viaggio en Italia* (have a good trip to Italy)!

MAMA MIA MINESTRONE

*Gluten Free (use gluten-free pasta and vegan cheese), **Soy Free (use soy-free vegan cheese)

Hearty minestrone is great as a starter as well as a main course. No matter what time of year, this soup fits in beautifully. Since I was a little girl I've loved this soup and could eat it just about every day. A terrific way to get your veggies!

2 tablespoons (30 ml) olive oil

1 medium-size white onion, diced

3 or 4 cloves garlic, chopped

3 medium-size carrots, cubed

1 cup (100 g) sliced green beans

2 stalks celery, sliced

2 large Yukon Gold potatoes, chopped

1½ cups (135 g) chopped cabbage

2 small zucchini, halved and sliced or cubed

2 cans (15 ounces, or 420 g each) peeled and crushed tomatoes

2 to 4 tablespoons (5 to 10 g) chopped fresh basil

2 tablespoons (8 g) chopped fresh parsley

1 teaspoon dried thyme

½ teaspoon dried sage

2 bay leaves

1 can (15 ounces, or 420 g) cannellini beans, rinsed and drained

6 cups (1,410 ml) vegetable broth, store-bought or homemade (page 16)

Salt and pepper, to taste

2 cups (280 g) cooked elbow, macaroni, or fusilli pasta

Shredded vegan mozzarella cheese, for serving (optional)

In a large pot over medium heat, heat the olive oil and sauté the onion, garlic, carrots, green beans, celery, and potatoes for 8 to 10 minutes, until the vegetables are soft and the onion and celery are translucent. Add the cabbage and zucchini and sauté for about 5 more minutes. Add the tomatoes, basil, parsley, thyme, sage, bay leaves, and beans and stir. Add the vegetable broth and then season with salt and pepper to taste. Bring to a boil over high heat, then lower the heat and simmer until the vegetables are soft, 15 to 20 minutes. Remove the bay leaves and discard. Add ¼ cup (35 g) of the pasta to each of 8 soup bowls and ladle in the soup. Sprinkle with the cheese and serve.

YIELD: 8 servings

COOK'S NOTE

Minestrone is great fun when served in a bread bowl. Hollow out a sourdough roll, ladle in the soup, then sprinkle bits of the bread on top.

THE ITALIAN QUARTET: MARINARA, BOLOGNESE, ARRABIATA, AND ALFREDO SAUCES

*Gluten Free (use gluten-free vegan meats and cheeses), **Soy Free (use soy-free vegan meats and cheeses; for the alfredo, substitute cashew cream for heavy cream and soy-free vegan butter), ***Low Fat (opt for the base marinara)

Sauce or gravy, whatever you want to call it, you can't do Italian without it! These will be your base sauces for most of the upcoming Italian recipes, so it wouldn't hurt to make big batches and freeze them for future use.

MARINARA SAUCE:

2 tablespoons (30 ml) olive oil

3 to 4 tablespoons (30 to 40 g) minced fresh garlic

4 cups (720 g) canned peeled plum tomatoes, coarsely crushed

1 cup (40 g) chopped fresh basil

¼ cup (12 g) dried oregano

½ cup (30 g) chopped Italian parsley

Salt and pepper, to taste

1¼ teaspoons fennel seed

2 tablespoons (30 ml) dry red wine

1 tablespoon (13 g) sugar

To make the marinara: In a medium-size saucepan, heat the oil over medium-high heat. Add the garlic and cook, stirring, for 30 seconds. Add the tomatoes (crush them down with a fork), making sure they do not burn. Add the basil, oregano, parsley, salt, pepper, fennel, wine, and sugar and bring to a boil, stirring, being careful not to burn. Lower the heat and simmer, stirring occasionally, until thickened, 20 to 30 minutes. Remove from the heat.

BOLOGNESE SAUCE:

1 to 2 tablespoons (15 to 30 ml) olive oil

1 cup (130 g) diced carrot

¾ cup (90 g) diced celery

1 cup (160 g) finely chopped white onion

Salt and pepper, to taste

2 cups (450 g) cooked and minced vegan meatballs or vegan ground beef

3 cloves garlic, minced

1 recipe Marinara Sauce (above)

½ cup (120 ml) plain soymilk

½ cup (120 ml) vegan heavy cream, store-bought or homemade (page 15)

To make the Bolognese: In a saucepan over medium heat, heat the olive oil and sauté the carrot, celery, and onion for about 3 minutes, or until translucent, then season with salt and pepper. Add the ground beef and brown, stirring well, 2 to 3 minutes, then stir in the garlic. Add the marinara and reduce the heat to low. Simmer for 30 minutes, slowly adding the soymilk little by little until well incorporated by the end of the 30 minutes. Stir in the heavy cream, season with salt and pepper to taste, and serve.

ARRABIATA SAUCE:

1 recipe Marinara Sauce (page 136)

2 teaspoons crushed red pepper flakes, or more to taste

ALFREDO SAUCE:

2 cups (470 ml) vegan heavy cream, store-bought or homemade (page 15)

½ cup (112 g) vegan butter, softened

1 tablespoon (10 g) minced garlic

½ cup (60 g) shredded vegan mozzarella cheese

¼ cup (32 g) nutritional yeast

Salt and pepper, to taste

Chopped fresh flat-leaf parsley, for garnish

To make the arrabiata: When making the marinara, add the red pepper flakes when you add the herbs, wine, and sugar.

To make the Alfredo: Heat the heavy cream in a deep sauté pan over medium-low heat. Add the butter and whisk gently to melt. Sprinkle in the garlic, cheese, and nutritional yeast and stir to incorporate well. Season with salt and pepper. Garnish with chopped parsley just before serving.

YIELD: 4 to 8 servings

fun fact

Marinara means "sailor's" tomato sauce. Alfredo is named after a real Alfredo, Alfredo di Lello, who whipped up this cream-based sauce for his finicky pregnant wife. And Bolognese sauce, from Bologna, also known as ragù, didn't call for tomatoes in its original incarnation!

BATTISTA'S GARLIC KNOTS

*Gluten Free (use gluten-free flour), **Soy Free (use soy-free butter), ***Low Fat (limit the garlic sauce)

It's another delicious favorite that my good family friend Joe Battista created, and I just had to adjust per my vegany specifications.

FOR DOUGH:

1 package (2¼ teaspoons, or 9 g) active dry yeast

1 cup (235 ml) warm water, at least 110°F (43°C)

1½ tablespoons (23 ml) olive oil, plus more to coat bowl

1½ teaspoons salt

Pinch of sugar

2½ to 3 cups (300 to 360 g) all-purpose flour, divided, plus more if needed

FOR KNOTS AND SAUCE:

1 tablespoon (15 ml) olive oil

1 teaspoon salt

½ cup (112 g) vegan butter

3 to 4 tablespoons (30 to 40 g) minced garlic

¼ cup (32 g) nutritional yeast or (20 g) grated vegan Parmesan cheese

1 tablespoon (2 g) dried basil

1 tablespoon (3 g) dried oregano

1 tablespoon (1.3 g) dried parsley

To make the dough: In a large bowl, combine the yeast, water, olive oil, salt, and sugar and stir well until dissolved. After 5 minutes, and a little swelling, add 1¼ cups (150 g) of the flour and mix well. Add 1¼ cups (150 g) more flour and mix well with your hands. Transfer the dough to a lightly floured work surface and knead for at least 5 and up to 7 minutes, adding a little of the remaining ½ cup (60 g) flour as necessary to form a smooth and elastic dough; it should not be sticky. Transfer the dough to a large, lightly oiled 2- or 3-quart (1.8 or 2.7 L) bowl and turn in the bowl to coat with oil. Cover with plastic wrap or tight foil and let rise in a warm place until doubled in size, at least 1 hour.

To make the knots and sauce: Lightly grease 2 large baking sheets. Remove the risen dough from the bowl and place on a lightly floured surface. Using a lightly floured rolling pin, roll the dough into a large rectangle, about 16 × 12 inches (40.6 × 30.5 cm). Brush the dough lightly with the olive oil. Cut the dough in half, lengthwise (up and down), and then cut crosswise (side to side) into strips about 1¼ inches (3 cm) wide. Do not make the strips too skinny or you'll get skimpy rolls. Working with floured hands, tie each strip loosely into a knot, stretching gently if necessary, and place on the prepared baking sheets about 2 inches (5 cm) apart. If you have trouble tying knots, roll the dough into balls, making sure they aren't too dense.

Preheat the oven to 375°F (190°C, or gas mark 5). Sprinkle the tops of the dough with a little salt. Cover tightly with plastic wrap or foil and allow the dough to rise in a warm, draft-free place for about 30 minutes. Bake the knots until golden brown and risen, about 20 minutes.

While the knots are baking, combine the butter and garlic in a small saucepan over low heat. Cook until the garlic is tender, 3 to 4 minutes. Remove from the heat, add the cheese and herbs, and set aside, covered, for the flavors to meld. When the rolls are almost done, transfer to a large bowl. While the rolls are still warm, toss gently with the warm garlic mixture. Add salt to taste if necessary and serve warm.

YIELD: 8 to 10 rolls

COOK'S NOTE

Get funky and try these out as mini pizza crusts!

YOU'LL BE STUFFED MANICOTTI

*Gluten Free (use gluten-free pasta and vegan cheese and choose the marinara option)

The manicotti won't be the only thing stuffed at the table! I think these are great fun for kids to help assemble, bringing the family into the kitchen and not just for the meal itself. Creamy ricotta baked inside tubes of pasta, slathered in herb-filled sauce—you'll think you've died and gone to Venice!

FOR RICOTTA CHEESE:

16 ounces (454 g) extra-firm tofu, pressed and drained

⅓ cup (83 g) light miso

½ cup (120 ml) water

⅓ cup (80 g) unsalted, raw cashew nut butter or tahini

1 tablespoon (8 g) nutritional yeast

¼ cup (60 ml) olive oil

5 to 7 large cloves garlic

1 tablespoon (15 ml) lemon juice

1 cup (40 g) fresh basil

½ cup (32 g) fresh oregano

Salt and pepper, to taste

FOR MANICOTTI:

3 cups (345 g) shredded vegan mozzarella cheese, divided

2 tablespoons (8 g) chopped fresh parsley or basil

2 teaspoons olive oil

3 cups (735 g) Marinara Sauce (page 136) or Bolognese Sauce (page 136), divided

1 package (8 ounces, or 225 g) vegan manicotti (about 12 tubes), cooked according to package instructions and drained, or vegan lasagna noodles, cooked according to package instructions, drained, and rolled into tubes (about 12)

2 tablespoons (28 g) vegan butter, chilled and cut into pieces

To make the ricotta: Place all the ingredients in a food processor and process until combined. For a chunky texture, pulse; for a creamy texture, purée. Taste and adjust the seasonings before it's too well blended.

To make the manicotti: Preheat the oven to 350°F (180°C, or gas mark 4).

Combine the ricotta mixture with 1½ cups (173 g) of the mozzarella and the parsley. Brush the bottom of a glass casserole of or baking dish with the olive oil and then top with 1½ cups (368 g) of the sauce. Fill the tubes with the ricotta mixture and line up the manicotti in a single layer of organized rows in your casserole dish. Cover the pasta with the remaining 1½ cups (368 g) sauce and sprinkle with the remaining 1½ cups (173 g) cheese. Scatter the butter pieces all over the cheese.

Bake, uncovered, for 10 to 15 minutes, or until the cheese has melted and the sauce on the sides is bubbling, being careful not to burn. Let cool for about 5 minutes, then serve.

YIELD: 6 servings

COOK'S NOTE

Have fun with this recipe by replacing the manicotti with jumbo pasta shells!

WHO NEEDS CHICKEN EGGPLANT PARMESAN

*Gluten Free (use gluten-free bread crumbs and vegan cheese)

Who needs cheesy chicken when you can have cheesy eggplant?! This dish is a fabulous way to introduce omnivores to plant-based fare, one that hearkens back to all the flavors of the original.

3 cups (345 g) bread crumbs

3 tablespoons (12 g) finely chopped flat-leaf parsley

1 tablespoon (4 g) finely chopped fresh oregano

1 tablespoon (2.5 g) finely chopped fresh thyme

1½ teaspoons salt, plus extra for seasoning

½ teaspoon pepper, plus extra for seasoning

3 recipes vegan egg wash (page 13)

All-purpose flour, for dredging

2 or 3 medium-size eggplants, cut into ½-inch (1.3 cm) thick rounds (about 18 slices)

Coconut oil, for frying (or preferred high-heat oil)

1 recipe Marinara Sauce (page 136)

1 recipe Ricotta Cheese (page 140)

1½ cups (173 g) shredded vegan mozzarella cheese

1 cup (40 g) fresh basil leaves, torn

Preheat the oven to 375°F (190°C, or gas mark 5). Lightly butter the bottom and sides of a 15 × 10 × 2-inch (38 × 25 × 5 cm) baking dish.

Place the bread crumbs in a large shallow bowl. Add the herbs, salt, and pepper and stir to combine. Pour the egg wash into a separate large bowl and spread the flour on a shallow plate.

Season each eggplant slice on both sides with salt and pepper. Dredge each eggplant slice in the flour, tapping off the excess, then dip into the egg wash, and finally dredge in the bread crumb mixture. Shake off any excess breading and place the eggplant on a baking sheet. Pour the oil to a depth of about ½ inch (1.3 cm) in a large sauté pan or skillet over medium heat. Heat until the oil reaches 385°F (196°C). Working in small batches, fry a few of the eggplant slices, turning once, until golden brown, about 3 minutes total. Do not crowd the pan. When done, place the eggplant on a paper towel–lined baking sheet.

Cover the bottom of the baking dish with some of the marinara sauce. Arrange one-third of the eggplant over the sauce, then cover with some more of the sauce. Next, place 1 heaping tablespoon (16 g) ricotta on top of each eggplant. Finally, top with one-third of the shredded cheese and some of the basil. Repeat to make 3 layers, ending with the sauce. Top with the remaining mozzarella and bake until just beginning to brown, about 20 minutes. Let stand about 10 minutes to set before serving.

YIELD: 8 to 10 servings

COOK'S NOTE

Feel free to substitute the eggplant with portobello mushrooms. Yum!

BOLOGNESE BAKED GNOCCHI WITH SPINACH (POTATO DUMPLING PASTA)

*Gluten Free (use gluten-free flour and vegan cheese, and use marinara sauce instead of Bolognese),
**Soy Free (use soy-free vegan cheese and use marinara sauce instead of Bolognese)

The soft dumplings melt in your mouth while the tangy tomato sauce zings you!

FOR GNOCCHI:

3 pounds (1,362 g) russet potatoes, diced into 1-inch (2.5 cm) pieces

6 quarts (5.4 L) water

Ice bath of 6 cups (1,350 g) ice and 6 cups (1,410 ml) water

2 cups (240 g) all-purpose flour

Salt, to taste

1 egg replacer, mixed, store-bought or homemade (page 13)

½ cup (120 ml) olive oil

FOR ASSEMBLY:

1½ cups (368 g) Bolognese Sauce (page 136)

1 cup (30 g) chopped fresh spinach

1 cup (115 g) shredded vegan mozzarella cheese

2 tablespoons (28 g) vegan butter, chilled and cut into pieces

¼ cup (10 g) chopped basil, for garnish

To make the gnocchi: Place the potatoes in a large pot of salted water and bring to a boil. Cook until soft, about 15 minutes. While still warm, peel them and pass through a vegetable mill or potato ricer or grate on the large holes of a grater onto a well-floured cutting or pasta board. Bring the water to a boil in a large pasta pot and set up the ice bath.

Make a well in the center of the potatoes and sprinkle all over with the flour and salt. Add the egg replacer to the center of the well and, using a fork, stir into the flour and potatoes. Once well incorporated, bring the dough together and, with floured hands, knead gently until a ball is formed. Knead gently for about another 4 minutes, until the ball is dry to the touch. Scoop about ½ to ¾ cup (112 g to 170 g) onto the center of the board and set the rest aside. Dust with flour and dust your hands generously too, then roll into a finger-thick snake. Cut it into little pillows (rub the knife in flour to prevent it from sticking to the dough). Place each gnocchi on a floured board or parchment paper–lined baking tray. Repeat until all the dough has been used. Try to move quickly, otherwise the gnocchi will get soggy and stick to the paper/board.

Drop the gnocchi into the boiling water and stir once so they don't stick to the bottom. Cook until they float to the surface, 2 to 4 minutes. Remove them to the ice bath. Let cool for 5 to 7 minutes, then drain. Toss with the olive oil and store, covered, in the refrigerator until ready to serve or up to 48 hours.

Warm the Bolognese sauce in a saucepot over medium heat. Remove from the heat, add the spinach, and stir to combine. Add the gnocchi to the sauce mixture and toss.

Preheat the oven to 350°F (180°C, or gas mark 4). Pour the gnocchi/sauce mixture into a glass or ceramic casserole dish. Top with the cheese and butter pieces and bake for about 15 minutes, or until the cheese is melted. Garnish with the chopped basil and serve.

YIELD: 8 servings

COOK'S NOTE

To make sweet potato gnocchi, use sweet potatoes in place of the russets.

HOMEMADE RICOTTA RAVIOLI

*Gluten Free (use gluten-free flour, chickpea flour, or soy flour in place of semolina and use marinara or alfredo sauce)

Ravioli is a favorite of many since childhood, and is definitely one of mine! Kids and adults alike can't deny the fun of eating these; this healthified version will make anyone who tries them very happy indeed!

FOR PASTA:

1½ cups (180 g) unbleached white flour (or 1 cup [120 g] unbleached white flour with ½ cup [60 g] whole wheat flour), plus extra for rolling

1½ cups (113 g) fine semolina flour

1 teaspoon olive oil

½ to ¾ teaspoon salt

⅔ cup (160 ml) water, plus more as needed

FOR FILLING:

1 teaspoon olive oil

1 cup (70 g) stemmed and chopped mushrooms

2 cloves garlic, minced

½ cup (120 ml) white wine

1 cup (250 g) Ricotta Cheese (page 140)

¼ cup (10 g) finely chopped basil, plus extra for garnish

FOR SERVING:

1 recipe Marinara Sauce (page 136) or Italian sauce of choice

To make the pasta: Mix the flour, semolina, oil, and salt in a medium-size bowl. Pour in the water and stir with a fork until the dough comes together into a ball. Knead the dough, with floured hands, on a lightly floured surface for about 10 minutes, or until the dough is smooth. The dough should not be sticky, so add tiny amounts of flour until you reach the desired consistency. It should be easily workable, so add tiny amounts of water until you reach the desired consistency. Place the dough in a plastic bag or greased bowl, seal tightly, and let rest for 10 to 30 minutes, to allow the gluten to settle for increased elasticity. Divide the dough into 8 portions. Keep the dough you aren't working with in the plastic bag or bowl. Roll each piece out on a floured surface until it is ⅛ inch (3 mm) thick, flouring as you go to prevent sticking. Make it thin, make it flat!

To make the pasta easier to cut, try hanging the rolled pieces to dry for 5 to 10 minutes. If you have a clothes drying rack or high-back chairs, you may want to hang the rolled-out portions of dough over them (unless you have a pasta rack).

To make the filling: Heat the olive oil in a skillet over medium heat and sauté the mushrooms and garlic until the mushroom liquid evaporates, 2 to 3 minutes. Add the wine and cook over high heat until it evaporates, 2 to 3 minutes. Remove from the heat and stir in the ricotta and basil.

Lay out your dough sheets and begin to cut out the pasta. You can make them circular with a cookie cutter or the rim of a glass, making 2½- to 3-inch (6.4 to 7.5 cm) disks. To make them square, cut the lengths of rolled-out dough into 2½-inch (6.4 cm) wide strips and cut 2½-inch (6.4 cm) squares with a ravioli stamp, pasta cutter, or pastry cutter. As you cut your disks or squares, gather up the leftover dough, roll into a ball, roll it out thin, and cut more disks or squares until you have no more dough, about 48 pieces.

Bring a pot of salted water to a boil so you can cook your raviolis as soon as they are assembled so they won't dry out. Place a heaping teaspoon of filling in the center of half the disks. To seal, brush water around the edge of the disk and cover with a second disk. Don't overfill, and make sure that no filling gets into the seal on the edges or it may break open when cooking. Crimp the edges with a fork, pastry wheel, or fluted pasta cutter. You can also cut bigger disks and place the filling on one side, and then fold it over to make a half-circle ravioli. Just be sure not to overfill the half and leave room for the fold and seal, so the filling won't ooze out. Repeat with the remaining dough and filling to make about 24 ravioli. Cover with waxed paper or paper towels to keep them from drying out. Do not stack them or place them too close together, because they will stick and break apart.

Cook the ravioli in 2 or 3 batches by dropping them one at a time into rapidly boiling water. They need to cook no longer than 3 to 4 minutes once the water has come back to a gentle boil. Don't let the water boil violently because the big bubbles will cause the ravioli to come apart.

Meanwhile, gently heat the sauce in a saucepot over medium-low heat. Remove the ravioli with a slotted spoon, place on warmed plates or a serving platter, cover lightly with the sauce, and garnish with the extra basil.

YIELD: 6 to 8 servings

COOK'S NOTE

Instead of making your own pasta, you can use store-bought or homemade vegan wonton wrappers (page 18). Place 1 tablespoon (15 g) of the mixture in the center of a wonton wrapper. Wet, crimp, and seal the edges of the wrapper well so that it doesn't open in the pan, causing the filling to spill out. Cook a few at a time in a vegetable steamer, being careful not to crowd them or they will stick to each other and become gluey. Keep warm in a covered dish while the remainder steam and toss with a bit of olive oil when they are cooked to prevent sticking.

Fun Fact

Vegetarian ravioli are quite popular on Fridays and during Lent in Italy because meat it not consumed on these holy days. *Ravioli* means "to stuff," so when making them, feel free to stuff with a variety of your favorite things. Butternut squash, mushrooms, spinach, or whatever your heart desires, these little guys are delish no matter what!

BUONA LASAGNE

*Gluten Free (use gluten-free pasta)

A classic dish, a tasty dish, a festive dish. Everyone knows it's a special occasion when a hot dish of lasagne is set on the table! Honestly, it is hard for omnivores to know the difference between this and the meat variety.

5 tablespoons (70 g) vegan butter, plus 2 tablespoons (28 g), chilled

½ cup (60 g) all-purpose flour

4 cups 940 ml) plain soymilk, at room temperature

Pinch of nutmeg

1½ cups (368 g) Marinara Sauce (page 136)

Salt, white pepper, and black pepper, to taste

¼ cup (60 ml) olive oil

2 cups (450 g) vegan ground beef

1 pound (454 g) lasagna noodles, cooked according to package instructions

2½ cups (625 g) Ricotta Cheese (page 140)

1¼ cups (38 g) chopped fresh spinach

3 cups (345 g) shredded vegan mozzarella cheese

¼ cup (20 g) grated vegan Parmesan cheese or (32 g) nutritional yeast (optional)

Preheat the oven to 375°F (190°C, or gas mark 5).

In a 2-quart (1.8 L) pot, melt the 5 tablespoons (70 g) butter over medium heat. Add the flour and whisk until smooth, about 2 minutes. Gradually add the milk, whisking constantly to prevent lumps. Continue to simmer and whisk over medium heat until the sauce is thick and creamy, 2 to 3 minutes. Remove from the heat and add the nutmeg and marinara sauce. Stir until well combined and season with salt and white pepper. Set aside and allow to cool completely.

In a sauté pan, heat the olive oil over medium heat. Add the ground beef, season with salt and black pepper, and cook until brown, 2 to 3 minutes. Remove from the heat and set aside to cool.

In the bottom of a 13 × 9-inch (33 × 23 cm) glass or ceramic baking dish, spread one-third of the sauce. Arrange the noodles side by side, covering the bottom of the baking dish. Evenly spread a layer of all the ricotta, then a layer of all the spinach. Arrange another layer of noodles on top and spread all the ground beef on top. Sprinkle half of the mozzarella cheese on top of the beef. Spread on another one-third of the sauce. Arrange the last layer of noodles and top with the remaining third of the sauce, the remaining half of the mozzarella, and the Parmesan cheeses. Cut the remaining 2 tablespoons (28 g) chilled butter into ¼-inch (6 mm) pieces and scatter on top so that when it melts, each cube will evenly cover the lasagne.

Line a large baking sheet with aluminum foil. Place the lasagna dish on top, cover it with foil or a lid, and place on the middle rack of the oven. Bake until bubbling, 15 to 20 minutes. Remove the cover and for about 15 minutes longer, or until the cheese is beginning to brown and the center is cooked through.

YIELD: 8 to 10 servings

COOK'S NOTE

Get creative with your lasagne and make them into single serving rolls or rouladen. Go a step further and bread the lasagne rolls and fry them up in a good high heat oil for a delicious fried lasagne entrée!

CALZONE PERSONALIZZATO

*Gluten Free (use gluten-free flour and vegan cheese), **Soy Free (omit the ricotta and use soy-free vegan cheese)

**If you love pizza, you'll love calzones! Stuff them any which way you like and enjoy.
This is a great dish to get the kids to help assemble and personalize. Fun to make and fun to eat!**

FOR DOUGH:

1 package (2¼ teaspoons, or 9 g) active dry yeast

1 cup (235 ml) warm water, heated to 110°F (43°C)

1½ teaspoons salt

1½ tablespoons (23 ml) olive oil

2½ to 3 cups (300 to 360 g) all-purpose flour, divided, plus more if necessary

FOR FILLING:

1 cup (245 g) Marinara Sauce (page 136)

½ cup (125 g) Ricotta Cheese (page 140)

½ cup (60 g) shredded vegan mozzarella cheese

Fillings of choice: mushrooms, fresh basil, fresh diced tomatoes, fresh chopped garlic, chopped onion, artichokes, spinach, vegan pepperoni, vegan sausage, etc., ¼ to ½ cup of each

To make the dough: In a large bowl, combine the yeast, water, salt, and olive oil and stir well until dissolved. After 5 minutes, and a little swelling, add 1¼ cups (150 g) of the flour and mix well to combine. Add another 1¼ cups (150 g) flour and mix well with your hands. Transfer the dough to a lightly floured work surface and knead with floured hands for at least 5 and up to 7 minutes, adding as much of the remaining ½ cup (60 g) flour as necessary to form a smooth and elastic dough; it should not be sticky. Transfer the dough to a lightly oiled 2- or 3-quart (1.8 or 2.7 L) bowl and turn to coat with oil. Cover with a clean towel or plastic wrap and let rise in a warm place until doubled in size, about 1 hour.

Preheat the oven to 475°F (240°C, or gas mark 9). Place a pizza stone in the oven to preheat.

Divide the dough into 4 equal portions and form into 4 balls. Place on a lightly oiled baking sheet and cover with a damp towel. Let rest for 15 minutes, then transfer to a lightly floured surface and roll out into four 6-inch (15 cm) circles.

To make the filling: Place the fillings of choice in the center of one side of each circle. You'll be filling the half-moon, leaving about 1 inch (2.5 cm) from the edge. Spread a little more than 1 tablespoon (15 g) sauce, then 2 tablespoons (30 g) ricotta, then top with 2 tablespoons (14 g) cheese and the toppings of choice, being careful not to overstuff. Spoon a little sauce on top of the pile. Fold the dough over the filling to meet the other side. Crimp the edges with a fork or your fingers, then cut a small slit in the top of the calzone to allow steam to escape while cooking. Transfer carefully (spatulas help here) onto the preheated pizza stone and bake for 8 to 10 minutes, or until well browned. Remove from the oven with a metal peel or spatula and serve hot with the remaining sauce for dipping.

YIELD: 4 calzones

Fun Fact

Calzones most likely date back to the creation of pizza. The pizza as we know it today was first made in Naples. However, flatbreads go as far back as ancient Egypt, when they were topped with herbs and served at birthday celebrations for pharaohs.

TIRAMISU FOR ME, TIRAMISU FOR YOU

*Gluten Free (use gluten-free flour)

Meaning "pick-me-up" in Italian, tiramisu is definitively my favorite dessert, ever! Whether served as a cake or a parfait, it is a decadent confection. And no one will know it's vegan, what with that creamy, rummy custard layered in light, flaky, espresso-dipped cookies.

FOR LADYFINGERS:

2 cups (240 g) all-purpose flour

1 cup (200 g) sugar

1 tablespoon (14 g) baking powder

1 teaspoon arrowroot powder

⅓ cup (75 g) vegan butter

2 teaspoons vanilla extract

1 cup (235 ml) soymilk

FOR MASCARPONE:

¼ cup (60 ml) vegan heavy cream, store-bought or homemade (page 15)

1 tablespoon (8 g) agar powder or arrowroot flour

1 cup (230 g) vegan cream cheese

¼ cup (60 g) vegan sour cream

2 tablespoons (30 ml) Amaretto or 1 tablespoon (15 ml) almond extract

⅓ cup (40 g) confectioners' sugar

2 teaspoons vanilla extract

FOR ASSEMBLY:

1½ cups (353 ml) strong espresso, divided, cooled

2 teaspoons dark rum

½ cup (50 g) vegan dark chocolate shavings, for garnish (shave cold chocolate with a potato peeler)

To make the ladyfingers: Preheat the oven to 350°F (180°C, or gas mark 4) and line a 9 × 12-inch (23 × 30.5 cm) baking sheet with parchment paper. Sift together the flour, sugar, baking powder, and arrowroot powder, and stir just to combine. Add the butter, vanilla, and soymilk. Stir until you get rid of most of the lumps. Spread the mixture evenly on the baking sheet, like making a sheet cake. Bake for 25 minutes, until light golden brown. Let cool for 5 minutes and transfer the baked cake with parchment paper to a cutting board. Cut the cake lengthwise (up and down) into 3 pieces, and then cut crosswise (side to side) into 8 pieces to make 24 finger-size cookies. Place on the baking sheet and bake for another 15 minutes, or until slightly golden. Remove from the oven and let cool completely.

To make the mascarpone: Bring the heavy cream to a boil in a small saucepan, remove from the heat, add the agar, stir until dissolved, then let cool to room temperature. Add the cream cheese, sour cream, Amaretto, confectioners' sugar, and vanilla and whisk until well incorporated and fluffy. Cover and refrigerate for at least 3 hours. If it solidifies, stir to soften before using.

Add 1 tablespoon (15 ml) of the espresso to the mascarpone cheese and mix until thoroughly combined. In a small shallow dish, combine the remaining 1 cup and 3 tablespoons (338 ml) espresso and the rum. Dip each ladyfinger into the espresso mixture for 3 to 5 seconds, but no longer or they will fall apart. Place 12 of the soaked ladyfingers on the bottom of a 13 × 9-inch (33 × 23 cm) baking dish, cutting them in if needed to fit the bottom. Spread half of the mascarpone mixture evenly over the ladyfingers. Arrange of the remaining 12 soaked ladyfingers on top and spread with the remaining half mascarpone mixture. Cover the tiramisu with plastic wrap and refrigerate for at least 2 hours or up to overnight. Sprinkle with the chocolate shavings just before serving.

YIELD: 8 to 12 servings

COOK'S NOTE

This dessert can be made as a cake but is just as terrific when served as individual parfaits. In a glass, layer the ladyfingers, the mascarpone, more ladyfingers, more mascarpone, and then top with chocolate shavings.

ANISE COOKIES WITH ALMOND ICING

*Gluten Free (use gluten-free flour), **Soy Free (use soy-free vegan butter, shortening, and alternative rice/nut milk)

These cookies are synonymous with the holidays and rightfully so, because they are pretty and fun. I like them as is or doused in icing.

FOR COOKIES:

½ cup (112 g) vegan butter

½ cup (112 g) vegan shortening

1½ cups (300 g) sugar

4 egg replacers, mixed, store-bought or homemade (page 13)

1 teaspoon anise extract

1 teaspoon lemon extract

1 teaspoon vanilla extract

4 cups (480 g) all-purpose flour

2 teaspoons baking powder

½ teaspoon baking soda

FOR GLAZE:

2 cups (240 g) confectioners' sugar

2 tablespoons (30 ml) soymilk, plus more as needed

½ teaspoon almond extract

½ teaspoon vanilla extract (or a full teaspoon of vanilla if you want to omit the almond extract)

Vegan colored sprinkles

To make the cookies: Preheat the oven to 350°F (180°C, or gas mark 4). Line 3 baking sheets with parchment paper or silicone baking mats.

In a double boiler or saucepan, melt the butter and shortening. Remove from the heat and let cool. In a large bowl, combine the sugar, egg replacers, anise, lemon, and vanilla. Add the melted butter mixture and stir to combine. In a separate bowl, combine the flour, baking powder, and baking soda, then add to the butter mixture and combine until it forms a soft dough (it will be easier to work with when cool). Spoon about 1 tablespoon (15 g) of dough per cookie onto the prepared baking sheets and bake for 15 to 20 minutes, until golden. Let cool on the pans, then transfer to a wire rack to cool completely. You will get ball-like cookies because the dough doesn't flatten out like sugar cookies do.

To make the glaze: Combine the confectioners' sugar, milk, and extracts in a bowl. Add a little more milk or a little more sugar to achieve the desired consistency. Dip half of each cooled cookie into the glaze, or spread the glaze with an offset spatula. Top with the sprinkles while still warm.

YIELD: 36 cookies

COOK'S NOTE

If you like, add natural food coloring to your glaze for a festive look.

Fun Fact

Anise and star anise are not related, despite having the same aromatic characteristics. In addition, neither is the source of licorice, which is its own plant entirely.

Chapter 10

GERMANY

WE'VE ENTERED THE LAND of brats and beer! Due to the fertile terrain for grazing livestock and access to many water sources, the German diet mainly consists of meat and dairy. Smoking, marinating, and salting techniques were developed in the Middle Ages to help preserve meat, a practice that is used today in sausage making and other popular dishes.

The Romans made significant contributions to German cuisine and food culture. Latin literature records that German cuisine had been pretty tame, but by the time the Romans completed their colonization of southern Germany, the Germans took to Roman eating and drinking habits quickly. Over time, Germany has picked up myriad French and Italian cooking techniques and has incorporated more fruits, vegetables, rice, and potatoes into their diet.

Simple yet substantial food is the crux of German cuisine. Traditional foods obviously include meat, sausages (wurst), and cheese, but they've come to include juniper berries with horseradish, hazelnuts, sauerkraut, and pumpernickel bread.

As one would expect, geographical differences and neighboring countries have an influence on regional cuisine. Cooking in the north tends to reflect the customs of the nearby Scandinavian countries. The diet here is much heavier than that in the south, with an emphasis on meat and potatoes. In the south, a lighter cuisine can be found with strong influences from nearby Italy and Austria. Also, grain products are often substituted for potatoes in many instances, such as with spaetzle, which is a special type of pasta noodle.

Although Germany no longer holds the title for the biggest beer-drinking nation, you can rest assured that there are a slew of sloshy steins at any get-together, along with oodles of heavy food.

So grab your frosty mug, fill it with pilsner, and get your non-meaty German grub on. *Gut essen* (eat well)!

TRADITIONAL HOMEMADE PRETZELS

*Gluten Free (use gluten-free flour), **Soy Free (use soy-free vegan butter)

If this doesn't scream "German food," I don't know what does. (Okay, besides beer and brats.) Your kids or the kid in you will have loads of fun with this recipe. How can you beat fresh, homemade, thick salty pretzels?

2 packages (2¼ teaspoons, or 9 g each) active dry yeast

1 cup plus 3 tablespoons 280 ml) lukewarm water

4 cups (480 g) all-purpose flour

2 teaspoons salt

1 teaspoon sugar

3 tablespoons (42 g) vegan butter, softened

Coarse salt (optional)

½ cup (112 g) baking soda

Melted vegan butter, for brushing

Mustard, for serving

Dissolve the yeast in the lukewarm water. Mix the flour and salt together in a large mixing bowl. Form a well in the flour mixture, then add the sugar to the center of the well. Pour the yeast/water mixture into the well. Let it rest for 15 minutes before mixing. Add the softened butter to the mixing bowl and knead into a smooth dough, and then let the dough rest for 30 minutes. Cut the dough into 12 equal portions, then roll each piece on a flat, dry surface until about 20 inches (51 cm) long (shorter ropes will yield fatter pretzels, and they are harder to tie), tapering toward the ends. Place the pretzels, uncovered, in the fridge for about 1 hour.

Preheat the oven to 400°F (200°C, or gas mark 6). Line a baking sheet with parchment paper and sprinkle with the coarse salt.

Fill a large pot three-fourths full with water and bring to a boil. Carefully and slowly add the baking soda to the boiling water. When the baking soda hits the water, it will bubble like crazy for a moment and then go down. Be very cautious not to get burned, so stand back until the bath has simmered down. Using a slotted spoon, gently drop each pretzel into the bath for 10 seconds, then turn over for another 10 seconds. Transfer to the prepared baking sheet and bake for about 12 minutes, or until golden brown. Brush with the melted butter and serve with the mustard.

YIELD: 12 pretzels

fun Fact

Invented by a monk about 1,400 years ago who was looking for a creative way to bake unleavened bread for Lent, pretzels were meant to mimic the monks who, back then, prayed with their hands crossed over their chests. They were made soft for children's treats, and given to them if they memorized their prayers. They named them *pretiola*, which in Latin means "little reward."

POTATOEY PICKERT
(POTATO HASH)

*Gluten Free (use gluten-free flour)

A bite of this version of hash browns and you'll know why they're so popular in Deutschland.

2 packages (2¼ teaspoons, or 9 g each) active dry yeast

2⅛ cups (500 ml) soymilk, warm

6 large potatoes, peeled and grated

4½ cups (540 g) all-purpose flour

2½ cups (500 g) puréed silken tofu

1 tablespoon (18 g) salt

1 tablespoon (13 g) sugar

2 cups (290 g) raisins

Safflower oil, for frying (or preferred high-heat oil)

Jam, applesauce, vegan butter, and/or syrup, for serving

Put the yeast in a very large pot and add the warm milk and grated potatoes; stir to combine. Add the flour and tofu and mix well. Add the salt and sugar and stir to combine. Stir in the raisins and mix until well combine. It should have the consistency of soft cookie dough; add a little milk or flour to adjust if necessary. Let sit for 30 minutes, until doubled in size.

Heat 1 inch (2.5 cm) of oil in a large skillet over low heat. Drop palm-size amounts (small pancakes) into the oil, being careful not to crowd the pan, and fry until golden brown and cooked through, 2 to 3 minutes. Drain on a paper towel–lined plate. Serve with jam, applesauce, vegan butter, and/or syrup.

YIELD: About 24 cakes

Fun Fact

Did you know that potatoes have an okay amount of protein? Yep, about 2 grams! And fiber too—not too shabby!

SEITAN WIENERSCHNITZEL
(BREADED SEITAN)

*Gluten Free (use tempeh or tofu and gluten-free bread crumbs)

**Schnitzel is the original breaded meat of the world. This version is
so tasty, however, that even avowed carnivores will be satisfied.**

Coconut oil, for frying (or preferred high-heat oil)

¼ cup (30 g) all-purpose flour

Salt and pepper, to taste

4 seitan steaks, store-bought or homemade (page 19),
pounded to ¼-inch (6 mm) thickness

2 recipes vegan egg wash (page 13)

½ cup (60 g) bread crumbs

Lemon slices, for serving

Heat at least ¼ inch (6 mm) of oil in a large skillet or pan
to 350°F (180°C).

Spread the flour on a shallow plate and season with salt
and pepper. Dredge the cutlets in the flour, shaking off the
excess. Dip into the egg wash to coat, allowing the excess
to drip back into the bowl, and then roll quickly in the bread
crumbs until well coated. Place 2 cutlets in the oil, and fry
for 3 to 4 minutes on one side, moving them around a little
with your fork so they don't stick. Turn them over once and
fry for 3 to 4 minutes, or until golden brown. Repeat with
the remaining 2 cutlets. Let cool on a paper towel–lined
plate. Serve with lemon slices.

YIELD: 4 servings

COOK'S NOTE

Try making a schnitzel sandwich! On a
good-sized crusty roll, slather on some
vegan garlic aioli, squeeze on the lemon
and perhaps some leafy greens, and
go to town. Go nuts and add some
sauerkraut while you're at it!

fun fact

Kaiser Basileios I (867–886
CE) liked his meat covered in
sheets of gold. This got
expensive, so they replaced the
gold with bread crumbs.

VEGGIE-STYLE GERMAN POTATO SOUP

*Gluten Free (use gluten-free vegan bacon)

An oh-so-good classic from Deutschland! If you haven't noticed, I'm a sucker for soups, and this one is freakin' delicious and chock-full of creamy flavor!

2 tablespoons (28 g) vegan butter

1 large leek, trimmed and chopped

2 large carrots, peeled and diced

1 stalk celery, diced

1 cup (90 g) chopped cabbage

1 large white onion, chopped

¼ cup (15 g) chopped fresh parsley, plus more for garnish

2 cups (220 g) peeled, diced potatoes

½ teaspoon caraway seed

¼ teaspoon grated nutmeg

1 bay leaf

4 cups (940 ml) vegan beef broth (make with vegan beef bouillon)

Salt and pepper, to taste

½ cup (115 g) vegan sour cream

1 pound (454 g) vegan bacon, cooked and diced (about 2 cups [160 g])

Splash of white vinegar

Heat the butter in a large soup pot. Add the leek, carrots, celery, cabbage, onion, and parsley and fry until the onion becomes transparent, 2 to 3 minutes. Add the potatoes, caraway, nutmeg, bay leaf, and broth. Add salt and pepper to taste, stir well, and cook until the potatoes are tender all the way through and almost done, 8 to 10 minutes.

Remove and discard the bay leaf. Remove about a third of the potatoes from the pot. Mash the remaining two-thirds and return the reserved potatoes to the pot. Add the sour cream and reheat the soup. Stir in the bacon and cook for a few more minutes to be sure the flavors have married well and the soup has thickened. Season with salt and pepper, add just a hint of vinegar, garnish with the chopped parsley, and serve.

YIELD: 4 to 6 servings

Fun fact

Soup is one of the best meals you can have to win the battle of the bulge. A hearty soup like this one is not only filling and satisfying, but it's also packed with essential vitamins and nutrients from all the delicious veggies. You've also got a little protein and some good fiber to keep you on the go!

GOOD FOR YOU GOULASH
(BEEF STEW)

*Gluten Free (use gluten-free vegan beef and bacon), **Soy Free (use soy-free vegan beef, bacon, and butter)

**This is the German version of the famous Hungarian dish. It's super
hearty and savory, so even omnivores will ask for seconds!**

½ cup (56 g) vegan butter, divided

3 packages (8 to 10 ounces, or 225 to 280 g each)
vegan beef chunks

½ cup (40 g) finely chopped vegan bacon

2 cups (320 g) diced white onion

3 cloves garlic, finely chopped

2 teaspoons sweet paprika

3 tablespoons (48 g) tomato paste

5¼ cups (1,235 ml) vegan beef broth
(make with vegan beef bouillon)

Zest of 1 lemon

1 medium-size red bell pepper, cut into bite-size chunks

1 medium-size green bell pepper, cut into bite-size chunks

½ cup (16 g) finely chopped fresh marjoram

Salt and pepper, to taste

Cooked macaroni noodles, for serving

In a large pot, melt 2 tablespoons (28 g) of the butter over medium heat. Add the beef chunks in small portions and brown on all sides (but do not cook all the way through yet); remove each batch as it browns to a covered dish and set aside. In the same pan, add the bacon, onion, and garlic and sauté for a few minutes until starting to brown, about 5 minutes. Return the beef to the pan, and sprinkle with the paprika.

Add the tomato paste and stir until blended. Add just a little of the broth and bring to a boil, stirring. Repeat with a little more broth, then after it boils, add the rest of the broth along with the lemon zest. Reduce the heat to low, cover, and let simmer for about 1 hour. In the last 5 minutes of cooking time, add the bell peppers and marjoram and season with salt and pepper to taste. Divide the noodles among 8 to 10 bowls, place a bit of the remaining 2 tablespoons (28 g) butter on each, stir to coat, then ladle the stew on top.

YIELD: 8 to 10 servings

fun fact

Okay, so goulash isn't really German. While Germans have their version, its famed birthplace is Hungary. It was made popular by Hungarian herdsmen, called *gulyas*, who cooked it out in the fields in large cast-iron kettles over open fires.

SEITAN STEAK AND MUSHROOM ROULADEN (SEITAN AND MUSHROOM ROLLS)

*Soy Free (use soy-free vegan butter)

Here's a tasty and fun way to kick dinner up a notch! These are an incredibly satisfying and flavorful dish for omnivores to sink their teeth into without missing the meat.

FOR FILLING:

½ cup (112 g) vegan butter

4 cups (280 g) finely diced mushrooms

2 shallots, minced

3 cloves garlic, minced

2 teaspoons minced fresh thyme or tarragon

1 egg replacer, mixed, store-bought or homemade (page 13)

½ cup (60 g) bread crumbs

Salt and pepper, to taste

FOR SEITAN STEAKS:

8 thin seitan steaks, store-bought or homemade (page 19), about 3 ounces (85 g) each, pounded to ¼-inch (6 mm) thickness

Salt and pepper, to taste

½ cup (60 g) flour mixed with salt and pepper

2 to 3 tablespoons (30 to 45 ml) coconut oil, for frying (or preferred high-heat oil)

1 medium-size white onion, diced

2 teaspoons dried thyme

1 cup (235 ml) red wine

1 quart (945 ml) vegan beef broth (make with vegan beef bouillon)

To make the filling: Melt the butter in a large frying pan. Add the mushrooms, shallots, garlic, and thyme. Simmer until the mushrooms are very well cooked, 2 to 3 minutes. Place in a mixing bowl and add the egg replacer and bread crumbs; season with salt and pepper. Let the mixture chill in the fridge while you prepare the seitan steaks.

To make the steaks: Season the pounded steaks with salt and pepper, then spread on about 1 heaping tablespoon (15 g) mushroom filling. Roll up the steak and secure with a toothpick, weaving it like a safety pin. This way you can brown it easily and the toothpick won't get in the way. Roll the steaks in the seasoned flour.

In a large, deep pan, over medium heat, heat the oil, then add the rouladen and fry until beginning to brown, 1 to 2 minutes. Add the onion and thyme and continue to fry, turning, until brown on all sides, 2 to 3 minutes longer. Transfer to a plate. To the pan, add the remaining flour that was used for breading and stir to combine with the onion; cook for 1 minute. Add the wine and broth, blend until smooth, and bring to a simmer. Add the rouladen back to the pan and simmer, covered, over low heat, for 30 to 40 minutes, or until fork-tender and the flavors have melded.

YIELD: 8 servings

COOK'S NOTE

You may also use seitan strips to make smaller, appetizer-size rouladen.

Fun Fact

Rouladen is French for "rolled." The Germans liked the technique, applied it to their beloved meats, and voilà— German rouladen!

JUST LIKE OMA'S APFELSTREUDEL
(APPLE STRUDEL)

*Gluten Free (use gluten-free flour), **Soy Free (use soy-free vegan butter)

Flaky, in a good way. Apple-y in an awesome way! All the work that goes into this dessert is worth the yumma-liciousness! If you don't want to make the dough, you can use store-bought vegan phyllo or puff pastry dough (see Cook's Note).

FOR PASTRY DOUGH:

1½ cups (180 g) flour

Pinch of salt

¼ to ⅓ cup (60 to 80 ml) lukewarm water

1 egg replacer, mixed, store-bought or homemade (page 13)

1 tablespoon (15 ml) oil

Fun Fact

While the oldest strudel recipe dates back to 1696, the pastry has a much older history, having originated in the Middle East.

To make the dough: In a large bowl, mix together the flour and salt. Make a well in the center of the flour and pour in ¼ cup (60 ml) of the water, the egg replacer, and the oil. Stir the wet ingredients into the flour with a spoon, adding more water as needed to form a soft, pliable dough. Turn out the dough onto a lightly floured work surface and knead until smooth and elastic, 3 to 5 minutes. Cover with plastic wrap and set aside to rest for at least 1 hour.

To make the filling: Preheat the oven to 400°F (200°C, or gas mark 6). Lightly grease a 13 × 18-inch (33 × 46 cm) baking pan or line it with parchment paper or a silicone baking mat.

Cover a work surface approximately 4 feet × 4 feet (1.2 × 1.2 m) with a clean piece of cloth and make sure it's securely fastened. Your work area should be open (like a table you can walk around instead of a counter). The cloth is used to facilitate stretching and rolling the dough, so you don't want it sliding around. Then dust the cloth lightly with flour. Place the rested dough in the center of the cloth.

Using a rolling pin, roll the dough into a large, thin rectangle. When the dough is as thin as it will go from rolling, it's time to begin stretching and pulling the dough. This is done by placing your lightly floured hands under the dough, and gently pulling and stretching the dough, working your way around the table. Do this until it is a good-size rectangle, about 24 × 18 inches (61 × 46 cm). Be very careful when you are pulling and stretching not to tear the dough, but if you do, just pinch it back together and smooth it out. Try not to make it super thin or it will tear when you fill and roll it. Trim off any thick edges or thin them out, being sure to keep the dough in its rectangular shape. Let the dough rest for a few minutes.

CONTINUED ON NEXT PAGE ▶

FOR APPLE FILLING:

2 pounds (905 g) baking apples, peeled and thinly sliced (Granny Smith are best)

½ cup (60 g) coarsely chopped walnuts or almonds

¼ cup (75 g) raisins, soaked in warm water and drained

½ cup (100 g) granulated sugar

3 tablespoons (45 ml) rum or orange juice

1 tablespoon (7 g) ground cinnamon

1 teaspoon vanilla extract

½ to 1 cup (112 to 225 g) vegan butter, melted

½ cup (60 g) dry bread crumbs

¼ cup (30 g) confectioners' sugar

To make the filling: In a large bowl, mix together the apples, walnuts, raisins, granulated sugar, rum, cinnamon, and vanilla. Brush the dough with the melted butter, leaving an unbuttered border of about 2½ inches (6.3 cm) on all sides. Sprinkle the buttered section of the dough with the bread crumbs, then spread the apple mixture evenly over the bread crumbs.

Use the cloth to help you gently lift one of the long sides of the dough and roll it over the apple filling, brushing the exposed parts with more melted butter. Repeat with the other long side, making them overlap and forming a big cigar-shaped roll. Don't forget to brush all exposed parts with butter. Gently lift the strudel (use the cloth to help you move and roll it) and place seam side down on the prepared baking pan. You may have to bend the strudel into a crescent shape to fit it on the baking pan.

Bake for 40 to 60 minutes, or until cooked through and golden brown on top. Brush the top of the strudel with some more melted butter once or twice during baking and be careful not to burn. Remove from the oven and sprinkle with the confectioners' sugar. Slice and serve warm.

YIELD: 12 to 14 servings

COOK'S NOTE

Try making savory strudel with vegan cheese, spinach, mushrooms, and your favorite herbs.

If using phyllo dough, thaw and lay out 5 sheets, brushing each sheet generously with melted butter and laying them on top of one another. Fill the center as described above, leaving a 2-inch (5 cm) border. Fold the short sides over the filling, then the long sides. This will be a lot smaller than the homemade strudel.

Fun Fact

Even though strudel dates back hundreds of years, it was the Austrians who created the first apple strudel, or *Wiener Apfelstrudel* (Viennese Apple Strudel).

Chapter 11

GREECE

LIKE THEIR ITALIAN NEIGHBORS, the Greeks love to mix food and company, and each meal is planned with guests in mind. Greek food is fresh, light, and very close to its roots. Greek cuisine is exactly what it has been for centuries; in fact, it has not changed since ancient times. The flavors, ingredients, and traditions have stood the test of time.

Greek food is synonymous with healthy dining because traditional meals are largely comprised of fresh fruit and vegetables, legumes, and olive oil, with less meat and more fish than most other European cuisines. In fact, the famous Mediterranean Diet is largely based on Greek cuisine.

Some of the more common spices found in Greek cooking are mint, dill, oregano, and bay leaves. They also like to use cinnamon and cloves for spicing meats, while showcasing nuts and honey in their desserts. The basic grain is wheat and the more popular vegetables are tomatoes, potatoes, eggplant, and okra. Citrus is also widely used. Greek dishes are not heavily spiced, showing simplicity, and the natural, fresh flavors of the Mediterranean come through in the food.

One of the more influential philosophers in Greek history was Epicurus. In the Hellenistic period, he taught the importance of pleasure, simplicity, and good friends, which are all central to Greek cooking. Interestingly, the first known cookbook was written by a Greek named Archestratus in 320 BCE. Greece's 4,000-year-old culinary history spread through ancient Rome and into the rest of the world via Europe.

The Greeks make eating an event, so much so that they love to move meals to taverns and restaurants to incorporate more guests into the fray. They usually begin with mezes, small plates such as dolmas and a variety of salads, along with a glass of wine or ouzo (a liqueur made from anise), followed by an array of main dish, and then a fresh dessert. There is simply no stopping a Greek feast.

Grab your friends, pour some ouzo, and break some plates, 'cause it's going to be a big Grecian feast! *Opa* (hooray)!

HORIATIKI (GREEK SALAD)

*Soy Free (omit the feta)

The epitome of light, fresh Greek fare. Nothing beats a good Greek salad on a warm, breezy day. Close your eyes, take a bite, and be transported to the Greek Isles!

FOR FETA CHEESE:

¼ cup (60 ml) olive oil

2 tablespoons (30 g) tahini

½ cup (120 ml) red wine vinegar or apple cider vinegar

1 teaspoon minced garlic

1 tablespoon (8 g) nutritional yeast

1 tablespoon (2 g) dried basil

½ teaspoon dried oregano

Salt and pepper, to taste

1 pound (454 g) extra-firm tofu, pressed, drained, and cubed or crumbled

FOR SALAD:

3 tablespoons (45 ml) olive oil

1½ tablespoons (23 ml) lemon juice

1 clove garlic, minced

Salt and pepper, to taste

½ teaspoon dried oregano

3 tomatoes, cut into wedges

¼ red onion, sliced into rings

½ cucumber, sliced into thick half-moons

½ green bell pepper, julienned

16 kalamata olives

To make the feta cheese: Place the oil, tahini, vinegar, garlic, nutritional yeast, basil, oregano, salt, and pepper in a bowl and whisk together. Add the tofu, mix well, and let sit for at least 1 hour.

To make the salad: Place the olive oil, lemon juice, garlic, salt, pepper, and oregano in a small jar with a screw-top lid and shake to combine. Place the tomatoes, onion, cucumber, bell pepper, olives, and feta in a large bowl. Pour the dressing over the salad and toss gently to combine just before serving. Garnish with a grind of black pepper.

YIELD: 4 servings

fun fact

Horiatiki salad means "country" or "village" salad. What we know as the widely popular salad can be found on virtually every restaurant menu in Greece.

COOK'S NOTE

For a more traditional salad, nix the lettuce and really chunk up the veggies.

GYRO PITA SANDWICHES

*Soy Free (use soy-free yogurt and omit the sour cream)

Bring the food court into your own kitchen, the healthy way! When I was young, my dad and I lived for these and I have to say that this recipe brings me right back. So convincing and bursting with flavor! If you want to make your own pita bread, check out healthyvoyager.com for a great recipe.

FOR TZATZIKI SAUCE:

1 cup (230 g) plain vegan yogurt

1 cup (230 g) vegan sour cream

1 large cucumber

1 tablespoon (18 g) salt, plus more as needed

2 cloves garlic, minced

2 tablespoons (30 ml) lemon juice

1 tablespoon (15 ml) white wine vinegar

2 teaspoons finely chopped fresh or dried dill

Freshly ground pepper, to taste

FOR GYRO:

1 tablespoon (15 ml) olive oil

½ cup (80 g) minced onion

2 cloves garlic, minced

8 ounces (225 g) seitan, store-bought or homemade (page 19), cut into thin strips or slices

2 tablespoons (30 ml) lemon juice

½ teaspoon dried oregano

½ teaspoon ground cumin

½ cup (23 g) shredded romaine and iceberg lettuce

½ cup (90 g) diced tomato

4 regular-size, store-bought pita rounds

To make the sauce: Blend the yogurt and sour cream until creamy. Peel the cucumbers, then cut in half lengthwise and scrape out the seeds with a small spoon. Slice the cucumbers, then put in a colander, sprinkle with the salt, and let stand in the sink or over a bowl for 30 minutes to draw out the water. Drain well and wipe dry with paper towels.

In food processor, combine the cucumbers, garlic, lemon juice, vinegar, dill, and a few grinds of black pepper. Process until well blended, then stir into the yogurt mixture. Taste before adding any extra salt, then season as needed. Place in the refrigerator for at least 2 hours before serving so the flavors can marry. This will keep for a few days or more in the refrigerator, covered, but you will need to drain off any water and stir each time you use it.

To make the gyro: Preheat the broiler. Heat the oil in a skillet over medium-low heat and sauté the onion and garlic until soft, 5 to 6 minutes, stirring constantly. Add sautéed onion and garlic to a mixing bowl along with the seitan, lemon juice, oregano, and cumin and mix thoroughly. Place on a baking sheet and broil for 3 to 5 minutes on each side, turning once, or until desired doneness, being careful not to dry it out.

Cut around one edge of 4 pita breads and pull open to form a pocket. Fill each pita with one-fourth of the lettuce and tomato, place one-fourth of the seitan on top, and drizzle with the tzatziki sauce.

YIELD: 4 servings

Fun Fact

George Apostolou is the grandfather of gyros in the United States. In 1965, he was the first to successfully bring this hundred-year-old Greek recipe to the States and manufacture them on a mass scale. What Papa George created at his small Parkview Restaurant in Chicago has since become a fast-food favorite with ancient roots.

COOK'S NOTE

Check out how to make your own pita from scratch in the "In the Kitchen" recipe section at HealthyVoyager.com!

DIVINE DOLMAS
(STUFFED GRAPE LEAVES)

I have to say that these are one of my favorite dishes—refreshing, full of nutty, dilly flavor, and mega satisfying. Not to mention healthy, good for you, and perfect for a snack or a side!

1¼ cups (295 ml) olive oil, divided

1 medium-size white onion, finely chopped

4 scallions, finely chopped

3 cloves garlic, minced

½ cup (68 g) pine nuts

2 cups (330 g) cooked long-grain or brown rice

1 teaspoon salt

2 tablespoons (12 g) minced fresh mint

Juice of 2 lemons, divided

1 jar (8 ounces, or 225 g) grape leaves
or 30 medium-size fresh leaves

In a large sauté pan over medium-high heat, heat ¼ cup (60 ml) of the olive oil. Add the onion and scallions and sauté until translucent, 5 to 6 minutes. Add the garlic and pine nuts and sauté for another 2 minutes. Transfer to a large mixing bowl and allow to cool slightly. Add the cooked rice, salt, mint, and juice of 1 lemon to the bowl, mix well, and set aside.

Bring a medium-size pot of water to a simmer over medium heat. Drop the grape leaves in batches of 4 or 5 into the hot water and blanch for 30 seconds. Quickly remove them from the water and spread flat on a towel-lined work surface. Cut the stem from each grape leaf, as needed.

To assemble the dolmas, place 1 grape leaf on the work surface, dull side up. Place 1 to 2 teaspoons of rice filling near the stem end of the leaf. Fold the stem (bottom) end up over the filling, fold the sides in toward the center, then roll up into a small cylindrical package, being careful not to fold too tightly, because the rice will expand during cooking. Place the dolmas in a large Dutch oven or wide sauté pan, seam side down. Combine the remaining 1 cup (235 ml) olive oil and remaining juice of 1 lemon, and pour over the dolmas. Cover with a lid, heavy plate, or baking dish and add water up to the level of the lid so that the dolmas remain submerged. Bring to a boil, lower the heat, and simmer for 1 hour, or until the dolmas are tender. Let cool in the liquid before removing them with a slotted spoon. Serve at room temperature.

YIELD: About 30 dolmas

fun fact

Greek mythology mentions that dolmades were served on Mount Olympus, but it seems that they date back to the time of Alexander the Great. The poor, with little to eat, took what meat they could, mixed it with leftover rice, and rolled it up in grape leaves.

MORE MOUSSAKA, PLEASE!
(VEGETABLE CASSEROLE)

*Gluten Free (use gluten-free bread crumbs and flour), **Soy Free
(make cashew heavy cream and mix with plain alternative rice/nut milk)

Creamy, veggie-packed Greek lasagne. Mmm!

FOR BÉCHAMEL SAUCE:

3 tablespoons (42 g) vegan butter

3 tablespoons (23 g) all-purpose flour

2 cups (470 ml) plain soymilk

1 package (12 ounces, or 340 g) silken tofu

1 vegetable bouillon cube

Pinch of grated nutmeg

Pepper, to taste

FOR MOUSSAKA:

1½ pounds (680 g) eggplant (about 2 medium size),
sliced into ¼-inch (6 mm) rounds

Salt and pepper, to taste

8 ounces (225 g) zucchini (2 small),
sliced into ¼-inch (6 mm) rounds

5 tablespoons (75 ml) olive oil, divided

2 teaspoons minced fresh thyme, divided

1 cup (160 g) finely chopped onion

2 large portobello mushrooms, stemmed and chopped

8 ounces (225 g) seitan, store-bought
or homemade (page 19), or vegan ground beef

4 cloves garlic, minced, divided

1 teaspoon ground cumin

½ teaspoon ground cinnamon

¼ teaspoon ground allspice

1 cup (180 g) crushed, drained tomatoes

2 tablespoons (32 g) tomato paste

1 teaspoon lemon juice

1 cup (115 g) bread crumbs

1½ pounds (680 g) russet potatoes, peeled, cooked,
and mashed with a little salt and pepper

In a medium-size saucepan, melt the butter over medium heat and add the flour. Whisk for 2 to 3 minutes, until smooth. Blend the milk and tofu together, then slowly add it to the pan, along with the bouillon, whisking constantly until the sauce has thickened, 2 to 3 minutes. Lower the heat to very low and simmer, stirring occasionally, for 15 to 30 minutes, or until thickened. Season with nutmeg and pepper.

Arrange a single layer of eggplant on a baking sheet. Sprinkle each with salt, turn, and repeat. Let sit for 30 minutes, then rinse, dry, and return to sheet. Arrange zucchini in a single layer on another baking sheet.

Preheat the oven to 375°F (190°C, or gas mark 5).

Combine 1 tablespoon (15 ml) of the olive oil with some black pepper and 1 teaspoon of the thyme. Brush this mixture over both sides of the eggplant and zucchini, then bake both until softened, about 20 minutes. Remove from the oven (leave oven on) and set aside.

Heat 2 tablespoons (30 ml) of the oil in a frying pan, add the onion, and sauté over medium-low heat until soft, about 10 minutes. Place the portobellos and seitan in a food processor and pulse to combine. Add to the onion and increase the heat to medium; fry, stirring occasionally, until the pan is dry, 2 to 3 minutes. Add 3 cloves of the garlic, cumin, cinnamon, allspice, tomatoes, and tomato paste, stirring occasionally, until fairly dry, about 15 minutes. Stir in the lemon juice, season with salt and pepper, and set aside.

Reduce the oven to 350°F (180°C, or gas mark 4).

Combine the bread crumbs with the remaining garlic, thyme, and olive oil. Arrange half the eggplant in the bottom of a 13 × 9-inch (33 × 23 cm) baking dish, followed by a layer of half of the seitan mixture, then a layer of half of the mashed potatoes. Continue layering with the remaining eggplant, zucchini, seitan mixture, and mashed potatoes. Pour the béchamel over the top. Sprinkle with the bread crumb mixture. Bake until golden brown and not jiggly, about 30 minutes. Let sit for 5 minutes before serving.

YIELD: 6 to 8 servings

HEAVENLY SPANAKOPITA TRIANGLES

Gluten Free (use gluten-free phyllo dough)

Warm, cheesy, savory pastries? I'm in! These are perfect as appetizers or even a meal on their own. This recipe really gives the original a run for its money!

3 tablespoons (45 ml) olive oil

1 medium-size white onion, finely diced

1 or 2 cloves garlic, minced

¾ teaspoon dried dill

1 package (14 ounces, or 392 g) extra-firm tofu, pressed and drained

3 tablespoons (24 g) nutritional yeast

2 tablespoons (30 ml) lemon juice

Salt and pepper, to taste

2 cups (360 g) coarsely chopped steamed spinach

1 pound (454 g) vegan phyllo dough, thawed

½ cup (112 g) vegan butter, melted

Heat the olive oil in a skillet over medium heat and sauté the onion and garlic, for 2 to 3 minutes, until translucent. Add the dill and remove from the heat.

In a large bowl, mash the tofu, nutritional yeast, lemon juice, salt, and pepper with a fork until lumpy, then add the onion mixture and the steamed spinach.

Unroll the thawed phyllo, handling with care. With a sharp knife, cut the phyllo into 3 × 11-inch (7.5 × 28 cm) strips and cover with waxed paper and a slightly damp dish towel to keep moist. Make sure they don't get too wet or too dry. Take a strip of phyllo and lay it in a lightly oiled 9 × 13-inch (23 × 33 cm) pan or baking sheet. Brush lightly all over with the butter. Add another layer, brushing it as well. Spread about 1 tablespoon (15 g) of the filling on one end of the strip, being careful to leave a 1-inch (2.5 cm) border from the edge. Fold, starting from the filling end, into a triangle, as if folding a flag, until you reach the end of the strip. Brush the top with melted butter. Repeat with the remaining phyllo and filling. Cover them as you finish so they do not dry out while you're assembling the rest. Refrigerate for 30 minutes, covering layers of triangles with waxed paper to prevent sticking.

Preheat the oven to 375°F (190°C, or gas mark 5). Bake for 20 to 30 minutes, or until golden brown.

YIELD: 36 pieces

COOK'S NOTE

If you'd rather make pillows, you can wrap them up like little square packages. Or make them more like baklava by layering the phyllo and filling in a baking pan and then cutting all the way through after baking.

VEGGIE-FRIENDLY PATATOPITA
(VEGETARIAN SOUVLAKI)

*Gluten Free (use gluten-free pita), **Soy Free (omit the tzatziki or make it with plain coconut milk yogurt and no sour cream)

This dish is one that has many incarnations worldwide, but throw these grilled veggies into a pita and drown it in tzatziki and it's inherently Greek.

½ large eggplant, cubed

12 portobello mushrooms, stemmed and cubed

1 green bell pepper, stemmed, seeded, and cubed

6 pineapple rings, each cut into 4 chunks

2 tablespoons (30 ml) balsamic vinegar

1 tablespoon (4 g) chopped fresh oregano or 1 teaspoon dried

2 teaspoons (30 ml) olive oil

1 teaspoon minced garlic

1 recipe Gyro (page 165, optional)

8 large pita breads, store-bought or homemade

1 recipe Tzatziki Sauce (page 165)

In a large bowl, combine the eggplant, mushrooms, bell pepper, pineapple, vinegar, oregano, oil, and garlic. Let marinate for 20 minutes at room temperature, stirring frequently.

Preheat a grill or grill pan. Thread the vegetables, gyro, and pineapple onto 8 metal or presoaked wooden skewers, alternating ingredients. Grill for 10 minutes, turning once, or until the veggies are tender and lightly browned, basting with any leftover marinade. Be careful not to burn. Warm the pita rounds on the grill, turning once. Enjoy on the skewer or wrap 1 pita around each shish kebab and carefully remove the skewer. Top with tzatziki sauce.

YIELD: 4 to 8 servings

Fun Fact

The origins of souvlaki can be traced to an exact recipe from ancient Greece. Found in *The Deipnosophists* by Athenaeus, these skewers were originally called *kandaulos*.

COOK'S NOTE

If you don't have a grill, feel free to panfry your veggies for about 3 to 5 minutes, depending on how crisp you like them.

MELT IN YOUR MOUTH BAKLAVA
(STICKY NUT PASTRY)

*Gluten Free (use gluten-free phyllo dough), **Soy Free (use soy-free vegan butter)

This dessert is literally nuts! Gooey, spicy, nutty, and flaky—MMMMM!!

3 cups (360 g) walnuts

1 cup (145 g) almonds

1 teaspoon ground cinnamon

½ teaspoon ground cloves

12 sheets vegan phyllo dough, thawed

½ cup (112 g) vegan butter, melted

1¼ cups (250 g) sugar

¼ cup (60 ml) lemon juice

2 tablespoons (30 g) maple syrup

1 teaspoons vanilla extract

½ teaspoon almond extract

Preheat the oven to 350°F (180°C, or gas mark 4). Lightly grease a 9 × 13-inch (23 × 33 cm) baking pan.

Place the walnuts in a food processor and pulse until finely chopped, but not pasty or powdery. Place the almonds in the food processor and pulse until finely chopped, but not pasty or powdery. In a bowl, combine the chopped walnuts and almonds, cinnamon, and cloves, stirring well to combine.

Place the stacked sheets of phyllo dough flat on a cutting board and cut them in half widthwise to make 24 sheets that are 9 × 13 inches (23 × 33 cm). Stack the cut sheets on top of each other and remove 6 sheets from the stack to begin working on. Cover the remaining with a clean kitchen towel or waxed paper to keep them from drying out.

Place 1 sheet of phyllo dough in the prepared pan and brush lightly with a little butter. Repeat the layering and buttering procedure for the remaining 5 sheets of phyllo dough (each layer of phyllo will consist of 6 buttered sheets). Sprinkle one-third of the reserved nut mixture evenly over the top of the stacked phyllo dough. Repeat the layering and buttering procedure with the next 6 sheets of phyllo dough, sprinkle with another third of the nut mixture, and repeat the process, ending with a layer of 6 buttered phyllo sheets. Using a sharp knife, carefully cut into 12 or 16 squares.

Bake for 20 minutes, then lower the heat to 300°F (150°C, or gas mark 2). Bake 25 to 30 minutes longer, or until golden brown. Let cool on a rack for up to 2 hours.

Toward the end of the baklava cooling time, make the glaze. In a saucepan, combine the sugar, lemon juice, and maple syrup, and cook over medium heat until thick and syrupy, 2 to 3 minutes. Remove from the heat and stir in the vanilla and almond extracts.

Go over the cuts in the baklava to make sure that the grooves go all the way through. Pour the syrup mixture over the baklava, making sure it goes into all the cracks and crevices. Cover and let stand for a few hours or overnight before serving.

YIELD: 12 or 16 pieces

Fun Fact

Baklava is the source of some Middle Eastern drama. The Greeks, Lebanese, Turks, and Armenians all claim rights to this dessert, although it seems that the Assyrians dished it up first in the eighth century.

LOUKOUMADES OF CHAMPIONS
(LEMONY DOUGHNUT HOLES)

*Gluten Free (use gluten-free flour)

All I have to say is, Greek doughnut holes! These are fan-freakin'-tastic when they're fresh and hot. Lemony and sweet, they melt in your mouth.

2½ cups (300 g) all-purpose flour

½ teaspoons salt

½ package (about 1⅛ teaspoons, or 4.5 g) active dry yeast

1 cup (235 ml) lukewarm water

½ cup (170 g) light agave nectar

1¾ cups (411 ml) water

¾ cup (150 g) sugar

2 teaspoons lemon juice

2 cups (470 ml) coconut oil (or preferred high-heat oil)

2 teaspoons ground cinnamon

Sift the flour and salt together into a bowl. Sprinkle the yeast into the lukewarm water and stir to dissolve. Add the yeast mixture to the flour and beat or knead for 5 minutes, or until the dough is smooth and elastic. Cover the bowl with plastic wrap and a dry dish towel on top. Let rise until the dough has doubled in size, about 1 hour.

In a saucepan, combine the agave, water, sugar, and lemon juice and bring to a boil. Cook, stirring, until the sugar dissolves and the mixture is thick and syrupy, 2 to 3 minutes. Set aside.

Heat the coconut oil in a deep fryer or large saucepan, filled one-quarter to half full, to 350°F (180°C). Pinch off small pieces of dough, roll into a ball about the size of a Ping-Pong ball, and fry for about 3 minutes, or until golden brown, being careful not to crowd the pan. Drain on a paper towel–lined plate and keep warm. Repeat with the remaining dough. Pour the syrup over the hot puffs and sprinkle with the cinnamon.

YIELD: About 24 doughnut holes

Fun Fact

Talk about a sweet reward! Loukoumades were given as awards to the victors of the ancient Olympic games. Because they were made with honey, they were named "honey tokens," and were presented at the awards ceremony to all the winners.

Chapter 12

RUSSIA

AS ONE WOULD IMAGINE, Russian cuisine is hearty and warming. The large, chilly country offers up a great many stews and soups. Such foods were a great way to preserve and make use of meats, poultry, and fish while giving cooks the ability to prepare one-pot meals. Even today at Christmastime, Russians center the festive dinner around a number of soups.

Russia was a very grain-centric nation for some time. Wheat, rye, oats, and millet were made into beautiful pastries, breads, pies, pancakes, and baked puddings. Blintzes are extremely popular, along with a multitude of berries and mushrooms found in the ample forests that cover much of Russia. Traditionally, Russian food is not heavily spiced; however, mustard and horseradish are plentiful on Russian menus.

Neighboring countries brought their influences as well, from the Nordic Vikings to Asian and Western European nations. The New World introduced potatoes to Russia. Of course, that means lots of potato-heavy dishes, but the spud's biggest claim to Russian fame is vodka, surely an invention that came from necessity; after all, the inclement weather was probably best handled with a stiff drink. And what better way to create a national liquor than to use your most abundant vegetable? *Priyatnogo appetita* (eat well)!

APPLE DZYAD
(APPLE PASTRY)

*Gluten Free (use gluten-free flour), **Soy Free (use alternative rice/nut milk and soy-free vegan butter)

You'll love this Russian version of a large, shareable Pop-Tart! It's fun to make and fun to eat, perfect for breakfast or dessert, and there are lots of ways to change it up.

FOR DOUGH:

6 cups (720 g) flour

1 cup (200 g) sugar

Salt, to taste

4 teaspoons (16 g) active dry yeast

1¼ cups 295 ml) warm soymilk

½ cup (112 g) vegan butter, melted

3 egg replacers, mixed, store-bought or homemade (page 13)

FOR FILLING:

1¼ cups (400 g) apple jam

⅓ cup (50 g) raisins

3 tablespoons (35 g) finely chopped dates

½ cup (112 g) vegan butter, melted

To make the dough: Combine the flour, sugar, and salt in a bowl and mix well. In a small bowl, dissolve the yeast in the milk, allow it to get frothy for 10 minutes, and then add it along with the butter and egg replacers to the flour mixture. Knead the dough until smooth and elastic, 5 to 6 minutes, cover with a clean towel, and set it aside to double in size, about 1 hour.

To make the filling: In a saucepot over medium-low heat, warm the apple jam, then add the raisins and dates and stir to combine. Let cool.

Preheat the oven to 350°F (180°C, or gas mark 4). Grease a 13 × 18-inch (33 × 46 cm) baking sheet.

Turn the dough out onto a floured work surface, divide in half, and roll out each half into a thin sheet. Place 1 sheet on the prepared baking pan, then spread the filling evenly over it and cover with the other sheet of dough. Pinch the edges to seal. Brush the top with the melted butter and bake for 25 to 30 minutes, or until the top is golden brown. Let cool, then cut and serve.

YIELD: 12 to 16 servings

COOK'S NOTE

Get creative with the fillings if you're not a fan of raisins, dates, and apples. Have fun with your dzyad!

BEET YOU TO IT BORSCHT
(BEET SOUP)

You may be familiar with the cold serving of this soup. But we're going to pretend we're in Moscow at the height of winter. Doesn't hot soup sound good right now? Tart and savory, chunky and sweet, it's like a tasty, warm hug!

2 tablespoons (30 ml) olive oil

1 pound (454 g) seitan, store-bought or homemade (page 19), cut into ½-inch (1.3 cm) cubes

1 onion, finely chopped

3½ quarts (3.2 L) vegan beef broth (make with vegan beef bouillon)

¼ cup (60 ml) red wine vinegar

2 tablespoons (30 ml) lemon juice

2½ cups (175 g) cored and shredded cabbage

3 cups (540 g) diced tomatoes

4 cups (900 g) peeled and diced beets, tops chopped and reserved

2 bay leaves

Salt and pepper, to taste

1 cup (225 g) vegan sour cream

¼ cup (16 g) chopped fresh dill, or more to taste

Heat the oil over medium-high heat in a large stockpot. Add the cubed seitan, and sear until well browned, 1 to 2 minutes. Stir in the onion, and cook until tender and translucent, about 2 minutes. Pour in the broth, vinegar, and lemon juice; add the cabbage, tomatoes, beets, bay leaves, salt, and pepper. Bring to a boil over high heat, then reduce the heat to medium-low, cover, and simmer until the seitan and beets are tender, about 2 hours. Stir the beet tops into the borscht, and simmer for 15 minutes longer, then season to taste with salt and pepper. Garnish with a generous dollop of sour cream and a sprinkling of dill.

YIELD: 8 servings

Fun Fact
Beets, while having the wonderful staining power that they do, are quite good for you. Rich in natural sugar, sodium, sulphur, chlorine, iodine, copper, vitamins B_1, B_2, and C, and bioflavonoids, beets are fabulous for kidney and gallbladder cleansing.

MINSKY SALAD
(POTATO AND SAUERKRAUT SALAD)

Talk about a fresh take on salad! The ingredients may sound a little unorthodox, but I can assure you that this salad is mega yum!

2 cups (20 g) quartered potatoes

2 tablespoons (30 ml) olive oil, divided

1 cup (70 g) chopped mushrooms

1½ teaspoons apple cider vinegar

1½ teaspoons sugar or agave nectar

Salt and pepper, to taste

⅔ cup (95 g) sauerkraut

¼ cup (45 g) finely chopped white or red onion

Place the potatoes in a medium-size pot, cover with water, and bring to a boil; cook until soft enough to grate but not so soft that they will mush up or fall apart, 10 to 15 minutes. Drain, let cool, grate, and set aside.

In a medium-size pan, heat 1 tablespoon (15 ml) of the oil and sauté the mushrooms over medium heat until tender, about 2 minutes. Set aside.

Combine the remaining 1 tablespoon (15 ml) oil, vinegar, sugar, salt, and pepper in a bowl and set aside. In a large salad bowl, combine the potatoes, sauerkraut, onion, and mushrooms. Pour in the dressing, toss to coat, and serve.

YIELD: 2 to 4 servings

fun Fact

Sauerkraut is terrific for a healthy digestive system. Filled with lactic acid bacteria due to the fermentation process, you get all the benefits of the raw cabbage plus that of the fermentation.

PRIZE-WINNING PIROZHKI
(BEEF-FILLED ROLLS)

*Gluten Free (use gluten-free flour and vegan ground beef), **Soy Free
(use TVP instead of vegan ground beef and alternative rice/nut milk)

**How can anyone go wrong with meat-filled bread balls?
These are a delicious way to start any Russian-themed meal.**

1 tablespoon olive oil

1 onion, finely chopped

1½ pounds (680 g) vegan ground beef

1 tablespoon (18 g) salt, plus more to taste, divided

Ground pepper, to taste

1¼ teaspoons chopped fresh dill, or more to taste

1 cup (235 ml) soymilk

3 egg replacers, mixed, store-bought
or homemade (page 13)

½ cup (120 ml) olive oil

2 tablespoons (25 g) sugar, divided

1 package (2¼ teaspoons, or 9 g) active dry yeast

¼ cup (60 ml) warm water

4 cups (480 g) all-purpose flour

3 cups (705 ml) safflower oil, for frying
(or preferred high-heat oil)

In a medium-size skillet over medium heat, heat the oil and cook the onion and ground beef until the meat is evenly browned and the onion is translucent, 4 to 5 minutes. Season with salt, pepper, and dill to taste. Set aside to cool.

In a medium-size saucepan over low heat, warm the milk and gently whisk in the egg replacers, olive oil, 1 table-spoon (12.5 g) of the sugar, and the 1 tablespoon (18 g) salt. Remove from the heat.

Combine the yeast, warm water, and remaining 1 table-spoon (12.5 g) sugar in a mixing bowl (or stand mixer). Set aside and wait about 15 minutes for the yeast to proof. Then add the warm milk mixture to the yeast mixture. With the dough hook attachment on low speed, add the flour, 1 cup (120 g) at a time. If you are not using a mixer, knead until the dough forms a ball and does not stick to the bowl. Cover the bowl with a clean cloth. Set in a warm location and allow to rise until doubled in size, about 1 hour. Turn out the dough onto a lightly floured work surface. Pinch off golf ball–size pieces and press into disks about 3½ to 4 inches (9 to 10 cm) in diameter. Fill the center of each disk with a heaping tablespoon of the cooled meat mixture. Fold the disk over the mixture and firmly pinch the edges to seal. Arrange on a flat surface and allow to rest for 10 minutes.

In a large skillet or deep fryer, heat the safflower oil to 375°F (190°C). Fry the pirozhki in batches until golden brown on one side, about 2 minutes, then gently turn and fry on the other side for 2 to 3 minutes longer. Remove and drain on a paper towel–lined plate.

YIELD: About 24 pirozhki

Fun Fact

Pirozhki are common fast food in Central and East Asia because the Russians introduced them to this doughy delight.

SURE TO LOVE STROGANOFF
(BEEF AND NOODLES)

*Gluten Free (use gluten-free vegan beef, flour, and noodles)

This stroganoff is so convincing that your meat-eating friends won't know the difference! I've always loved the combo of stew and noodles, and this dish has it all.

1½ pounds (680 g) vegan beef or seitan, store-bought or homemade (page 19)

Salt and pepper, to taste

3 tablespoons (42 g) vegan butter, divided

2 tablespoons (15 g) all-purpose flour

2 cups (470 ml) vegan beef broth (make with vegan beef bouillon)

2 teaspoons Dijon mustard

¼ cup (56 g) vegan sour cream

1 tablespoon (15 ml) olive oil

½ small white or yellow onion, sliced

1 pound (454 g) wide noodles, cooked according to package instructions

Chopped fresh parsley, for garnish

Slice the beef into strips ½ inch (1.3 cm) thick by 2 inches (5 cm) long and season with salt and pepper. Set in the refrigerator.

Heat a skillet over medium heat. Melt 2 tablespoons (28 g) of the butter, add the flour, and cook, stirring constantly, for about 1 minute. Whisk in the broth and cook for 1 minute to thicken. Stir in the mustard and sour cream and cook for 2 to 3 minutes. Remove from the heat, season with salt and pepper, and set aside.

Heat a second skillet over high heat. Add the oil and the remaining 1 tablespoon (14 g) butter, then add the meat strips and onion and cook until brown on both sides, 2 to 3 minutes total. Arrange the meat on a bed of noodles, ladle the sauce on top, and sprinkle with the parsley.

YIELD: 4 to 6 servings

Fun Fact

This dish is the subject of Russian food lore. My favorite story is that this famous dish was named after Count Pavel Stroganoff in the nineteenth century. Although there were versions in existence before the count or the chef committed it to paper in 1891, stroganoff didn't make it into English cookbooks until the late 1930s.

Chapter 13

THE MIDDLE EAST

SOME OF THE MOST TRADITIONAL cuisine can be found in Middle Eastern nations. Tradition is what defines these countries, and what they eat goes hand in hand with those traditions. Known as the cradle of civilization, the Middle East was once a very fertile place. What we see now as a barren and dry region was once a land of farmers who grew a variety of food in the Fertile Crescent, which was naturally irrigated by the Nile, the Tigris, and the Euphrates rivers. Some of the more popular cultivations were barley, pistachios, figs, dates, and pomegranates.

In addition to being powerful traders, Middle Easterners also discovered fermentation for making beer and leavening bread. Over thousands of years and as different tribes and religions moved in and out of the area, the cuisine evolved. Exotic spices from the Orient and the addition of many more fruits and vegetables increased their cooking repertoire. The Turks brought in phyllo and sweet coffee; yogurt came from Russia, okra from Africa, and tomatoes from the Moors of Spain.

Nowadays, due to religious observances within the region, many Middle Eastern citizens do not drink alcohol or consume pork. However, many Middle Eastern dishes, such as hummus and shish kabob, have become staples in countries around the world.

In many areas of the Middle East, it is common to serve from a platter in the center of the table, where diners scoop up food with pita bread as opposed to using utensils. And for many, the left hand is reserved for hygiene and typically not used for handling food, and especially not for hand shaking.

Enjoy your travels through the flavorful Middle East and ‏اذا بردن از موام داوغیی خود را (enjoy your food)!

MIDEAST MUST-HAVES: HUMMUS, FALAFEL, TABBOULEH, AND BABA GHANOUSH SAMPLER

*Gluten Free (use quinoa in lieu of bulgur wheat in tabbouleh, gluten-free flour in falafel, and gluten-free pita)

It's a party on a platter—or at least a good excuse to throw one! And I'm pretty sure that this is a vegan and vegetarian staple. Serve up a platter with each of these dishes alongside warm pita bread, lemon wedges, and tahini (to make store-bought tahini creamier, blend it with olive oil, 1 tablespoon [15 ml] at a time, until you've reached the desired consistency).

FOR GARLIC HUMMUS:

1 can (15 ounces, or 420 g) chickpeas, drained and rinsed

2 tablespoons (20 g) minced garlic

1 tablespoon (15 ml) olive oil

½ tablespoon (7.5 ml) lemon juice

½ teaspoon dried oregano

Salt and pepper, to taste

Cayenne, for garnish (optional)

To make the hummus: In a food processor, process the chickpeas, garlic, olive oil, lemon juice, and oregano until the desired consistency is achieved. Season with salt and pepper. If the hummus is too thick, add more olive oil ½ teaspoon at a time until the desired consistency is achieved. Spread on a plate and sprinkle with the cayenne.

FOR BABA GHANOUSH:

1 medium-size eggplant

3 or 4 cloves garlic

¼ cup (60 ml) fresh lemon juice

Pinch of ground cumin

2 tablespoons (30 g) tahini

¼ to ½ cup (15 to 30 g) chopped fresh parsley leaves

Salt and pepper, to taste

Agave nectar, to taste (optional)

To make the baba ghanoush: Preheat a grill to medium-high or preheat the oven to 375°F (190°C, or gas mark 5). Pierce holes in the skin of the eggplant and grill or roast, turning every 7 minutes, until blackened and soft, about 30 minutes. Remove from the grill and let cool. Once the eggplant is cool enough to handle, peel away the skin and discard. Place the eggplant flesh in a colander and drain for about 10 minutes.

In a food processor, combine the garlic, lemon juice, cumin, tahini, and parsley and pulse to combine. Then add the eggplant, season with salt and pepper, and pulse to combine. If it's too bitter, drizzle with agave.

FOR FALAFEL:

1 can (15 ounces, or 420 g) chickpeas, drained and rinsed

2 cloves garlic, chopped

1 large onion, chopped

3 tablespoons (12 g) chopped fresh parsley

1 teaspoon ground coriander

1 teaspoon ground cumin

Salt and pepper, to taste

2 tablespoons (15 g) all-purpose flour

Coconut oil, for frying (or preferred high-heat oil)

FOR TABBOULEH:

⅔ cup (122 g) bulgur wheat or cooked and cooled quinoa

½ cup (48 g) chopped fresh mint

1½ cups (90 g) chopped fresh parsley

1 large tomato, diced

1 medium-size cucumber, peeled, seeded, and diced

⅔ cup (65 g) chopped scallion

¼ cup (60 ml) olive oil

⅓ cup (80 ml) fresh lemon juice

Salt and pepper, to taste

To make the falafel: Place the chickpeas in a pan with water to cover and bring to a boil over high heat. Allow to boil for 5 minutes, then simmer over low heat for about 1 hour. Drain and set aside to cool for 15 minutes. Combine the chickpeas, garlic, onion, parsley, coriander, cumin, salt, and pepper in a medium-size bowl. Add the flour and stir to combine. Add this mixture to a food processor, process into a thick paste, and form into Ping-Pong-size balls.

Pour about 2 inches (5 cm) of oil into a deep skillet and preheat to 350°F (180°C). Add the falafel in batches, being careful not to crowd the pan, and fry until golden brown, 5 to 7 minutes. Transfer to a paper towel–lined plate to drain. Or if you'd like to bake the falafel, preheat the oven to 400°F (200°C, or gas mark 6) and bake on a greased baking sheet for 10 to 15 minutes, turning halfway through.

To make the tabbouleh: Soak the bulgur wheat in cold water to cover for 2 hours (or as directed on the package). Drain well, squeezing out any excess water. Combine the bulgur, mint, parsley, tomato, cucumber, scallion, oil, lemon juice, salt, and pepper in a large bowl. Cover and chill.

YIELD: 4 to 6 appetizer-size servings

COOK'S NOTE

Don't forget, you can make pita pocket sandwiches filled with these mid-east must haves for a delicious and healthy meal to go!

Fun Fact

Hummus is one of the oldest foods, dating back to ancient Egypt. Both hummus and falafel could even be more than 20,000 years old, because chickpeas have been grown and used by people in the Middle Eastern region since then.

BETTER WITH BÉCHAMEL MACARONI AND BEEF

*Gluten Free (use gluten-free pasta and vegan ground beef or TVP), **Soy Free
(use soy-free vegan ground beef or TVP, alternative rice/nut milk, and soy-free butter)

Move over, mac n' cheese, here comes something creamier (and heartier). It's so delicious, all you need is a good-size helping and you've got a really satisfying meal.

1 tablespoon (15 ml) olive oil

1 medium-size onion, chopped

2 cloves garlic, minced

4 cups (900 g) vegan ground beef

2 tablespoons (8 g) chopped parsley

1 tablespoon (4 g) plus 1 teaspoon dried thyme, divided

1 teaspoon ground cinnamon

1 can (8 ounces, or 225 g) tomato sauce

3 egg replacers, mixed, store-bought or homemade (page 13), divided

6 tablespoons (84 g) vegan butter

6 tablespoons (48 g) all-purpose flour

2 quarts (1.8 L) cold soymilk

Salt, white pepper, and black pepper, to taste

½ teaspoon grated nutmeg

1 package (16 ounces, or 454 g) penne or elbow pasta, cooked according to package instructions

2 tablespoons (16 g) nutritional yeast (optional)

Heat the olive oil in a skillet and sauté the onion over medium-high heat until soft, 3 to 5 minutes. Add the garlic and sauté another 2 minutes. Add the ground beef and brown for 2 to 3 minutes. Add the parsley, 1 tablespoon (4 g) of the thyme, and cinnamon and stir to combine. Stir in the tomato sauce and simmer over low heat for about 10 minutes. Remove from the heat and let cool. Once it has cooled stir in 1 of the egg replacers and set aside.

Melt the butter in a large saucepan over medium-high heat. Add the flour and whisk until smooth; continue whisking for 2 minutes. Slowly whisk in the milk, making sure there are no lumps, and season with salt, white pepper, and black pepper. Continue whisking until the milk is almost boiling. Whisk in the remaining 1 teaspoon thyme and the nutmeg and whisk until the sauce thickens, 2 to 3 minutes. Quickly whisk in the remaining 2 egg replacers and remove from the heat.

Preheat the oven to 400°F (200°C, or gas mark 6).

Mix half the sauce into half of the pasta and pour this mixture into a baking dish. Layer the entire meat mixture over the pasta. Top with a little nutritional yeast. Add the rest of the pasta and pour on the remaining sauce, spreading it evenly to cover and coat the pasta. Bake for 45 to 60 minutes, or until the top is golden brown. Let cool, then cut and serve.

YIELD: 6 to 8 servings

fun fact

Another recipe shrouded in culinary mystery is béchamel sauce. There are a number of stories depicting the creation of this creamy sauce, but here are just a few: (1) Chefs to Catherine de' Medici, the Italian-born French queen, created it for her; (2) it was named after its French inventor, the Marquis de Béchamel, in the 1600s, who created it for King Louis the XIV; (3) chef François Pierre de la Varenne also created it for King Louis XIV, and he has also been credited as the inventor of "haute cuisine."

Egypt, Israel, Turkey

DATE NUT BREAD

*Gluten Free (use gluten-free flour)

Whether it's the holidays or not, a warm slice of this will put a smile on anyone's face. Nothing is as indulgent as warm bread straight from the oven. Heavenly!

2 cups (240 g) all-purpose flour

1 teaspoon baking powder

½ teaspoon salt

1 teaspoon ground cinnamon

¼ teaspoon ground cloves

1 cup (200 g) sugar

1 egg replacer, mixed, store-bought or homemade (page 13)

1 tablespoon (15 ml) vanilla extract

2 cups (356 g) finely chopped dates

1 cup (120 g) finely chopped walnuts

1 cup (235 ml) boiling water

Preheat the oven to 350°F (180°C, or gas mark 4) and grease a loaf pan.

In a mixing bowl, combine the flour, baking powder, salt, cinnamon, cloves, and sugar. Mix in the egg replacer and vanilla, then set aside.

In a large mixing bowl, combine the dates and walnuts. Pour the boiling water over and set aside for about 10 minutes. Add the flour mixture to the date/nut mixture, stirring to combine. Spoon into the greased loaf pan and bake for 55 minutes to 1 hour, or until golden and a toothpick inserted into the center comes out clean. Remove from the oven and let cool slightly before slicing.

YIELD: 10 to 12 servings

fun fact

Dates are rich in vitamins and minerals and is said to help fight constipation, intestinal disorders, weight gain, heart problems, diarrhea, and abdominal cancer.

COOK'S NOTE

These are also fun as mini muffins!

OODLES OF KUGEL
(POTATO AND CHEESE CASSEROLE)

*Gluten Free (use gluten-free flour and vegan cheese)

Potatoes and cheese? I'm in! There are all sorts of kugel variations, but this is the one I enjoy most.

1 cup (200 g) silken tofu blended with
2 teaspoons arrowroot powder

2 cloves garlic, minced

½ cup (120 ml) olive oil

¼ cup (30 g) all-purpose flour

Salt and pepper, to taste

8 medium-size baking potatoes, peeled

2 medium-size white or yellow onions

2 cups (225 g) shredded vegan cheddar cheese

Preheat the oven to 400°F (200°C, or gas mark 6). Grease a 9 × 13-inch (23 × 33 cm) baking dish.

In a large bowl, combine the tofu, garlic, oil, flour, salt, and pepper. Set aside.

Coarsely grate the potatoes and onions, by hand or in a food processor. Let stand for 3 to 5 minutes, and then squeeze out any excess liquid. Add the grated potatoes, grated onions, and cheese to the tofu/flour mixture. Mix by hand until smooth. Pour into the prepared baking dish and bake, uncovered, for 1 hour, or until golden brown on top.

YIELD: About 15 servings

Fun Fact

Historians believe that kugel "popped" up more than 800 years ago and was named for its "roundness" after baking, because it began mainly as a bready dish. Nowadays, you can kugel almost anything!

SWARM FOR SHAWARMA
(CHICKEN PITA)

*Gluten Free (use gluten-free vegan chicken and pita), **Soy Free (use soy-free vegan chicken)

I love the combination of lemony, garlicky goodness on warm pita. Lunch, anyone?

FOR SAUCE:

5 cloves garlic

1 to 1½ cups (240 to 360 g) tahini, to taste

2 cups (470 ml) cold water

½ to ¾ cup (120 to 175 ml) lemon juice

Salt and pepper, to taste

FOR SHAWARMA:

10 cloves garlic, chopped

Juice of 2 lemons

½ cup (120 ml) olive oil

2 teaspoons curry powder

Salt and pepper, to taste

1 teaspoon ground turmeric

8 vegan chicken cutlets

4 pita breads, warmed and cut in half

1 medium-size tomato, chopped

1 red onion, chopped

To make the sauce: Add the garlic to a food processor or blender and pulse to chop. Add the tahini and pulse to combine. On a low setting, slowly add the cold water and blend until frothy. Add the lemon juice until the mixture is the desired creaminess, then season with salt and pepper.

To make the shawarma: Whisk together the garlic, lemon juice, and oil in a medium-size bowl. Add the curry powder, salt, pepper, and turmeric and whisk to combine. Add the chicken, turn to coat with the marinade, and marinate overnight in the refrigerator, turning occasionally.

Preheat a grill or grill pan to medium heat. Remove the chicken from the marinade and grill for 5 to 7 minutes on each side, until cooked through. Divide among the 8 warm pitas and top with the tomato, onion, and sauce.

YIELD: 8 servings

fun fact

Shawarma comes from the Turkish word that means "turning," seeing as how the original dish features kebab style meat.

HALVA PIECE OF THE MIDDLE EAST
(SEMOLINA CANDY)

*Gluten Free (use spelt or amaranth in lieu of semolina), **Soy Free (use alternative rice/nut milk and soy-free vegan butter)

Here's a delicious way to impress your friends without having to spend hours working at a candy factory. It has just the right touch of sweet and crunch and lots of healthy deliciousness!

1¾ cups (411 ml) soymilk

3 tablespoons (45 ml) rosewater

1 to 2 teaspoons vanilla extract

1 teaspoon ground cardamom seeds

¼ cup (500 g) sugar

1 cup (75 g) coarse semolina

3½ tablespoons (32 g) raisins

1 teaspoon slivered almonds

Heat the milk, rosewater, vanilla, cardamom, and sugar in a pan over medium heat for 4 to 5 minutes. Add the semolina and raisins and cook, whisking continuously, for 5 to 10 minutes, or until the mixture has thickened. Remove from the heat and mix in the slivered almonds. Spoon the mixture into a deep 9 × 13-inch (23 × 33 cm) baking tray, smoothing it out to fill the pan evenly. Set aside and allow to cool. Once cooled, place in the freezer for at least 10 minutes and up to 1 hour; this extra setting time will make it easier to slice. Remove from the freezer and cut into squares.

YIELD: 12 servings

fun fact
There are also a great many varieties of Indian halva. From fruit to veggies and even cakes and nuts, there are many faces of halva!

Chapter 14

AFRICA

A LARGE, BEAUTIFUL, and sometimes wild continent, Africa has a distinctive culinary history, one that is very much the same now as it was thousands of years ago. While American soul food was born from African Americans, African food itself is entirely different due to the continent's resources, geography, economy, and peoples.

Wildlife dominated the African diet for centuries, so farming didn't take off for some time. The men hunted while the women gathered wild fruit and vegetables. But as the Sahara Desert began to grow in size, this changed the availability of animals and naturally growing vegetation for folks in northern Africa. The Africans learned how to cultivate wheat and barley from the Egyptians in order to supplement their dwindling diet. Northern Africans, as well as those in coastal regions, incorporated fish into their diet as local wild animals migrated south, where grasslands still remained.

Much of Africa is underdeveloped and the economy plays a major role in what is eaten by its inhabitants. Families tend to eat their largest meal at lunch, which normally consists of vegetables and legumes with a small amount of meat. Stews are very popular because they are efficient to make in small spaces, require only one pot, and make use of local vegetables, grains, and spices.

Due to the size of the continent, dishes vary from region to region. West African cuisine is very tropical and starchy, heavily filled with root vegetables such as cassava and fruits such as plantains. Southern Africa has many European and Asian influences and incorporates a variety of local seafood into its cuisine. North Africa shares its culinary history with Egypt and the Middle East, retaining a lot of the spices and flavors that the Ottoman Empire brought in. East Africa showcases corn, or maize, as well as many Arabic and Indian cooking techniques. Central African cuisine has remained the most traditional, probably because the vast rainforest makes it impervious to outside influences. A great many vegetables and stews as well as local game make up its fare.

Because this is not the most well-known world cuisine, I am so glad to include some of my favorite African dishes from all around the continent. It's fun, it's fresh, and it's frill-free. *Jambo* (greetings)!

SUKUMA WIKI WITH UGALI
(GREENS, TOMATOES, AND CORNMEAL)

We're takin' it over to East Africa. And don't be afraid to eat with your hands to get the full effect. This just may be the perfect dish to get your kids to eat their greens!

FOR SUKUMA:

2 tablespoons (30 ml) olive oil

1 medium-size white onion, chopped

1 medium-size tomato, diced

1 heaping cup (70 g) chopped kale or collard greens

½ cup (120 ml) vegetable broth, store-bought or homemade (page 16), or water

Salt, to taste

FOR UGALI:

4 cups (940 ml) water

2 cups (275 g) finely ground white cornmeal

Salt, to taste

Vegan butter, for serving

To make the sukuma: Heat the oil in a medium-size pot over medium-high heat. Add the onion and sauté for 1 to 2 minutes. Add the tomato and sauté for 1 minute. Add the greens and sauté for about 1 minute. Add the broth and salt to taste. Let the mixture simmer until the vegetables have reached the desired tenderness, 3 to 5 minutes.

To make the ugali: Bring the water to a boil in a saucepan. Slowly pour in the cornmeal and season with salt. Cook for 3 or 4 minutes, stirring continuously to avoid forming lumps, and mash any lumps that do form, until the mixture is thicker than mashed potatoes. Form into 2 large balls, place on 2 serving plates, and top with a pat of vegan butter. Cover and keep warm.

Serve immediately with the sukuma. To eat, grab a small handful of ugali, shape it into a ball and make a dent in it, and use it to scoop up the vegetables and sauce.

YIELD: 2 servings

COOK'S NOTE

You may also make the ugali into little grilled rolls (as pictured). Pinch off pieces and roll into Ping-Pong-size balls, then flatten them into fat little disks between the palms of your hands. In a greased skillet or griddle, grill over medium heat, cooking evenly on both sides until crispy and done, about 2 minutes per side. Serve with vegan butter.

Fun fact

Sukuma wiki means to "push the week," because the dish is a way to stretch the amount of food to last the week.

ALL BUT THE KITCHEN SINK KOUSHARI
(LENTILS, PASTA, AND RICE)

*Gluten Free (use gluten-free pasta)

A virtual hodgepodge of ingredients, this dish is basically fun with Egyptian leftovers! It reminds me of quick dinners as a kid—heating and mixing up leftovers and curling up on the couch with my folks.

1 cup (192 g) lentils

5 cups (1,175 ml) salted water

2 tablespoons (30 ml) olive oil

1 large onion, diced

2 cloves garlic, minced

1 teaspoon ground coriander

½ teaspoon ground cumin

1 can (15 ounces, or 420 g) tomato sauce

1 tablespoon (15 ml) white or apple cider vinegar

1 cup (165 g) cooked brown rice

1 cup (140 g) cooked elbow pasta

¼ teaspoon red chile pepper flakes

Salt and black pepper, to taste

Rinse the lentils, and combine them and salted water in a pot, bring to a boil, reduce the heat to medium, and simmer, covered, for 15 to 30 minutes, depending on the type of lentils you are using. Keep checking and add more water if needed.

Meanwhile, heat the oil in a skillet over medium heat and sauté the onion and garlic until golden, 4 to 6 minutes. Add the coriander and cumin and stir to combine. Add the tomato sauce and simmer for 8 to 10 minutes. Remove from the heat and stir in the vinegar.

Combine the cooked lentils, rice, and pasta in one pot and gently reheat. Place some of the lentil mixture on each plate and top with the sauce. Sprinkle with the chile flakes and salt and pepper.

YIELD: 4 servings

fun fact
Commonly a vegetarian dish in Egypt, this recipe reflects the meatless diet of the Coptic Christians of the region during their many fasting holidays.

INJERA (SOURDOUGH FLATBREAD)

*Gluten Free (use gluten-free flour)

The process of making this sourdough flatbread is not only interesting but fun, too!

2 cups (240 g) teff or quinoa flour

3 cups (705 ml) lukewarm water

1 teaspoon active dry yeast

Safflower oil, for griddle (or preferred high-heat oil)

In a large bowl, combine the flour, water, and yeast. Cover with a clean towel and set aside overnight to ferment. It will look like thin pancake batter.

Lightly oil and preheat a pan or griddle over medium heat. Ladle the injera batter onto the pan, in a circular shape and motion, like a crepe or thin pancake. Cook for 2 minutes, or until holes form and the surface is dry, then transfer to a plate to cool; *do not* flip over to cook on the other side. Continue with more oil and the remaining batter, placing waxed paper or plastic wrap in between injeras so they don't stick together. Serve warm and enjoy with your favorite African meal.

YIELD: 12 to 15 breads

KELE WELE (SPICY PLANTAINS)

Doin' plantains Ghana style! Who knew bananas could pack such a punch? Spicy, sweet, and garlicky, they serve it up as dessert.

1 teaspoon ground red chile pepper

1 teaspoon salt

1 piece (2 inches, or 5 cm) fresh ginger, finely chopped, or 1 teaspoon ground ginger

3 cloves garlic, minced

1 medium-size onion, finely chopped

3 tablespoons (45 ml) olive oil, divided

2 or 3 well-ripened yellow plantains

Combine the chile pepper, salt, ginger, garlic, onion, and 1 tablespoon (15 ml) of the oil in a small bowl.

Peel the plantains and cut on the diagonal into ½-inch (1.3 cm) thick slices. Place in a large bowl; add the spice mixture and mix well to coat. Refrigerate for about 2 hours.

Heat 1 tablespoon (15 ml) of the oil in a large skillet over medium-high heat. Add the plantains in a single layer. Sauté until browned, 1 to 2 minutes, turn over, and brown on the other side for 1 to 2 minutes longer. Repeat with the remaining 1 tablespoon (15 ml) oil and plantains.

YIELD: 2 to 4 servings

Morocco

BIRYANI B'STILLA
(CHICKEN PASTRY)

**This is a chickeny, cinnamony, and warm pastry. I like saying that
this is a sweet, spicy, and fun Moroccan take on chicken potpie!**

4 vegan chicken cutlets

2 tablespoons (12 g) vegan chicken bouillon

2 cups (470 ml) water

½ cup (100 g) silken tofu blended with
1 teaspoon arrowroot powder

2 tablespoons (8 g) chopped fresh parsley

1 teaspoon ground cinnamon

2 teaspoons sugar

1 package (17½ ounces, or 490 g)
frozen puff pastry, thawed

Salt and pepper, to taste

¼ cup (56 g) vegan butter, melted

Preheat the oven to 350°F (180°C, or gas mark 4).

Place the chicken in a small saucepan and add the bouillon and water. Poach over medium-low heat, 5 to 7 minutes, or until cooked through. Remove the chicken, reserving the cooking liquid. Dice the chicken and set aside.

In a small bowl, whisk the tofu mixture with ½ cup (120 ml) of the reserved cooking liquid and the chopped parsley. In a separate bowl, mix together the cinnamon and sugar.

Roll out 1 sheet of the pastry into a 12-inch (30.5 cm) square. Cut another sheet of pastry in half and roll out into two 8-inch (20.3 cm) squares. Fit the 12-inch (30.5 cm) square of pastry into a 9-inch (23 cm) pie pan; there will be a little overhang. Spread half of the diced chicken evenly across the bottom. Pour half of the tofu mixture over the chicken. Sprinkle with half of the cinnamon and sugar mixture, then season with salt and pepper. Cover with the 8-inch (20.3 cm) square of pastry. Cover this pastry square with the remaining chicken, tofu mixture, and cinnamon and sugar, seasoning with more salt and pepper. Cover with the remaining 8-inch (20.3 cm) pastry square. Fold the edges of the bottom pastry over the top of the pie to seal and brush with the melted butter. Bake for 30 to 40 minutes, or until golden brown.

YIELD: 4 to 6 servings

fun fact

A classic Moroccan dish, this pie normally features pigeon or squab. Not in this book, it doesn't!

CHUNKY SWEET POTATO STEW

This dish features the flavors of Africa with the comfort of home! It contains lots of veggies, vitamins, and nutrients, but you would never know it with a bowl of this savory sweetness!

2 tablespoons (30 ml) peanut oil

1 tablespoon (6 g) curry powder

2 medium-size onions, finely diced

2 medium-size carrots, peeled and diced

4 stalks celery, diced

2 teaspoons minced garlic

2 pounds (905 g) sweet potatoes (about 2 large), peeled and chopped into chunks (about 4 cups [440 g])

2 cups (470 ml) vegetable broth, store-bought or homemade (page 16)

1 can (28 ounces, or 784 g) whole tomatoes, drained and quartered

Salt and pepper, to taste

¼ teaspoon cayenne

½ to 1 cup (130 to 260 g) chunky peanut butter

3 tablespoons (27 g) roasted peanuts

½ cup (120 ml) coconut milk

Heat the oil in a large Dutch oven or stockpot over medium-high heat. Add the curry powder and cook, stirring constantly, for 1 minute. Add the onions, carrots, and celery and cook, stirring occasionally, for 2 minutes. Add the garlic and cook for 1 minute longer. Stir in the sweet potatoes, broth, and tomatoes, and bring the soup to a boil. Simmer, covered, for 20 to 30 minutes. Season with salt and pepper and add the cayenne, peanut butter, peanuts, and coconut milk, stirring to combine. Return the mixture to a simmer and cook for an additional 20 minutes. Serve hot.

YIELD: 6 servings

Fun Fact

Rich in vitamin A, vitamin C, and other powerful antioxidants, sweet potatoes are a great way to beat the under-the-weather blues.

COUSCOUS SALAD

*Gluten Free (use quinoa instead of couscous), **Soy Free (use soy-free vegan butter)

A North African favorite, this salad is simple, flavorful, and great any time of the day.

FOR DRESSING:

½ cup (120 ml) orange juice

⅓ cup (80 ml) olive oil

⅓ cup (80 ml) white wine vinegar

2 tablespoons (40 g) agave nectar

Salt and pepper, to taste

FOR COUSCOUS:

3 cups (705 ml) vegan chicken broth

3 cups (525 g) couscous

1 tablespoon (14 g) vegan butter

¾ teaspoon ground cinnamon

⅔ cup (65 g) sliced scallion

1 cup (140 g) chopped dried apricots and golden raisins

½ cup (55 g) toasted, slivered almonds

2 large oranges, supremed (plus any juice)

To make the dressing: Whisk together all the dressing ingredients in a small bowl. Set aside.

To make the couscous: Bring the broth to a boil in a large saucepan. Stir in the couscous, butter, and cinnamon; cover and remove from the heat. Let stand for 5 minutes, then fluff with a fork and let cool. Place the scallion, apricots, raisins, almonds, and oranges with juice in a bowl; add the cooled couscous and drizzle with the dressing, tossing well to coat. Cover and chill for about 1 hour.

YIELD: 2 to 4 servings

AHH-VOCADO ICE CREAM

Healthy, sweet, and scrumptious! Give it a shot—you'll be pleasantly surprised.

3 medium-size ripe avocados, pitted and peeled

1½ to 2 tablespoons (23 to 30 ml) lemon juice

1½ cups (353 ml) soymilk

1 cup (200 g) sugar

1 cup (235 ml) vegan heavy cream, store-bought or homemade (page 15)

Put the avocados, lemon juice, milk, and sugar in a blender and purée. Add the heavy cream and pulse to combine. Place the mixture in the refrigerator in a container with a lid and chill until it reaches 40°F (4.5°C) or below, 4 to 6 hours.

Process in an ice-cream maker, per manufacturer's instructions, or mix well and place in the freezer. Mix every 30 to 45 minutes so it stays smooth and doesn't get too hard. Freezing should take 2 to 3 hours.

YIELD: 6 to 8 servings

Chapter 15

INDIA

THE ORIGINS OF INDIAN CUISINE are most likely as old as mankind itself. Despite the country's revolving door of travelers and reigns, Indian food never lost its original identity; rather, it has become richer after assimilating the myriad influences over time.

The Ayurvedic tradition of cooking, which follows a holistic approach, began around 2000 BCE. Ayurveda posits that everything we eat affects both our body and our mind, so everything we consume should be pure, from nature, and balanced, incorporating the six tastes of sweet, sour, salty, pungent, bitter, and astringent. Hinduism developed somewhere around 1000 BCE, and it divided food habits of people broadly by caste. The Brahmins, for the most part, were vegetarians, and the Kshatriyas were nonvegetarian. Buddhism and Jainism came about in 600 BCE and have had a lasting effect on Indian cuisine, as the Jains do not consume meat. About a third of modern India is vegetarian.

A traditional Indian meal usually consists of two or three main courses with many accompaniments such as chutneys, bread, and rice. The staples of Indian cuisine are rice, flour, or *atta*, and various legumes, such as masoor (red lentils), chana (Bengal ram), toor (pigeon pea), urad (black gram), and mung (green gram).

Cuisine styles are divided into four distinctive regions: northern, southern, eastern, and western. The northern Indian diet consists of a lot of dairy products. They utilize ghee (clarified butter) and yogurt, and the region is also the birthplace of the popular samosa. Southern cooking includes a lot of coconut and snacks such as dosa, idli, vada, bonda, and bajji, which are all eaten at breakfast. Eastern cuisine is well known for its desserts. Lastly, western cuisine is broken down into four groups: Rajasthani, Gujarati (mostly vegetarian with a lot of sugar used), Maharashtrian (some fish and wheat), and Goan (with mainly rice and coconut used).

Get ready to embark on a colorful, ancient, and delicious culinary adventure! *Namaste* (I bow to you)!

GANESH'S FAVORITE GARLIC NAAN
(FLATBREAD)

*Gluten Free (use gluten-free flour), **Soy Free (use soy-free vegan butter and vegan yogurt)

Perfect with any meal, this warm garlicky bread has lots of fun flavors. I devour naan at any Indian meal (so much so that I sometimes spoil my dinner!).

½ teaspoon sugar

¼ cup (60 ml) warm soymilk

1½ teaspoons (6 g) active dry yeast

1¾ cups (210 g) all-purpose flour

½ teaspoon salt

1 clove garlic, minced

½ teaspoon ground cumin

½ cup (115 g) plain vegan yogurt

¼ cup (56 g) vegan butter, melted

Garlic powder, for sprinkling

Dissolve the sugar in the milk and then add the yeast. Stir to combine and allow to rest for 5 to 10 minutes.

In a large bowl, blend the flour, salt, minced garlic, and cumin. Pour in the milk mixture and yogurt and stir with a spoon until you are unable to do so. Turn out onto a floured work surface and knead until all the flour is incorporated and the dough is soft and elastic. Form the dough into a ball, return to the bowl, and cover with a clean, damp towel for 2 to 3 hours, or until it has doubled in size. Divide into 5 golf ball–size pieces and roll out into ⅛-inch (3 mm) thick disks.

Slather the naan with butter and place, butter side down, in a hot skillet or pan (you can grill them, too!). When large bubbles begin to form, about 2 to 3 minutes, slather the non-buttered side with butter and flip over. Cook for 2 to 3 minutes, or until browned. Sprinkle with a little garlic powder and serve.

YIELD: 5 naan

COOK'S NOTE

If you'd like to bake the naan instead, preheat the oven to 400°F (200°C, or gas mark 6), place on a foil-lined baking sheet, brush the dough with the melted butter, and bake until the dough begins to bubble and brown, about 2 minutes. Brush the nonbuttered side with butter, flip over, and bake until brown, about 2 more minutes.

Fun Fact

The first documentation of naan goes back to 1300 CE. It was a popular menu item at the imperial court in Delhi for hundreds of years.

MASALA DOSAS (LENTIL CREPES)

Move over, pancakes, here comes the dosa! If you get the hang of it, rolling these savory crepes is not only impressive but also a great deal of fun. And if you can't, they're still just as tasty!

FOR DOSAS:

3 cups (570 g) brown rice

1 cup (250 g) urad dal

¾ teaspoon fenugreek seeds

Salt, to taste

½ teaspoon olive or sesame oil

FOR MASALA FILLING:

1 tablespoon (15 ml) olive oil

½ teaspoon mustard seed

1 medium-size white or yellow onion, chopped

½ teaspoon split yellow peas

½ teaspoon ground turmeric

1 or 2 green chiles, stemmed, seeded if desired, and minced

Salt, to taste

2 large potatoes, peeled and finely diced

FOR TAMARIND CHUTNEY:

1 tablespoon (15 ml) olive oil

1 teaspoon cumin seeds

1 teaspoon ground ginger

½ teaspoon cayenne

½ teaspoon fennel seeds

½ teaspoon asafoetida powder

½ teaspoon garam masala

2 cups (470 g) water

1 cup plus 2 tablespoons (225 g) sugar

3 tablespoons (45 g) tamarind paste

To make the dosas: Soak the brown rice, urad dal, and fenugreek seeds in water to cover for at least 6 hours or overnight.

In a food processor, grind together the soaked ingredients until a smooth batter is achieved, adding water if needed. This may take a while. Transfer the batter to a large bowl. Add the salt and oil, stir to combine, and allow the dough to ferment in a warm place overnight or for at least 12 to 15 hours before making the dosas.

To make the filling: Heat the oil in a pan over medium heat. Add the mustard seed, onion, peas, turmeric, chiles, and salt and sauté for about 5 minutes, or until the onion is golden brown. Add the potatoes and cook until fork-tender, 10 to 12 minutes.

To make the chutney: Heat the oil in a saucepan over medium heat. Add the cumin seeds, ginger, cayenne, fennel seeds, asafoetida powder, and garam masala and sauté, stirring, for about 2 minutes. Stir in the water, sugar, and tamarind paste. Bring to a boil, then simmer over low heat until the mixture thickens and turns a deep chocolaty brown, 20 to 30 minutes. It will thicken as it cools.

Spray a griddle with nonstick cooking spray and heat to medium-high. Pour a ladleful of batter and spread to the desired thickness with the back of the ladle. Repeat with the remaining batter. Transfer to a plate, spread on some filling, and roll into a cigar shape. Serve with the chutney.

YIELD: 10 to 12 dosas

Fun Fact

Masala dosas have a ton of variations. They can be filled with mushrooms, cauliflower, peas, paneer, onion, and so on.

POTATO AND PEA SAMOSAS WITH MINT CILANTRO DIPPING SAUCE (POTATO FRITTERS)

*Gluten Free (use gluten-free flour), **Soy Free (use soy-free vegan butter)

Flaky, crispy, a bit spicy, and dense, these tasty fritters make any Indian meal complete. They are fun as a snack or an appetizer, and folks will be blown away by the flavor and your craftiness.

FOR DOUGH:

1½ cups (180 g) all-purpose flour

¾ teaspoon salt

¼ cup (56 g) vegan butter, melted

6 to 8 tablespoons (90 to 120 ml) cold water

FOR FILLING:

¼ cup (56 g) vegan butter

1 teaspoon ground coriander

½ cup (80 g) chopped yellow onion

2 teaspoons minced ginger

2 teaspoons minced garlic

2 green chile peppers, stemmed, seeded if desired, and minced (optional)

1 teaspoon garam masala

1 teaspoon salt

½ teaspoon ground turmeric

⅛ teaspoon cayenne

2 large baking potatoes, peeled, diced, and boiled until fork-tender

½ cup (65 g) partially cooked green peas

2 tablespoons (2 g) chopped fresh cilantro

2 teaspoons fresh lemon juice

Salt and pepper, to taste

To make the dough: Sift the flour and salt into a medium-size bowl. Add the melted butter and rub the mixture between your hands until the flour is evenly coated. It will look and feel like coarse bread crumbs. Add 6 tablespoons (90 ml) of the water and work until the dough forms, adding the remaining 2 tablespoons (30 ml) water if needed. Turn out the dough onto a lightly floured surface and knead for 4 minutes, until firm. Cover with a clean, dry kitchen towel and let rest for 30 minutes.

To make the filling: Heat the butter in a medium-size skillet over medium-high heat. Add the coriander and cook, stirring, for 10 seconds. Add the onion and ginger and cook for about 5 minutes, stirring continuously. Add the garlic, chile peppers, garam masala, salt, turmeric, and cayenne, and stir for 30 to 45 seconds. Add the potatoes and cook, stirring, until the potatoes start to color and dry, about 3 minutes. Stir in the peas and cook for 1 minute, then remove the pan from the heat, add the cilantro and lemon juice, and stir to combine. Season with salt and pepper to taste, then set aside and let cool.

On a lightly floured surface, knead the dough for about 1 minute. Divide into 2 equal portions and roll each into a ½-inch (1.3 cm) thick rope. Cut each rope into 8 equal portions and roll into smooth balls. Place each ball on the floured surface and roll out into a thin 6-inch (15 cm) circle. Cut each circle in half, so you end up with 2 semicircles. Take a semicircle and fold it into the shape of a cone, using water to seal the edges. Spoon about 2 teaspoons of the potato filling into the center of each little cone. Brush the open edges with water and fold the dough over the filling to seal, pressing them together to get a fat little triangle. Place on a baking sheet or waxed paper and repeat with the remaining dough and filling.

FOR MINT CILANTRO DIPPING SAUCE:

3 or 4 cloves garlic

¼ cup (40 g) minced white onion

½- to 1-inch (1.3 to 2.5 cm) piece fresh ginger, to taste

2 cups (120 g) chopped fresh mint

2 cups (32 g) chopped fresh cilantro

1 jalapeño pepper, stemmed and seeded (optional)

1 teaspoon sugar

Salt, to taste

Juice of 2 limes

1 tablespoon (15 ml) water

1 tablespoon (15 ml) olive oil

Safflower or peanut oil, for frying (or preferred high-heat oil)

To make the sauce: Place the garlic, onion, and ginger in a food processor and pulse until finely chopped. Add the mint, cilantro, jalapeño pepper, sugar, salt, and lime juice and purée. Add the water and olive oil and pulse to combine.

Preheat 2 inches (5 cm) of oil in a large pot to 350°F (180°C). Add the samosas in batches, being careful not to crowd the pot, and fry, turning to cook evenly, until golden brown, about 5 minutes. Remove with a slotted spoon and drain on a paper towel–lined plate. Return the oil to temperature and repeat with the remaining samosas. Serve with the dipping sauce.

YIELD: 32 samosas

fun fact

Although samosas did not originate in India, but rather in Central Asia, the Indian variety became quite popular and has been a favorite ever since.

PAKORA POPPERS
(FRIED VEGETABLES)

*Soy Free (use soy-free vegan yogurt)

This is the spice-filled Indian cousin of Japanese tempura. They are easier to prepare than you think, and your dining companions will think you spent all day in the kitchen!

FOR MINT YOGURT DIPPING SAUCE:

1 cup (230 g) plain vegan yogurt

Juice of 1 lime

3 cloves garlic

1 cup (60 g) chopped fresh mint

1 teaspoon ground coriander

1 teaspoon ground cumin

1 teaspoon paprika

Salt and pepper, to taste

FOR PAKORA:

1 cup (120 g) chickpea flour

½ teaspoon ground coriander

1 teaspoon salt

½ teaspoon ground turmeric

½ teaspoon chili powder

½ teaspoon garam masala

2 cloves garlic, minced

¾ to 1 cup (180 to 235 ml) water

Safflower or peanut oil, for frying (or preferred high-heat oil)

2 white or yellow onions, sliced into rings

1 cup (132 g) cauliflower florets

1 cup (110 g) peeled and cubed sweet potato

1 cup (71 g) broccoli florets

To make the sauce: Place the yogurt, lime juice, and garlic in a blender and purée on high speed until smooth. While blending, slowly add the mint, coriander, cumin, and paprika. Season with salt and pepper.

To make the pakora: Sift the chickpea flour into a medium-size bowl. Mix in the coriander, salt, turmeric, chili powder, garam masala, and garlic. Make a well in the center of the flour mix. Gradually pour the water into the well and mix to form a thick, smooth batter.

Heat 2 inches (5 cm) of oil in a large saucepan or fryer to 375°F (190°C). Dip the onions, cauliflower, sweet potatoes, and broccoli into the batter and fry in small batches until golden brown, 4 to 5 minutes. Drain on a paper towel–lined plate. Return the oil to temperature and repeat with the remaining vegetables and batter. Serve hot with the dipping sauce.

YIELD: 4 servings

Fun Fact

The word *pakora* is derived from the Sanskrit word *pakvavata*, a compound word comprised of *pakva*, meaning "cooked," and *vata*, meaning "a small lump."

CHANA MASALA WITH SAVORY SAFFRON RICE
(SPICED CHICKPEAS)

*Low Glycemic (limit rice portions)

So full of flavor and warmth, this is hands-down, Indian comfort food and by far my favorite Indian dish!

FOR CHANA MASALA:

1 medium-size white or yellow onion, peeled

6 tablespoons (90 ml) olive oil or (84 g) vegan butter

1-inch (2.5 cm) piece fresh ginger, minced

1 tablespoon (10 g) crushed garlic

1 or 2 green chiles, stemmed, seeded if desired, and minced

½ teaspoon red chile powder

1 tablespoon (6 g) ground coriander

1 teaspoon paprika

½ teaspoon ground cumin

½ teaspoon ground turmeric

1 cup (235 ml) water, divided

2 cups (360 g) drained, chopped tomatoes

3 cans (15½ ounces, or 435 g each) chickpeas, rinsed and drained

1 teaspoon garam masala

Juice of ½ to 1 lemon, to taste

FOR SAFFRON RICE:

2 tablespoons (28 g) vegan butter or (30 ml) olive oil

½ cup (80 g) diced white or yellow onion

2 cups (390 g) basmati rice

3½ cups (825 ml) vegetable broth, store-bought or homemade (page 16)

1 pinch saffron threads soaked in 2 tablespoons (30 ml) hot water for 10 minutes

1 teaspoon salt

To make the chana masala: Process the onion in a food processor until smooth. Pour off the extra liquid and set aside.

Heat the oil in a medium-size to large skillet over medium-high heat. Add the onion and cook until browned, 4 to 5 minutes. Adjust the heat as needed to avoid burning. Stir in the ginger and cook for 2 minutes. Add the garlic and cook for 1 minute longer. Add the chiles, chile powder, coriander, paprika, cumin, and turmeric, and mix well. Lower the heat to medium and add ½ cup (120 ml) of the water along with the tomatoes. Continue cooking and stirring for 2 minutes. Add the remaining ½ cup (120 ml) water and mix well. Stir in the chickpeas, lower the heat to medium-low, and cook for 10 minutes. Add the garam masala and lemon juice to taste and mix well. Cook for 2 more minutes and remove from the heat.

To make the rice: In medium-size to large pot, melt the butter over medium heat. Add the onion and fry for 3 minutes, or until tender and light brown. Stir in the rice, broth, saffron with the soaking water, and salt. Bring to a boil over high heat. Once it starts boiling, immediately cover and reduce the heat to low. Cook for about 20 minutes, or until most of the liquid has been absorbed. Remove from the heat and allow the rice to sit for 5 minutes, covered, to finish steaming. Fluff with a fork.

Scoop rice portions onto serving plates and top with a ladle of chana masala.

YIELD: 6 to 8 servings

GLUTEN FREE   SOY FREE   LOW FAT   LOW GLYCEMIC   KOSHER

ALOO GOBI
(SPICY CAULIFLOWER AND POTATOES)

You'll gob-ble up this aloo gobi! Make this dish to your taste and love it no matter the spice level. It's a fantastic blend of creamy cauliflower and hearty potatoes. Serve with warm naan and rice.

1 tablespoon (15 ml) olive oil or (14 g) vegan butter

1 small onion, chopped

1 clove garlic, minced

½-inch (1.3 cm) piece fresh ginger, grated

2 large potatoes, finely cubed

¼ teaspoon turmeric

½ teaspoon chili powder

¼ teaspoon cayenne

1 tablespoon (6 g) ground coriander

1 teaspoon ground cumin

5 tablespoons (75 ml) water

2 cups (200 g) cauliflower florets

Salt and pepper, to taste

½ teaspoon garam masala

Fresh cilantro, for garnish

Heat the oil in a medium-size saucepan over medium heat and sauté the onion, garlic, and ginger, about 2 minutes. Add the potatoes, turmeric, chili powder, cayenne, coriander, cumin, and water and cover the pot (make sure there is just enough water to cook the potatoes, so if you need more add 1 tablespoon [15 ml] at a time). Cook, stirring occasionally, until the potatoes are almost cooked but not fully tender, being careful not to burn, about 8 minutes. Add the cauliflower and mix well to coat. Cover again and cook, stirring every 3 to 4 minutes and making sure the cauliflower doesn't get mushy, just until soft, 8 to 10 minutes. Add the salt, pepper, and garam masala, mixing well. Garnish with cilantro and serve.

YIELD: 4 to 6 servings

fun fact

Surprise, surprise, *aloo gobi* means "potatoes and cauliflower"!

CHICKEN AND POTATO VINDALOO
(SPICY CURRY)

*Gluten Free (use gluten-free vegan chicken), **Soy Free (use soy-free vegan chicken)

The spice factor is up to you here, but whether it's kicked up or toned down, it's vinda-licious! Fun to say and great to eat, this dish is best served with rice or naan.

1 tablespoon (5 g) coriander seeds

½ to 1 teaspoon cardamom seeds

1 teaspoon whole black peppercorns

6 whole cloves

1 tablespoon (8 g) chili powder

4 cinnamon sticks

2 teaspoons fenugreek seeds

2 teaspoons minced fresh ginger

2 teaspoons cumin seeds

2 teaspoons mustard powder

2 teaspoons ground turmeric

2 teaspoons salt, plus more to taste

2 teaspoons minced garlic

1 cup (235 ml) white or apple cider vinegar

4 to 6 vegan chicken cutlets, sliced

4 red potatoes, peeled and cut into bite-size cubes

4 to 6 tablespoons (60 to 90 ml) olive oil, divided

4 bay leaves

2 medium-size white onions, chopped

1⅓ cups (315 ml) water

Fresh cilantro, for garnish

In a frying pan over low heat, gently roast the coriander seeds, cardamom seeds, peppercorns, cloves, chili powder, cinnamon sticks, fenugreek seeds, ginger, and cumin seeds for about 5 minutes. Place in a spice grinder and grind into a powder. Put the spice mixture in a blender and add the mustard powder, turmeric, salt, garlic, and vinegar and pulse to form a sauce. Place the chicken in a glass or ceramic bowl, pour the sauce over, stir to coat, and marinate in the refrigerator for at least 6 hours.

Boil the potatoes in lightly salted water until tender, about 10 minutes, drain, and set aside.

Heat 2 to 3 tablespoons (30 to 45 ml) of the oil in a skillet over medium heat, and sauté the bay leaves and onions until soft, 4 to 5 minutes, then remove from the pan and set aside. In the same pan, fry the marinated chicken for a few minutes, adding more oil of the if necessary. Add the remaining vindaloo sauce, sautéed onion, and water. Simmer, stirring well, until the chicken is tender and the sauce is thick, 3 to 5 minutes. With a few minutes left to cook, add the potatoes, coating well with the sauce. Add salt to taste, remove the bay leaves, and garnish with the cilantro.

YIELD: 4 servings

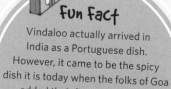

fun fact

Vindaloo actually arrived in India as a Portuguese dish. However, it came to be the spicy dish it is today when the folks of Goa added their fiery seasonings.

SACRED COW PALAK PANEER
(SPINACH AND CHEESE CURRY)

**Think of this as Indian spinach and cheese dip or a tasty main course. The texture
and flavors really complement each other in a mega awesome way. The cows can
go on vacation, because we can make our own paneer cheese without them!**

FOR PANEER:

1 pound (454 g) extra-firm tofu, pressed and drained

⅓ cup (80 g) light miso

½ cup (120 ml) water

⅓ cup (80 g) raw, unsalted cashew nut butter or tahini

1 tablespoon (8 g) nutritional yeast

¼ cup (60 ml) olive oil

5 to 7 large cloves garlic, to taste

1½ teaspoons ground coriander

2 sprigs fresh cilantro

1 tablespoon (15 ml) lemon juice

Salt and pepper, to taste

FOR CURRY:

5 tablespoons (75 ml) olive oil, divided

3 or 4 cloves garlic, chopped

1 tablespoon (8 g) grated fresh ginger, divided

2 dried red chile peppers (optional)

¾ cup (120 g) finely chopped white or yellow onion

2 teaspoons ground cumin

1½ teaspoons ground coriander

1 teaspoon ground turmeric

¾ cup (175 g) vegan sour cream

3 pounds (1,362 g) fresh spinach, torn

1 large tomato, quartered

4 to 8 sprigs fresh cilantro, to taste

Salt and pepper, to taste

To make the paneer: Toss all of the paneer ingredients into
a food processor and blend until well combined. Pulse for a
chunkier texture, or purée for a creamier texture. Taste and
adjust the seasonings before it's too well blended.

In a large saucepan, heat 3 tablespoons (45 ml) of the
oil and sauté the garlic, ½ tablespoon (4 g) of the ginger,
the red chiles, and the onion until browned, 5 to 6 minutes.
Add the cumin, coriander, turmeric, and sour cream and
stir to combine. Add the spinach, handfuls at a time, until it
is cooked down, about 15 minutes. Remove from the heat
and allow to cool a bit.

Pour the spinach mixture into a blender or food processor and add the tomato, the remaining ½ tablespoon (4 g)
ginger, and the cilantro. Blend until the spinach is finely
chopped. Pour back into the saucepan and keep warm over
low heat.

In a medium-size frying pan heat the remaining 2 tablespoons (30 ml) oil over medium heat, and fry the paneer
until browned, stirring to cook evenly, 3 to 4 minutes; drain
and add to the spinach, mixing well. Cook for about 10
minutes over low heat, then season with salt and pepper
to taste.

YIELD: 6 servings

Fun Fact

Also called saag paneer, paneer
(crumbly cheese) was created by
accident back in the times of the Mongols.
When riding long distances, they packed their
sacks full of food to sustain them for the
duration. At the time, they transported their milk
in rawhide bags. The heat of the desert
combined with the enzymes still present in
the leather curdled the milk into paneer.

Chapter 16

CHINA

CHINESE CUISINE IS A LOT MORE than little white take-out boxes and fortune cookies. In fact, this 5,000-year-old culture has had quite an influence on global food. For instance, pasta did not originate in Italy. Nope—it was invented by the Chinese! China also gave us soy sauce, tea, and chopsticks.

As you can imagine, cuisine evolves over the course of 5,000 years. During that time, China eventually divided itself into northern and southern styles of cooking. Throughout its evolution, food has also been an integral part of Chinese medicinal practice. For centuries, Chinese medicine has used the country's abundant herbs, mushrooms, and vegetables to heal people.

Two of the most popular schools of thought in China have been Confucianism and Taoism. Confucius believed that cooking and food should be enjoyable, emphasizing etiquette, social sharing, and beautiful presentation to delight the palate and the senses. Taosim focused on the healthful properties of food. Studying the physical and psychological effects of food was a way for them to understand how and which foods best nourished the body. Both belief systems have helped shaped Chinese cooking into the complex and delicious cuisine that it is today.

From the way food is prepared and served to how it is eaten, Chinese cuisine has a style all its own. Dining among family and friends is a key part of their culture, as is their incredibly detailed table etiquette. For example, chopsticks placed upright in rice is a no-no because it signifies death, and an empty plate means you are still hungry and the host must oblige by serving you more!

Whether you are dining with friends over dim sum or cooking up a feast for Chinese New Year or Mid-Autumn Festival, the look, feel, and meaning of food are vital. So what do you say we take a trip to the Orient and get stir-frying? Don't forget to pour yourself a glass of baijiu. *Gan bei* (bottoms up)!

CHICKEN'S DAY OFF VEGGIE EGG ROLLS

*Gluten Free (use wheat-free tamari and gluten-free wrappers), **Soy Free (use liquid aminos)

**Which came first? The spring roll or the egg? Hmmm, methinks
the spring roll! These are way better than delivery!**

FOR HOT SAUCE:

¼ cup (36 g) mustard powder

¼ cup (60 ml) water

FOR MILD SWEET SAUCE:

1 large peach

3 large plums

⅓ cup (50 g) diced red bell pepper

⅓ cup (55 g) coarsely chopped dried apricots

2 tablespoons (30 g) dark brown sugar

3 tablespoons (38 g) granulated sugar

¼ cup (60 ml) white vinegar

½ teaspoon minced candied ginger, or to taste (optional)

FOR EGG ROLLS:

2 tablespoons (30 ml) sesame oil

2 tablespoons (30 ml) olive oil

½ head green cabbage, shredded

1 cup (110 g) julienned or shredded carrot

1 cup (75 g) diced or julienned snow peas

1 cup (70 g) minced button mushrooms

1 tablespoon (8 g) cornstarch

¼ cup (60 ml) soy sauce or tamari

8 vegan egg roll wrappers, store-bought or homemade (page 18), or vegan spring roll wrappers, rice paper wrappers, or gyoza dumpling wrappers

Peanut or coconut oil, for frying (or preferred high-heat oil)

Salt and pepper, to taste

Paprika, to taste

Onion powder, to taste

Garlic powder, to taste

Fresh cilantro leaves, for garnish

To make the hot sauce: In a small bowl or ramekin, combine the mustard and water.

To make the mild sweet sauce: If using fresh fruit, skin the peaches and plums by plunging them into boiling water for a few seconds. Rinse and peel under cool water. Quarter the plums and divide the peach into eighths; discard the pits. Combine the peach, plums, bell pepper, apricots, both sugars, vinegar, and ginger in a saucepan and bring to a boil, stirring several times. Reduce the heat to low, and simmer, uncovered, for 30 minutes to 1 hour, stirring occasionally. Press the mixture through a coarse food mill or strainer. Cool and store in an airtight jar in the refrigerator.

To make the egg rolls: In a skillet over medium-high heat, heat the sesame and olive oils. Sauté the cabbage for 2 minutes, then add the carrot, snow peas, and mushrooms. Cook for 1 minute longer.

Whisk together the cornstarch and soy sauce until smooth and stir into the vegetable mixture. Cook until the sauce comes to a boil and is slightly thickened, about 2 minutes. Remove from the heat and let cool.

Lay the egg roll wrapper on a work surface and lightly brush the edges with water. Place one-eighth of the filling at one end of each wrapper, leaving a ¼-inch (6 mm) border at the top and sides. Roll the wrapper over the filling, tucking in the ends after the first roll.

Heat 3 inches (7.5 cm) of oil in a large, deep saucepan or deep fryer to 350°F (180°C) and fry the egg rolls until golden brown, 2 to 3 minutes, turning to cook all sides. Remove from the fryer and drain on a paper towel–lined plate. Season with salt, pepper, paprika, onion powder, and garlic powder to taste. Garnish with the cilantro leaves and serve with the sauces.

YIELD: 8 egg rolls

YOU KNOW YOU WANT SOME WONTON SOUP

*Gluten Free (use wheat-free tamari and gluten-free wrappers), **Soy Free (use liquid aminos)

Americans may turn to chicken noodle soup when they're feeling under the weather, but I'll cast my vote for a hot steaming bowl of wonton soup! This was always my go-to soup when out for Chinese with my parents, so I just had to include a vegan version. If you want to try making your own wonton wrappers, visit healthyvoyager.com for my recipe.

FOR WONTONS:

½ cup (45 g) finely chopped cabbage

½ teaspoon salt

¾ cup (150 g) minced seitan, store-bought or homemade (page 19), marinated tofu, tempeh, or (53 g) finely diced mushrooms

3 scallions, finely chopped

1 tablespoon (6 g) minced fresh ginger

1 teaspoon minced garlic

½ teaspoon lemon juice

1 teaspoon soy sauce or tamari

1 teaspoon toasted sesame oil

24 vegan wonton wrappers, store-bought or homemade (page 18)

FOR SOUP:

3¾ cups (880 ml) vegan chicken broth (make with vegan chicken bouillon) or vegetable broth, store-bought or homemade (page 16)

4 cups (940 ml) water

1 tablespoon (10 g) minced garlic

Salt, to taste

1 cup (70 g) thinly sliced bok choy

3 scallions, white and green parts, thinly sliced

2 to 3 teaspoons (10 to 15 ml) rice vinegar

½ teaspoon sesame oil

To make the wontons: In a medium-size bowl, toss the cabbage with the salt. Let stand for 10 minutes. Wrap the cabbage in a double layer of paper towels; firmly squeeze out the excess liquid. Return the cabbage to the bowl; add the seitan, scallions, ginger, garlic, lemon juice, soy sauce, and sesame oil. Mix well with a fork. Refrigerate the filling until it's time to make the wontons.

Work with 1 wrapper at a time, and keep the rest covered with a damp towel. Spoon 1 rounded teaspoon of filling into the center of a wrapper. With dampened fingers, wet the 4 edges. Fold the wrapper into a triangle over the filling, making sure the ends meet and the filling is centered; press the edges down firmly to seal. Moisten one tip on the long side of a triangle, then bring both tips together on the long side, overlapping them slightly; press the tips together to seal. Fold the remaining top corner back. Transfer to an oiled plate; cover with a damp towel to keep moist. Repeat with the remaining wrappers and filling.

To make the soup: In a large pot, combine the broth, water, garlic, and salt and bring to a boil. Add the boy choy and cook for about 2 minutes. Add the wontons one at a time; return to a boil. Reduce the heat to medium and simmer until the wontons are just cooked through, 4 to 6 minutes. Stir in the scallions, vinegar, and sesame oil; season with salt.

YIELD: 6 servings

fun fact

Won Ton is Cantonese for "swallowing a cloud!"

SOME LIKE IT HOT AND SOUR SOUP

*Gluten Free (use wheat-free tamari and omit the seitan), **Soy Free (use liquid aminos and omit the tofu)

If you like it hot, this is the soup for you! Make it as spicy as you like and this Taiwanese dish just may clear your sinuses. But even if you nix the spice, it's a tasty liquid meal.

FOR MEAT:

1 teaspoon soy sauce or tamari

½ teaspoon sesame oil

1 teaspoon tapioca starch or cornstarch

½ cup (100 g) thinly sliced seitan, store-bought or homemade (page 19)

FOR SOUP:

1 package (14 ounces, or 392 g) extra-firm tofu, pressed and drained

½ cup (50 g) bamboo shoots

3 or 4 Chinese dried black mushrooms or fresh mushrooms of your choice

5 cups (1,175 ml) water

1 cup (235 ml) vegan chicken broth (make with vegan chicken bouillon)

2 teaspoons minced fresh ginger

1 teaspoon sugar

2 tablespoons (30 ml) soy sauce or tamari

2 tablespoons (30 ml) red rice vinegar, white rice vinegar, or red wine vinegar

1 teaspoon sesame oil

1 teaspoon salt, or to taste

1 tablespoon (8 g) cornstarch dissolved in ¼ cup (60 ml) water

1 scallion, finely chopped

White pepper, to taste

Hot chile oil, to taste (optional)

Chopped fresh cilantro, for garnish

To make the meat: Combine the soy sauce, sesame oil, and tapioca starch in a large bowl, add the seitan, and stir to combine. Let marinate for 20 minutes.

Cut the tofu into small squares. Cut the bamboo shoots into thin strips and then into fine slices. If using dried mushrooms, soak in hot water to soften, then cut off the stems and cut into thin strips. If using fresh mushrooms, wipe clean with a damp cloth and slice.

Bring the water and broth to a boil in a large pot. Add the bamboo shoots, mushrooms, and ginger and stir to combine. Add the tofu. Return to a boil and add the marinated seitan. Stir in the sugar, soy sauce, vinegar, and sesame oil. Taste the broth and adjust the flavors, then season with salt to taste.

Slowly pour the cornstarch/water mixture into the soup, stirring all the while. Let the broth come back to a boil. As soon as it is boiling, remove from the heat. Add the scallion and the white pepper to taste. Drizzle with chile oil and garnish with chopped cilantro.

YIELD: 6 servings

COOK'S NOTE

Feel free to add more vegetables for a more healthful soup. Try bok choy, spinach, or carrots.

IT'S NOT DELIVERY VEGETABLE LO MEIN

*Gluten Free (use gluten-free noodles and wheat-free tamari and opt for cornstarch), **Soy Free (use liquid aminos)

If you have a yearning for noodles but are not in the mood for tomato sauce, this is a fabulously savory alternative. "Make-in" instead of "take-out"!

1 teaspoon sesame oil

3 cloves garlic, minced

3 cups (270 g) chopped bok choy

1 cup (70 g) sliced mushrooms

1 cup (75 g) sliced snow peas

¼ cup (25 g) chopped scallion, plus more for garnish

1 cup (235 ml) vegetable broth, store-bought or homemade (page 16)

2 tablespoons (30 ml) soy sauce or tamari, plus more for sprinkling

1 tablespoon (20 g) agave nectar

1 teaspoon grated fresh ginger

½ teaspoon red pepper flakes (optional)

½ cup (55 g) coarsely shredded carrot

½ cup (25 g) bean sprouts

1 can (15 ounces, or 420 g) baby corn, drained

1 tablespoon (8 g) all-purpose flour or cornstarch

6 ounces (170 g) vermicelli noodles, cooked and drained (lo mein or spaghetti is fine, too)

Coat a wok or large skillet with the sesame oil. Heat over medium-high heat until hot. Stir-fry the garlic for about 1 minute, then add the bok choy and stir-fry for 2 minutes. Add the mushrooms, snow peas, and scallion and stir-fry for 2 minutes. Add the vegetable broth, soy sauce, agave, ginger, and red pepper flakes and stir-fry for 1 minute. Add the carrot, bean sprouts, and baby corn and stir-fry for 2 minutes. Add the flour and cook until thickened, 2 to 3 minutes, then add the cooked noodles and toss gently to combine. Sprinkle with additional soy sauce to taste and toss again. Garnish with a little chopped scallion and serve.

YIELD: 4 servings

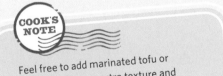

COOK'S NOTE

Feel free to add marinated tofu or tempeh for some extra texture and protein.

Fun Fact

It is believed that noodles originated in China as early as 5000 BCE. And by the way, *lo mein* is Cantonese for "stirred noodles."

GUILT-FREE VEGGIE FRIED RICE

*Gluten Free (use wheat-free tamari), **Soy Free (use liquid aminos and soy-free vegan butter)

Fried rice is a great accompaniment to any Chinese main course. But you know when it's super delish? For breakfast! (Hey, don't knock it 'til you try it!)

3 tablespoons (42 g) vegan butter

1 cup (195 g) uncooked rice, preferably brown

½ cup (50 g) chopped scallion

2 teaspoons minced garlic

½ cup (25 g) bean sprouts

½ cup (65 g) diced carrot

2 cups (470 ml) water

2 teaspoons vegan chicken bouillon

½ teaspoon sugar

¼ to ½ teaspoon grated fresh ginger

2 or 3 tablespoons (30 to 45 ml) soy sauce or tamari

1 tablespoon (15 ml) sesame oil, for sautéing tofu (if using)

½ cup (100 g) pressed, drained, and cubed extra-firm tofu (optional)

1 package (10 ounces, or 280 g) frozen sweet green peas, thawed

Melt the butter in a large skillet and sauté the rice, scallion, garlic, bean sprouts, and carrot for 4 to 5 minutes. Stir in the water, bouillon, sugar, ginger, and soy sauce, cover, and simmer for 20 minutes. Heat the sesame oil in a small skillet and sauté the diced tofu over medium heat for about 5 minutes, then add it and the peas to the rice. Stir and cook for 5 to 10 minutes.

YIELD: 4 to 6 servings

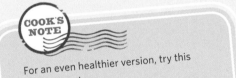

COOK'S NOTE

For an even healthier version, try this with quinoa!

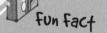

fun fact

Fried rice was essentially a way for the Chinese to use up leftover rice and create sustenance when they could not afford many vegetables or protein sources.

KILLER KUNG PAO CHICKEN

*Gluten Free (use wheat-free tamari and hoisin and use tofu or gluten-free vegan chicken),
**Soy Free (use liquid aminos, omit the hoisin and use agave or molasses to taste, and use seitan)

Putting the "pow" back into mealtime! Your dining companions will be in awe of the sweet and spicy authenticity of this dish.

8 vegan chicken cutlets, cut into 1-inch (2.5 cm) pieces

1 tablespoon (8 g) cornstarch

2 teaspoons sesame oil

3 tablespoons (18 g) chopped scallion, white and green parts

2 cloves garlic, minced

¼ to 1½ teaspoons red pepper flakes, to taste

½ teaspoon ground or grated fresh ginger

2 tablespoons (30 ml) rice wine vinegar

2 tablespoons (30 ml) soy sauce or tamari

2 tablespoons (30 g) hoisin sauce

2 teaspoons sugar

⅓ cup (50 g) dry-roasted peanuts

2 tablespoons (30 ml) vegetable broth, store-bought or homemade (page 16), mixed with 1 tablespoon (8 g) cornstarch to make a slurry

Cooked rice, for serving

Combine the chicken and cornstarch in a small bowl and toss to coat.

Heat the oil in large skillet or wok over medium heat and add the chicken. Stir-fry for about 5 minutes and remove from the skillet. Add the scallion, garlic, red pepper flakes, and ginger to the skillet and stir-fry for 15 seconds, then remove from the heat.

Combine the vinegar, soy sauce, hoisin sauce, and sugar in a small bowl, stirring well, then add to the skillet with the scallion mixture. Return the chicken to the skillet and stir until well coated. Stir in the peanuts and slurry mixture and heat thoroughly, stirring occasionally, until thickened a bit, 3 to 5 minutes. Serve over hot rice.

YIELD: 6 to 8 servings

fun fact

Unfortunately, *kung pao* has nothing to do with martial arts. It just means spicy stir-fried or deep-fried food.

GLUTEN FREE* SOY FREE** LOW FAT*** LOW GLYCEMIC KOSHER

SPICY MAPO DOUFU
(ZESTY TOFU AND SEITAN STEW)

*Gluten Free (use wheat-free tamari, and hoisin sauce and omit the seitan),
**Soy Free (use liquid aminos and replace the tofu with seitan), ***Low Fat (stir-fry with less oil)

This is a traditional Szechuan dish, sure to warm the soul. With lots of spices and a hearty, stewlike texture, it's a great way to wrap up your day.

FOR MARINADE:

1 tablespoon (11 g) Chinese salted black beans (they are fermented), rinsed

2 tablespoons (30 ml) soy sauce or tamari

2 tablespoons (30 ml) cooking wine, whiskey, or dry sherry

3 large cloves garlic, chopped

1-inch (2.5 cm) piece fresh ginger, minced or grated

1 medium-size white onion, roughly chopped

FOR STEW:

1 cup (200 g) sliced seitan, store-bought or homemade (page 19)

1 pound (454 g) firm tofu, pressed, drained, and cut into ½-inch (1.3 cm) cubes

2 to 3 tablespoons (30 to 45 ml) peanut or coconut oil for stir-frying (or preferred high-heat oil)

2 medium-size white onions, thinly sliced

3 large cloves garlic, thinly sliced

Salt, to taste

1 tablespoon (20 g) chili paste, or to taste

1 cup (235 ml) vegan chicken broth (make with vegan chicken bouillon)

1 medium-size red bell pepper, cored, seeded, and diced

1 leek or 3 scallions, rinsed well and finely chopped

1 tablespoon (8 g) cornstarch

2 tablespoons (30 ml) water

2 tablespoons (30 ml) light soy sauce or tamari

Freshly ground Szechuan pepper, to taste (you can use cayenne if you can't find Szechuan)

Cooked rice, for serving

To make the marinade: Combine all the marinade ingredients in a large bowl.

To make the stew: Add the seitan to the marinade and let sit for about 20 minutes. Bring a medium-size pot of water to a boil, add the tofu, and blanch for 2 to 3 minutes, then drain.

Heat the oil in a wok over medium-high heat. Add the onions and garlic and stir-fry until beginning to brown, 3 to 4 minutes. Add the marinated seitan and stir-fry until it darkens, 2 to 3 minutes. Stir in the salt and chili paste, stir-fry briefly, then add the broth and the tofu. Turn down the heat to medium and cook for 3 to 4 minutes. Add the bell pepper and the leek, and stir-fry for 2 to 3 minutes. Combine the cornstarch, water, and soy sauce in a small bowl, then add to the wok and stir gently. Sprinkle with the Szechuan pepper and serve over the cooked rice.

YIELD: 2 servings

Fun Fact

The direct translation of *mapo* is "old pockmarked-face lady." And this is her tofu dish! As legend has it, this unfortunate-looking woman lived on the outskirts of Chengdu. Her home happened to be by the road that traders used and so her dish became quite popular with folks passing through.

ALL FOR YOU FORTUNE COOKIES

*Gluten Free (use gluten-free flour)

No Chinese meal is complete without finding out what your future holds!

2 vegan egg whites, store-bought or homemade (page 13)

6 tablespoons (84 g) vegan butter, at room temperature

½ cup (100 g) sugar

½ cup (60 g) all-purpose flour

1½ teaspoons cornstarch

¼ teaspoon salt

½ teaspoon vanilla extract

½ teaspoon almond extract

COOK'S NOTE

Size matters! Smaller cookies are much harder to form. Shoot for a 3½- to 4-inch (9 to 10 cm) cookie because it is easier to fold and can fit in a muffin pan to cool and keep its shape so you don't have to hold it. A level tablespoon of batter will help you achieve a larger cookie size.

Write 15 fortunes on slips of paper that are 3½ inches (9 cm) long and ½ inch (1.3 cm) wide. Write these ahead of time because you need to be on your toes to get these right! You may also want to cut out a round stencil about 4 inches (10 cm) in diameter so your cookie size is accurate and uniform when placed on the baking sheet.

Preheat the oven to 300°F (150°C, or gas mark 2). Grease two 9 × 13-inch (23 × 33 cm) baking sheets and keep them cold. Have ready 2 muffin pans.

In a medium-size bowl, lightly beat the egg whites and chill in the fridge. In a large bowl, cream the butter and sugar with a mixer. Add the flour, cornstarch, and salt and beat to combine. Add the vanilla and almond extracts and beat again. Finally, add the chilled egg whites and beat until well incorporated and smooth. The batter should not be runny, but should drop easily off a wooden spoon.

Place level tablespoons of batter onto the baking sheets, through the stencil if you have it, spacing them at least 3 inches (7.5 cm) apart. If you need to get the size right without a stencil, gently tilt the baking sheet back and forth and from side to side so that each tablespoon of batter forms a circle about 4 inches (10 cm) in diameter. Tilting is much easier then trying to spread the batter, because it sticks to the spoon. You should get about 15 cookies.

Bake until the outer ½ inch (1.3 cm) of each cookie turns golden brown and they are easy to remove from the baking sheet with a spatula, 14 to 15 minutes. The inner part will still look light in color.

Speed is the key here, so recruit a helper. You have about 20 seconds at most before the cookies begin to harden. In addition, you may want to wear tight, close-fitting cotton gloves to avoid burning your fingers. Latex or rubber gloves may stick and might also be too bulky. Working quickly, remove a cookie with a spatula and flip it over in your hand. Place a fortune in the middle of the cookie. Fold the cookie in half, then gently pinch the pointy edges together. Place the finished cookie in the cup of the muffin pan so it keeps its shape. Repeat with the remaining cookies.

YIELD: About 15 cookies

Chapter 17

THAILAND AND VIETNAM

THAILAND, ONCE KNOWN AS SIAM, has a 4,000-year history. Because people migrated there from southern China, the cuisine is heavily influenced by Chinese as well as Indian foods. However, Thai food is unique all on its own.

As with Chinese and Japanese culinary culture, food is an art form in Thailand. Balance of flavors, such as sweet with sour, plays a major role in each dish, and harmony in flavor combinations is key. Fresh vegetables, herbs, and small portions of meat comprise the most popular meals, making Thai fare healthy and light. Dining has its traditional culture, as with the Chinese, and like the Japanese, rice, called *kaow*, is present at every meal.

Thai cooking can be labor-intensive and time-consuming because they are adamant about cooking everything from scratch and using fragrant spices, fresh herbs, and native fruits and vegetables. Some dishes can take all day to make, especially curry dishes, but every bite will tell you that it's worth it.

And as a quick bonus, I've thrown in two of my favorite Vietnamese dishes. Because Vietnam is so close to Thailand, its flavors and ingredients are similar. But be it deep-fried, stir-fried, boiled, or steamed, Vietnamese cooking is delish. Have fun in this part of the world, especially if you like spice. *Phelidphelin or thuong thuc* (enjoy)!

CREAMY AND CHUNKY COCONUT SOUP

*Soy Free (use liquid aminos and omit the tofu)

Savory and sweet all at once! Rich and creamy, with lots of chunky deliciousness, this soup will make you feel like you're sitting under a palm tree by the sea.

FOR RED CURRY PASTE:

10 to 12 dried red chiles, to taste

5 tablespoons (75 ml) hot water

5 cloves garlic, chopped

2 shallots, chopped

1 tablespoon (7 g) thinly sliced fresh lemongrass

3 thin slices fresh ginger

1 slice kaffir lime peel

6 to 8 coriander roots, coarsely chopped

White pepper, to taste

½ teaspoon ground cumin

½ teaspoon ground coriander

2 tablespoons (14 g) paprika

FOR SOUP:

1 tablespoon (15 ml) grapeseed oil

2 tablespoons (16 g) grated fresh ginger

1 stalk lemongrass, minced

2 teaspoons red curry paste, store-bought or homemade (above)

4 cups (940 ml) vegetable or vegan chicken broth (make with vegan chicken bouillon)

3 tablespoons (45 ml) vegan fish sauce, store-bought or homemade (page 17), soy sauce, or tamari

1 tablespoon (15 g) light brown sugar

3 cans (13½ ounces, or 378 g each) coconut milk

1 cup (70 g) sliced shiitake mushrooms

2 cups (400 g) pressed, drained, and cubed extra-firm tofu

2 tablespoons (30 ml) fresh lime juice

Salt, to taste

¼ cup (4 g) chopped fresh cilantro

To make the curry paste: Soak the chiles in the hot water for 1 to 2 hours. Combine the chiles and their soaking liquid with all the curry ingredients in a blender and process into a smooth paste.

To make the soup: Heat the oil in a large pot over medium heat. Add the ginger, lemongrass, and curry paste and sauté, stirring, for 1 minute. Slowly pour in the broth, stirring continually. Stir in the fish sauce and brown sugar and simmer for about 15 minutes. Add the coconut milk and mushrooms and cook, stirring occasionally, until the mushrooms are tender, about 5 minutes. Add the tofu and cook for 5 minutes longer. Remove from the heat, stir in the lime juice, season with salt, and garnish with the cilantro.

YIELD: 4 to 6 servings

Fun Fact

Coconut is highly nutritious and rich in vitamins, minerals, and fiber.

NOT FOR THE FAINT-OF-HEART SOM TAM
(SPICY PAPAYA SALAD)

*Soy Free (use liquid aminos and omit the tofu), **Raw (omit the tofu and rice)

**Looking for a salad with a kick? I introduce you to
som tam. It's super spicy, unique, and a hoot to make.**

1 cup (200 g) pressed, drained, and cubed extra-firm tofu

2 cups plus 3 tablespoons (515 ml) seaweed stock,
store-bought or homemade (page 16), divided

1 teaspoon umeboshi vinegar

2 to 5 chile peppers, to taste

3 cloves garlic, minced

1 medium-size tomato, sliced,
or 5 or 6 cherry tomatoes, halved

1 cup (100 g) sliced green beans

1 tablespoon (15 ml) vegan fish sauce,
store-bought or homemade (page 17)

2 thick lemon wedges

1 teaspoon palm or granulated sugar

1 cup (175 g) seeded and shredded or julienned papaya

¼ cup (35 g) coarsely chopped dry-roasted peanuts

Cooked rice, for serving

Cucumber slices, for serving

Combine the tofu, 2 cups (470 ml) of the stock, and the vinegar in a bowl and let marinate for at least 2 hours, then drain.

Pound the chile peppers and garlic together in a mortar and pestle. In a bowl, combine the tomato, green beans, and marinated tofu. Add the fish sauce, remaining 3 tablespoons (45 ml) seaweed stock, lemon wedges, sugar, and the chile/garlic mixture. Use a pestle to crush and mix all the ingredients together. Add the papaya and mix with the pestle or a spoon, then stir in the peanuts. Serve with the cooked rice and cucumber slices.

YIELD: 2 to 4 servings

Fun Fact

Did you know that spicy foods can actually speed up your metabolism? If you can deal with it, eat up!

PEANUTTY PAD THAI

*Soy Free (use liquid aminos and omit the tofu)

Noodles and creamy peanut sauce—so indulgent and oh so good. It's my Thai staple, hands down.

FOR PEANUT SAUCE:

½ to 1 tablespoon (8 to 16 g) red chile paste

1 cup (235 ml) coconut milk

1 tablespoon (15 ml) vegan fish sauce,
store-bought or homemade (page 17)

½ cup (130 g) peanut butter

1 tablespoon (13 g) sugar

FOR PAD THAI:

1 package (8 ounces, or 225 g) rice noodles

3 tablespoons (45 ml) peanut or sesame oil

3 cloves garlic, minced

¼ cup (60 ml) vegan fish sauce,
store-bought or homemade (page 17)

¼ cup (50 g) sugar

2 tablespoons (30 ml) vinegar

1 tablespoon (7 g) paprika

½ cup (100 g) pressed, drained, and cubed extra-firm tofu

1 teaspoon hoisin sauce or soy sauce

2 scallions, stems only, diced,
plus ½ cup (50 g) chopped, for garnish

¼ cup (35 g) dry-roasted peanuts, ground

1½ cups (75 g) bean sprouts, divided

6 lemon wedges, for garnish

To make the sauce: Combine the chile paste, coconut milk, fish sauce, and peanut butter in a saucepan and bring to a boil. Add the sugar and boil for about 2 minutes, or until thickened and well combined, then remove from the heat.

To make the pad Thai: Soak the rice noodles in cold water for 30 minutes, or until soft. Drain and set aside.

Heat the oil in a skillet or wok over medium heat. Add the garlic and stir-fry for 3 to 4 minutes, or until fragrant and golden. Add the noodles and stir-fry until the noodles are translucent, reducing the heat if the noodles begin to stick together, 2 to 4 minutes. Add the fish sauce, sugar, vinegar, and paprika and continue to stir-fry until combined, about 2 minutes longer. Stir in the tofu, reduce the heat to medium-low, and stir-fry for 2 minutes longer, or until most of the liquid has been reduced. Stir in the hoisin sauce, the 2 diced scallions, the ground peanuts, and 1 cup (50 g) of the bean sprouts. Mix well. Transfer to a serving plate, pour the peanut sauce over the top, and garnish with the remaining ½ cup (25 g) sprouts, the remaining ½ cup (50 g) chopped scallions, and the lemon wedges.

YIELD: 6 servings

fun fact

The *pad* in pad Thai means "stir-fried." Therefore, this dish means "Thai stir-fry."

CRISPITY, CRUNCHITY MEE KROB
(FRIED NOODLES)

*Soy Free (use liquid aminos and omit the tofu or substitute with soy-free vegan meat)

**Crispy noodles are fun and fabulous. Me grub! Making this dish
is super enjoyable, as is serving it up for friends and family.**

1 package (16 ounces, or 454 g) extra-firm tofu,
pressed and drained

4 cups (940 ml) peanut or safflower oil, for frying
(or preferred high-heat oil), divided

Salt and pepper, to taste

3 tablespoons (39 g) sugar

3 tablespoons (60 g) light agave nectar

¼ cup (60 ml) tamarind juice

3 tablespoons (45 ml) vegan fish sauce,
store-bought or homemade (page 17)

2 tablespoons (30 g) tomato paste or ketchup

1 cup (50 g) bean sprouts

1 package (8 ounces, or 225 g) vermicelli rice noodles

¼ cup (25 g) chopped scallion, for garnish

¼ cup (4 g) chopped fresh cilantro, for garnish

Preheat the oven to 250°F (120°C, or gas mark ½). Lay the tofu out on a tray in a single layer and bake until dry and hard on the outside, about a1 hour.

In a large, deep pot, heat 3 cups (705 ml) of the oil over high heat to 375°F (190°C). When the oil is hot turn down the heat to 350°F (180°C). Drop a piece of tofu in and if it puffs up and sizzles, the oil is ready. Add the rest of the tofu to the hot oil and cook briefly until slightly brown, about 1 minute or so. Remove with a slotted spoon and drain on a paper towel–lined plate. Season to taste with salt and pepper and set aside. Reserve the hot oil for the noodles.

Heat 1 tablespoon (15 ml) of the remaining oil in a pan over very low heat, add the sugar and agave, stir to combine, then add the tamarind juice and mix well. Add the fish sauce and ketchup and stir to combine, being careful not to burn. Simmer until the mixture is nice and thick, 2 to 3 minutes. Remove from the heat, add the fried tofu and bean sprouts, and stir to combine.

Add the remaining 1 cup (220 ml) oil to the reserved pot of oil and heat to 375°F (190°C). Open the package of vermicelli noodles and pry the tight bundles of noodles apart into several loose bundles. Test a piece of noodle in the hot oil to see if it is ready. If the noodle puffs up, the oil is hot enough. Put one small bundle of noodles into the hot oil and fry until it puffs up and expands, about 1 minute or so. As soon as it puffs up, flip the noodles over to fry the other side. Cook for a few seconds, and then remove and drain on a paper towel–lined plate. Repeat with the remaining noodle bundles and allow to cool.

Add the cooled noodles to the sauce, tofu, and bean sprout mixture, coating evenly with the sauce. Garnish with the scallion and cilantro and serve.

YIELD: 4 to 6 servings

Fun Fact
Mee krob means "crispy noodles" in Thai.

GREEN CURRIED TOFU AND VEGETABLES

Soy Free (use liquid aminos and omit the tofu)

This curry, tofu, and vegetable dish is a Thai classic that is simple yet flavorful.

FOR THAI GREEN CURRY PASTE:

1 stalk lemongrass, thinly sliced

2 teaspoons ground coriander

3 tablespoons (45 ml) vegan fish sauce, store-bought or homemade (page 17)

1 teaspoon brown sugar

1 to 3 green chiles, seeded if desired

1 small onion or 2 shallots

3 cloves garlic

2-inch (5 cm) piece fresh ginger, sliced

2 or 3 kaffir lime leaves, cut into small pieces

1 loose cup (16 g) fresh cilantro

1½ teaspoons soy sauce or tamari

½ cup (120 ml) water or unsweetened coconut milk, as needed

FOR TOFU AND VEGETABLES:

1 tablespoon (15 ml) sesame oil

8 ounces (225 g) extra-firm tofu, pressed, drained, and cubed

1 tablespoon (15 ml) grapeseed oil

2 red bell peppers, cored, seeded, and cut into strips

1 medium-size onion, thinly sliced

Salt and pepper, to taste

1 tablespoon (10 g) minced garlic

1½ tablespoons vegan Thai green curry paste, store-bought or homemade (above)

2 medium-size sweet potatoes, peeled and cut into 1-inch (2.5 cm) cubes

1 can (14 ounces, or 392 g) unsweetened coconut milk

½ cup (120 ml) water

8 ounces (225 g) snow peas

1 tablespoon (1 g) chopped fresh cilantro

Cooked rice, for serving

To make the curry paste: Combine the lemongrass, coriander, fish sauce, brown sugar, chiles, onion, garlic, ginger, lime leaves, cilantro, and soy sauce in a food processor or blender and process well. Add the water as needed to achieve the desired consistency.

Heat the sesame oil in a skillet and sauté the tofu over medium-high heat for about 5 minutes, or until browned on all sides. Remove from the pan and set aside.

Heat the grapeseed oil in the same skillet and sauté the bell peppers and onion over medium-high heat for about 5 minutes, or until soft and translucent. Season with salt and pepper. Add the garlic and curry paste and cook, stirring, for about 1 minute. Add the sweet potatoes, coconut milk, and water and simmer, covered, stirring occasionally, until the potatoes are almost tender, about 3 minutes. Add snow peas and simmer, uncovered, until the sauce is slightly thickened. Add the cilantro and tofu and warm through. Serve with the rice.

YIELD: 6 to 8 servings

fun fact

Originating in Asia, green curry paste has been changed to suit a variety of palates from mild to mega spicy. When Siam (Thailand) opened up to trade in the 1350s, the Indians and Moors added milk and cream to the basic paste of coriander seeds and roots, cumin, peppercorns, lemongrass, lime, garlic, shallots, and dried shrimp. The green curry we know today still has a lot of these base ingredients.

MEGA MANGO STICKY RICE

A good for you, guilt-free dessert. It's easier (and healthier) than you think to satisfy your sweet tooth with rich, coconutty rice and fresh, sweet mangoes!

2 cups (390 g) sticky rice (short-grain, glutinous rice), soaked in cold water for at least 1 hour and drained

1¼ cups (295 ml) coconut milk

Pinch of salt

2 tablespoons (15 g) sugar

1¼ cups (295 ml) water

2 large ripe mangoes, peeled and sliced

In a saucepan, bring the rice, coconut milk, salt, sugar, and water to a boil and stir. Lower the heat and simmer, uncovered, for 8 to 10 minutes, or until all the liquid is absorbed, then remove from the heat. Cover and let stand for 5 minutes. Transfer the rice to a steamer or double boiler and steam over boiling water for 15 to 20 minutes, or until the rice is cooked through. Transfer the cooked rice into 4 to 6 small bowls, mugs, or ramekins, lined with plastic wrap, to mold. Let cool to room temperature.

To serve, unmold onto a plate or into a bowl and top with the sliced mango.

YIELD: 4 to 6 servings

Fun Fact

What makes sticky rice sticky? It's a short-grain rice that has been bred to be especially sticky by being extremely low in starch, so the grains do not pull apart. It's the type of rice most often used in sushi.

VIETNAMESE TOFU BANH MI
(LEMONGRASS AND TOFU SANDWICH)

*Gluten Free (use gluten-free bread), **Soy Free (use liquid aminos and seitan),
***Low Fat (bake the tofu and omit the mayonnaise)

You can't get this sandwich at your local sub shop! The variety of flavors and textures—both sweet and savory, soft and crunchy—in banh mi may entice you to replace your usual ho-hum sandwich!

¼ cup (25 g) chopped fresh lemongrass

2 cloves garlic

½ cup (120 ml) grapeseed or olive oil

5 tablespoons (75 ml) soy sauce or tamari

Ground pepper, to taste

1 teaspoon sesame oil

1 package (14 ounces, or 392 g) extra-firm tofu, pressed, drained, and sliced into ¼-inch (6 mm) strips

Vegan mayonnaise (optional)

½ medium-size tomato, thinly sliced

2 baguettes (6 to 8 inches, or 15 to 20 cm each), sliced horizontally in half but not cut all the way through (sub style)

1 small to medium-size cucumber, peeled and thinly sliced

1 small white onion, thinly sliced (can be raw or sautéed)

¼ cup (4 g) chopped fresh cilantro

Jalapeño slices (optional)

Sweet relish (optional)

Kimchi (optional)

Place the chopped lemongrass in a mortar and pestle and crush until pulverized (you may also mince it if you don't have a mortar and pestle). Add the garlic and crush with the lemongrass. In a large plastic freezer bag, combine the crushed lemongrass and garlic, grapeseed oil, soy sauce, pepper, and sesame oil. Mix the marinade well, then add the tofu slices to the bag, being careful not to break them but coating well. Let marinate for at least 1 hour.

Heat a pan over medium-high heat and fry the tofu until both sides are golden brown and crispy, 2 to 3 minutes. Let cool. Spread the mayonnaise and tomato slices on the bottom half of the baguettes, then layer on the tofu, cucumber, onion, cilantro, jalapeño, relish, and kimchi.

YIELD: 2 sandwiches

Fun Fact

Banh mi means "bread" in Vietnamese. Although bread is not native to Vietnam, in the 1940s and 1950s these sandwiches were served in delis to French colonials and literally named French bread, or *bánh mì Tay*. They were served in French bread and came with a variety of fillings; however, they always featured a raw scallion. After the craze was over, the French bread sandwich stuck and is now sold in many Vietnamese markets and by mobile street vendors.

COLD VIETNAMESE SPRING ROLLS WITH PEANUT HOISIN DIPPING SAUCE

*Soy Free (use liquid aminos and omit the tofu)

These are a great way to start any meal. You'll love this light and crunchy, veggie-filled appetizer!

FOR DIPPING SAUCE:

1 cup (235 ml) hoisin sauce

¼ cup (65 g) smooth peanut butter

1 tablespoon (15 ml) rice vinegar

2 cloves garlic, crushed

1 chile pepper, stemmed, seeded if desired, and minced

FOR ROLLS:

8 ounces (225 g) extra-firm tofu, pressed, drained, and sliced into ¼-inch (6 mm) strips (8 strips)

½ cup (120 ml) soy sauce

Garlic powder or minced garlic, to taste

½ tablespoon sesame oil

8 rice wrappers (about 8½ inches [22 cm] in diameter)

2 ounces (56 g) rice vermicelli, cooked according to package instructions

1 cup (120 g) julienned cucumber

½ cup (55 g) julienned carrot

4 teaspoons (4 g) chopped fresh Thai basil

3 tablespoons (18 g) chopped fresh mint leaves

3 tablespoons (3 g) chopped fresh cilantro

2 leaves romaine lettuce, chopped

To make the dipping sauce: Mix all the ingredients together in a small serving bowl.

To make the rolls: Marinate the tofu slices in the soy sauce with a dash of garlic powder for 15 to 30 minutes. Heat the oil in a skillet over medium heat, then drain the tofu from the marinade and sauté for about 5 minutes. Set aside and let cool.

Fill a large bowl with warm water and dip 1 wrapper into the water for 1 second to soften. Shake off the excess water and lay the wrapper on a dry work surface. In single rows across the center, place 1 strip of tofu and one-eighth each of the vermicelli, cucumber, carrot, basil, mint, cilantro, and lettuce, leaving about 2 inches (5 cm) open on each side. Roll the wrapper up like a burrito, rolling away from you and tucking in the outside flaps to enclose completely. Don't roll too tightly, though, or the wrapper could split. Repeat with the remaining wrappers and ingredients, slice in half on the diagonal, and serve with the dipping sauce.

YIELD: 8 rolls

Fun Fact

This is called a spring roll (and often a salad roll) to refer to the freshness of the spring season, just like the roll's ingredients and cool temperature.

Chapter 18

JAPAN

DOMO ARIGATO (THANK YOU VERY MUCH) for turning to this chapter. Japan is comprised of many islands, large and small, with volcanic and mountainous terrain making the availability of farmland scarce. This geography reflects heavily on the cuisine, which is predominately reliant on the ocean.

Over the years, various religions and governments dominated the country's laws over eating meat. For some time, eating all animals except sea creatures was prohibited. When Buddhism became the official religion of Japan in the sixth century, meat was forbidden for the next 1,200 years. Although Japanese views on meat have changed quite a bit, seafood and rice are still very much staples in Japanese fare. They, like the Chinese, focus on food preparation and presentation as an art form so that is satisfies all the senses and promotes overall well-being.

The idea of yin and yang comes from Japan and is very much showcased in its cooking, because balancing the two is key. For instance, striking a balance of salty and sweet, and hot and cold, is essential because it creates a balance of mind, body, and soul. Ingredients are considered for their nutritional value and healthy properties. Season, region, and hot or cold properties are vital to the decision-making process; it is believed that too much cold food makes the stomach cold and can cause lack of appetite and lethargy, whereas too much hot food can cause inflammation.

The Japanese have perfected the art of knowing which foods contribute to hot and cold in the body as well as how to balance them. Macrobiotic cooking is meant to create harmony and balance in the body and is widely practiced in Japan. Meaning "large life," macrobiotic cooking is more than just a diet: it is a way of life. A macrobiotic meal is not only balanced to satisfy all our senses, but it also includes seasonal ingredients and is cooked and served in such a way as to create harmony. There is meaning and function in every aspect of macrobiotic foodways, down to the silverware.

Japanese dishes are fresh, healthy, low in fat, and very lightly seasoned so as to enhance the natural flavors of the ingredients in a particular dish. In Japan, healthy eating is a way of life. On that note, I wish you lots of fun in preparing the following Japanese dishes. May you live long and prosper—*banzai* (long life, hooray)!

SASSY SESAME AND SEAWEED SALAD

*Gluten Free (use wheat-free tamari), **Soy Free (use liquid aminos)

This salad is the perfect complement to any meal because it is light and tangy and packs a nutritious punch. Even if you're leery of trying seaweed, the fantastic blend of flavors and textures will convert you into a seaweed lover in seconds flat.

1 tablespoon (3 g) dried wakame

3 tablespoons (45 ml) rice vinegar

1 tablespoon (12 g) sugar

1 tablespoon (15 ml) soy sauce or tamari

½ cup (60 g) julienned cucumber

2-inch (5 cm) piece daikon radish, sliced
(use a potato peeler to get the slices extra thin)

1 teaspoon lemon zest

2 teaspoons roasted black and white sesame seeds

In a bowl, cover the wakame with water and let soak for 1 hour, then squeeze all the water from it. Mix the wakame with the vinegar, sugar, soy sauce, cucumber, and daikon. Sprinkle with the lemon zest and sesame seeds. Allow to sit at room temperature for 30 minutes before serving.

YIELD: 1 to 2 servings

COOK'S NOTE

These are great at cocktail parties as a light and fresh appetizer. Serve salads up in individual martini glasses and enjoy!

Fun Fact

Sea vegetables are full of calcium, iodine, iron, zinc, and potassium, to name a few essential minerals. It also boasts a full slate of B vitamins, including B_{12} and folic acid, and vitamins A and C.

HEARTY MUSHROOM AND TOFU MISO SOUP

*Gluten Free (use gluten-free miso), **Soy Free (use soy-free miso and omit the tofu)

Miso sure you will love this soup! Healthy, nutritious, warm, and savory, it features subtle yet enticing flavors.

½ teaspoon sesame oil

1 scallion, white and green parts, finely minced, plus extra for garnish

1½ teaspoons minced garlic

½ teaspoon grated fresh ginger (optional)

3 cups (705 ml) water, divided

6-inch (15 cm) piece dried kombu, rinsed and sliced into strips

2 tablespoons (32 g) light miso

2 or 3 dried mushrooms, thinly sliced

6 ounces (168 g) firm tofu, pressed, drained, and cubed

Heat the oil in a small pot, add the scallion, garlic, and ginger, and sauté for about 1 minute. Add 2½ cups (588 ml) of the water and the kombu.

Dissolve the miso in the remaining ½ cup (120 ml) water, add to the pot, and bring to a boil. Lower the heat and add the mushrooms and tofu. Garnish with extra chopped scallion and serve.

YIELD: 4 servings

COOK'S NOTE

Use a richer, darker miso if you'd like a heavier, heartier flavor.

Fun Fact

Miso paste, traditionally made from fermented soybeans, was introduced to the Japanese by Buddhist monks in the seventh century. It has been used for centuries as a healing food because it has a high concentration of B_{12}, zinc, and protein for very little calories.

NO-SEAFOOD NORI ROLLS

*Gluten Free (use wheat-free tamari), **Soy Free (use liquid aminos and substitute mushrooms for the tofu)

Whether you love sushi or have never tried it, these veggie rolls will be a great alternative or introduction. Get your chopsticks ready!

2 cups (390 g) uncooked brown rice

1 cup (235 ml) vegetable broth, store-bought or homemade (page 16)

1¼ cups (295 ml) water

¼ cup (60 ml) soy sauce or tamari, plus extra for dipping

2 teaspoons agave nectar

1 teaspoon minced garlic

3 ounces (84 g) pressed and drained extra-firm tofu or marinated tempeh, cut into ½-inch (1.3 cm) strips (8 strips)

2 tablespoons (30 ml) rice vinegar

4 sheets nori

½ medium-size cucumber, julienned

½ medium-size avocado, julienned

1 small carrot, julienned

Wasabi, for serving

Pickled ginger, for serving

In a large saucepan, combine the rice, broth, and water and let stand for 30 minutes.

In a shallow dish, combine the soy sauce, agave, and garlic. Add the tofu and let marinate for at least 30 minutes.

Bring the rice to a boil and then reduce the heat; simmer for about 20 minutes, or until thick and sticky. In a large bowl, combine the cooked rice and the rice vinegar, slicing and folding to mix well.

Place 1 sheet of nori on a bamboo mat, shiny side down. Working with wet hands (you may want to keep a bowl of water near you), spread one-fourth of the rice evenly over the nori; leave about ½ inch (1.3 cm) on the top edge of the nori. Place 2 strips of marinated tofu end to end, on top of the rice, about 1 inch (2.5 cm) from the bottom. Place 2 strips of cucumber next to the tofu, then follow with the avocado and carrot, all in tight rows on top of the rice. Roll the nori tightly, starting with the side nearest you and rolling away from you, using the mat to help make a tight cylinder. Be careful not to roll the mat into the nori; it is only a guide. Once the nori is tightly rolled, use the mat to squeeze it even tighter. Moisten the ½-inch (1.3 cm) flap at the top and fold over to seal. Repeat with the remaining 3 nori sheets and ingredients.

Slice each roll with a very sharp knife into 1-inch (2.5 cm) thick slices (about 6 per roll). Dip your knife in water between slices so the rice and nori don't stick to it. Serve with extra soy sauce mixed with a dab of wasabi for dipping and the pickled ginger.

YIELD: About 24 pieces

fun fact

Nori is a generic term used for seaweed. In the case of sushi nori, the thin sheets are made in a process similar to that of paper, most of which is cultivated and manufactured in Japan, Korea, and China.

COOK'S NOTE

As an alternative, lightly panfry the tofu with a little sesame oil, about 5 minutes, for extra flavor and texture. Or substitute tempeh and crisp it in a skillet before adding to the rolls.

GYOZA DUMPLINGS WITH SOY DIPPING SAUCE

*Gluten Free (use gluten-free wraps and wheat-free tamari), **Soy Free (use liquid aminos and seitan)

Sometimes known as pot stickers, these little dumplings will stick in your mind way after they have vanished from your plate. Gyozas are one of my favorite snacks.

FOR DIPPING SAUCE:

2 tablespoons (30 ml) soy sauce

1 tablespoon (15 ml) vinegar

1 teaspoon chili oil (optional)

FOR GYOZA:

1 cup (90 g) chopped napa cabbage, boiled until tender

¼ cup (12 g) chopped Chinese chives

1 teaspoon minced garlic

1 teaspoon grated fresh ginger

½ cup (35 g) minced button or shiitake mushrooms

4 ounces (112 g) extra-firm tofu, pressed, drained, and finely diced

Salt and white pepper, to taste

1 tablespoon (15 ml) sesame oil

1 tablespoon (15 ml) vegetable oil

20 vegan gyoza wrappers, store-bought or homemade (page 18)

2 tablespoons (30 ml) coconut oil, for panfrying

½ cup (120 ml) water, for steaming

To make the dipping sauce: Combine the ingredients in a small bowl or ramekin and set aside.

To make the gyozas: In a large bowl, combine the cabbage, chives, garlic, ginger, mushrooms, tofu, salt and white pepper to taste, sesame oil, and vegetable oil. Mix thoroughly with your hands until well combined. Place in the refrigerator for about 10 minutes to chill.

Lay out the gyoza wrappers on a dry work surface. Remove 1 from the stack and cover the rest with a clean kitchen towel to keep moist. Put about 1 tablespoon (15 g) of the mixture on one side of the wrapper. Moisten one side of the wrapper with a little water and then fold it in half, making a rectangle or semicircle, depening on the shape of your wrapper. Pinch the two sides together, sealing the wrapper all the way across like a small, sealed taco or crescent-shaped ravioli. Repeat with the remaining wrappers and filling.

The dumplings are cooked by panfrying, then steaming. You may have to do this in batches depending on the size of your skillet. Heat 1 tablespoon (15 ml) of the coconut oil in a large skillet over high heat. Once the skillet is hot, reduce the heat to medium, and place half the dumplings in the skillet, being careful not to crowd the skillet. Panfry for about 2 minutes without moving the dumplings, then lower the heat, add ¼ cup (60 ml) of the water, and cover. When the water has boiled off, about 2 minutes, uncover and remove from the pan. Keep warm while you repeat with the remaining dumplings, oil, and water.

Serve the dumplings hot with the dipping sauce.

YIELD: 20 gyozas

Fun Fact

The Japanese can't take the credit for inventing the gyoza; however, they have made it their own. In the 1940s, the Japanese brought the art of dumpling making back from China and stuck to this one specific style. Whereas the Chinese have various dumplings, the Japanese are very happy with their gyoza, so much so that there is even a gyoza museum in Osaka!

SWEET AND TANGY CHICKEN TERIYAKI

*Gluten Free (use gluten-free vegan chicken or tofu and wheat-free tamari),
**Soy Free (use liquid aminos and soy-free vegan chicken)

Anything is good when swimming in teriyaki sauce, so you're sure to love this dish.

4 vegan chicken cutlets

2 tablespoons (30 ml) sake (rice wine)

¼ cup (60 ml) soy sauce

¼ cup (60 ml) mirin (sweet rice wine)

2 tablespoons (15 g) sugar

1 tablespoon (15 ml) grapeseed, sesame, or olive oil

Grated fresh ginger, for garnish

Cooked rice, for serving

Poke the chicken with a fork and set aside. Combine the sake, soy sauce, mirin, and sugar in a bowl. Add the chicken and let marinate for 15 minutes in the refrigerator.

Heat the oil in a frying pan, drain the chicken, reserving the marinade, and fry the chicken over medium heat until lightly browned, about 2 minutes. Turn the chicken over to fry the other side and reduce the heat to low. Add the marinade, cover the pan, and steam until done, 5 to 7 minutes. Uncover the pan and simmer until the sauce thickens, 3 to 5 minutes. Remove from the heat. Transfer the chicken to a serving plate, pour the sauce over, garnish with the grated ginger, and serve with the rice.

YIELD: 4 servings

fun fact

In Japanese, *teri* means "glaze" and *yaki* means "broiled." The sauce was created by early Japanese settlers in Hawaii, who used the local pineapples and other ingredients to create marinades for their meat and fish.

COOK'S NOTE

Try using tofu, seitan, or mushrooms in lieu of the chicken. Or simply serve the sauce with rice and veggies.

SEITAN SUKIYAKI
(VEGETABLE, NOODLE, AND SEITAN HOT POT)

*Gluten Free (use wheat-free tamari and gluten-free noodles and omit the seitan),
**Soy Free (use liquid aminos and omit the tofu)

Bring the Japanese noodle house right into your own kitchen!

½ cup (120 ml) soy sauce or tamari

6 tablespoons (45 g) sugar, divided

1 cup (235 ml) vegetable broth,
store-bought or homemade (page 16)

¼ cup (60 ml) mirin

2 tablespoons (30 ml) sesame oil

1 pound (454 g) thinly sliced seitan,
store-bought or homemade (page 19)

2 medium-size onions, sliced

1 cup (100 g) sliced bamboo shoots

2 stalks celery, sliced

1 cup (70 g) shiitake mushrooms,
soaked in hot water, rinsed, and sliced

1 bunch scallions, cut into 2-inch (5 cm) lengths

2 leaves napa cabbage, sliced

1 package (14 ounces, or 392 g) extra-firm tofu,
pressed, drained, and cubed

2 ounces (56 g) shirataki or udon noodles,
cooked according to package instructions and drained

Red pepper flakes or chili sauce (optional)

Combine the soy sauce, 2 tablespoons (15 g) of the sugar, broth, and mirin in a bowl.

Heat the oil in a large skillet over medium heat. Add the seitan and brown on all sides, 1 to 2 minutes per side. Slowly add the remaining 4 tablespoons (30 g) sugar, stir to combine, then move the seitan to the corner of the skillet. Add the onions, bamboo shoots, celery, mushrooms, scallions, cabbage, and tofu to the skillet, keeping each in separate piles. Add the broth mixture and cover. Bring to a boil and cook for 2 minutes, uncover, turn over all the ingredients, and cook for 2 minutes longer.

Fill 1 or 2 bowls with the broth, then carefully spoon in the noodles, vegetables, tofu, and seitan, adding them as though you were filling in quadrants of the bowl with each ingredient. Sprinkle with red pepper flakes and serve.

YIELD: 1 or 2 servings

COOK'S NOTE

Feel free to experiment with your sukiyaki by trying out different combos of veggies.

MATCHA GREEN TEA ICE CREAM

Green tea has a variety of health benefits, and ice cream leads to optimum happiness. Just don't get brain freeze!

2 cups (470 ml) plain soymilk, divided

2 tablespoons (16 g) arrowroot powder

4 teaspoons (10 g) matcha powder (powdered green tea)

2 packages (12 ounces, or 336 g each) silken tofu

⅔ cup (210 g) agave nectar

1 teaspoon vanilla extract

Slowly whisk together ¼ cup (60 ml) of the soymilk and the arrowroot until well combined. Add the matcha and stir until there are no clumps. Set aside.

Blend the remaining 1¾ cups (410 ml) soymilk, tofu, and agave in a blender until very smooth. Pour into a saucepan and bring to a boil. As soon as it boils, remove from the heat immediately. Add the matcha mixture and vanilla, stir to blend, and let cool. Transfer to a container with a lid and chill in the refrigerator for at least 2 hours, then move to the freezer. As soon as ice crystals begin to form, remove and mix well to break up the crystals, and then return to the freezer. Freeze for 2 to 3 hours longer, mixing two or three times more to keep the ice cream smooth.

YIELD: 4 to 6 servings

Fun Fact

Ice cream that's good for you! Green tea contains polyphenols, which are powerful antioxidants. It is said that green tea has powerful healing benefits, boosts the immune system, and can fight against cancer, arthritis, high cholesterol and even headaches!

RECOMMENDATIONS AND RESOURCES

RECOMMENDED PRODUCTS

As time goes on, the availability of healthy and special diet products has increased tremendously. But navigating the product-line waters can be difficult. I've compiled a list of my absolute favorite products that help keep my kitchen stocked with healthy, yet time-saving goodies, making cooking time much easier!

Back to the Roots grow-your-own mushroom kits; www.bttrventures.com
Bob's Red Mill (flours, grains, beans, and more); www.bobsredmill.com
Bragg's Amino Acids; www.bragg.com
Daiya cheese (shredded vegan cheese); www.daiyafoods.com
Earth Balance (vegan butter, shortening, and nut butters); www.earthbalancenatural.com
Eat Cleaner (vegetable wash and wipes); www.eatcleaner.com
Edward and Sons (sauces, bouillons, and more); www.edwardandsons.com
Ener-G Egg Replacer; www.ener-g.com
Field Roast (sausages and cheese); www.fieldroast.com
Flanigan Farms (nuts and seeds); www.flaniganfarms.com
Follow Your Heart (Veganaise, sour cream, cream cheese, cheese); www.followyourheart.com
Gardein (vegan meat products); www.gardein.com
Helen's Kitchen (tofu steaks); www.thehelenskitchen.com
Lightlife tempeh; www.lightlife.com
Mary's Gone Crackers (gluten-free crackers and bread crumbs); www.marysgonecrackers.com
Match vegan meats (frozen ground vegan meat products); www.matchmeats.com
Nasoya (tofu and soy products); www.nasoya.com
Navitas Naturals (all-natural, organic cooking and baking products); www.navitasnaturals.com
Seelect natural food coloring; www.seelecttea.com
Soyatoo (vegan whipped cream and heavy cream); www.soyatoo.com
Tofurky (vegan deli meats); www.tofurky.com

RECOMMENDED RESOURCES

Over the years, I've truly enjoyed being a source for folks to get the best possible information on how to lead healthier lives, regardless of diet. I've compiled some of my favorite sites, products, books, and movies that are chock-full of great information that can help you start or continue down the path to optimum health.

The Healthy Voyager (www.healthyvoyager.com)

Ah yes, a little shameless self-promotion! But really, here you will find my travel show highlighting how to dine healthfully from Kansas City to Kenya, as well as a weekly radio show on all things healthy and green, recipes, health and green-living articles, fitness show, cooking show, giveaways, product reviews, and more! In fact, be sure to visit the Healthy Voyager Approved Directory for a more complete list of product recommendations for everything from food to travel items.

Cosmo's Vegan Shoppe (www.cosmosveganshoppe.com)

A great vegan online market! Perfect for when you can't find specialty items at your local grocer's and then some.

Food Fight Grocery (www.foodfightgrocery.com)

Another awesome vegan online grocer.

Food Revolution and *Diet for a New America* by John Robbins

Two books that really lay out the big-picture details as to why a plant-based diet will benefit not only our health but also the health of our society, our economy, and our planet. Must-reads!

Forks Over Knives (www.forksoverknives.com)

A revolutionary film highlighting in-depth scientific studies and real-world stories that prove a plant-based diet is key to healthy living and fighting disease.

Generation Rescue (www.generationrescue.org)

Autism is a subject that is very close to my heart, and it is a condition that can benefit tremendously from a plant-based and gluten-free diet. Generation Rescue is a fantastic organization that helps families affected by autism via "angels," conducts research, and aligns itself with Defeat Autism Now!—diet doctors and companies that are helping these families deal with and treat their children.

GlutenFree.com

A grocer for all things gluten free.

Gobble Green (www.gobblegreen.com)

Don't have time to cook? Need special diet–friendly "fast" foods? Get healthy, special diet–customized food delivered to your door! Specializing in vegan fare, Gobble Green offers meal plans for gluten-free folks as well as for weight loss. With an in-house fitness coach and nutritionist, Gobble Green will deliver your food to you with little to no prep required, and it will be good for you, too. They are great friends of the Healthy Voyager and I just love these guys!

Green Cooking Pots (www.greencookingpots.com)

Can't afford Le Creuset? These are just as pretty, a fraction of the cost, and eco-friendly! Enameled cast iron is the way to cook like a pro without needing to enroll in culinary school.

Green Pan (www.green-pan.com)

Get rid of your toxic nonstick pans and switch to this healthier, eco line.

Physicians Committee for Responsible Medicine (PCRM) (www.pcrm.org)

This organization with top-notch physicians promotes the importance of a plant-based diet, offers information on how to lead a healthy vegan life, and is changing the minds of lawmakers one initiative at a time.

Root Pouch (www.rootpouch.com)

No matter how much space you have, you can grow your own herbs and vegetables! This handy eco pouch can be hung indoors or out while housing your own organic garden. Made from 100 percent recycled materials, it is the easiest way to go organic and go local by growing your own produce!

SelectWisely special diet travel cards (www.selectwisely.com)

Translation cards for all special diets, in a wide variety of global languages, perfect for travelers. Pop the language card for the country you're visiting into your wallet and flash it at eateries to make sure you get the meal you need without the ingredients you don't. Don't leave home without it!

The China Study by T. Colin Campbell

Possibly the most comprehensive eye-opener on the vegan diet ever published. It is the story of a doctor and scientist who conducted a thirty-year study, the largest study on nutrition and its effects ever conducted, and the results it yielded prove that an animal protein–heavy diet is the cause for a large number of the world's deadliest diseases (cancer, heart disease, diabetes, etc.).

To-Go Ware (www.to-goware.com)

This line of eco utensils and containers are a must-have for the eco-minded traveler. Always be prepared with your very own set of bamboo utensils so you don't have to contribute to landfill waste when using the disposable alternative.

Vegan Essentials (www.veganessentials.com)

Yep, one more online vegan store.

Vegetarian Times (www.vegetariantimes.com)

The original publication for vegetarians, chock-full o' kitchen tips and veggie-based recipes.

Veggie Brothers (www.veggiebrothers.com)

Another vegan delivery service that is full of flavor and options. Again, there's no better excuse to go veg than when it's this tasty and convenient!

VegNews (www.vegnews.com)

A great-looking publication showcasing fun, entertaining, and informative content on all things vegan. From celebrity interviews to how to throw a vegan wedding, they've got it!

Vitamix (www.vitamix.com)

The Rolls-Royce of blenders. I highly recommend this brand for folks looking for a kitchen gadget that saves time and money and promotes health!

ACKNOWLEDGMENTS

To all of you who made this book possible (directly as well as indirectly), my sincerest gratitude and appreciation! Here are a few words just for you:

Dan ~ My husband and über-talented artiste, I wouldn't have the Healthy Voyager without you, and it definitely would not have the cool look it does without your magic touch! Thank you for all the long hours you put in to make this book look awesome. Oh yeah, and thanks for putting up with and taking care of me while I wrote for months on end! I love you and am looking forward to lots more fun projects together!

Mom ~ Thank you for being one of my great recipe testers, for being my biggest cheerleader, and for joining my vegan team! I'm so happy that you've embraced a plant-based diet and that you're promoting it in the best way possible, with yummy food!! I love you, Yach, you're the best mom in the world!! Thanks for everything, always!

Dad ~ Thank you for being excited when I decided to bail on med school! You have always been my biggest supporter when it comes to following my creative path. Traveling, writing, and storytelling is in our blood, and I'm finally doing it for the both of us! Love you!

Bella and Mom ~ My beloved, late grandmothers who I wish could have seen this book come to fruition. They were two great cooks who sparked my love of all things kitchen and cooking.

Joe ~ Thank you for showing me how fun cooking can be and how a good meal is a great way to bring people together!

Amanda, Meghan, and Will at Fair Winds Press ~ Thanks for making this book happen, making this book awesome, and most of all, putting up with me! You guys rock!

Celine Steen ~ My rad photographer and late-night foodie friend, thanks for the gorgeous pictures!

Michael Borys, Tracy Lee, and Thomas Worth ~ Thanks for your time, skill, tips, and tricks!

Gardein, Daiya, Earth Balance, Bob's Red Mill, Match Vegan Meats, Nasoya, Follow Your Heart, Helen's Kitchen, Mary's Gone Crackers, Tofurky, and Navitas Naturals ~ Thank you for providing your fabulous products for recipe testing!

And of course, my fabulous recipe testers who slaved over hot stoves and ovens for months to get the recipes in this book tasting great, THANK YOU!!

Hope Alexandria; SideshowDoug Allen, comedy writer, producer, and neologist at Dougtionary.com and SideshowDoug.com; Hope Atmore; Erin Calhoun-Dulaney; Lauren Cantrelle, caterer, foodie, blogger, and aspiring chef; Kelly Cavalier, home cook; Deborah Collupy (and Ichi the cat), home cook (and a cat with a sophisticated palate); Luke Dobie, owner and principal designer of LD Designs, LukeDobieDesigns.com; Kara Hunt, professional chef; Ron Husges, designer and developer of handmade websites, Superlotek.com; Whitney Lauritsen, filmmaker, journalist, EcoVeganGal.com; Sonia Lemoine, vegan health and fitness specialist, SoniaLemoine.Blogspot.com; Godiva Liu and Thomas J. Jroski, Jr., creator and owner of FoodieFlirt.com; Britny Lopez, artist, author, intuitive life coach, lover of life, and founder of LetUsBeOne.org; Alexandra McDougall, actress, writer, and experimental home cook; Marjorie Ohrnstein, chef/owner, FunFoodCatering.com and MarjorieWeddings.com; Stephanie Olivieri, writer and artist; Julianna Robbins, librarian, JuliannaRobbins.wordpress.com; Clara "Yach" Scott, mom of the Healthy Voyager; Tanya Slye, Suzanne Toro, food alchemist, shamanic broadcaster, and author of *Bare Naked Bliss . . . Loving from Within*; Elektra Tropoloc, blogger at CaliforniaBland.blogspot.com; and Liz Wyman.

ABOUT THE AUTHOR

The Healthy Voyager, a.k.a. Carolyn Scott-Hamilton, is the executive producer, creator, host, and writer of the Healthy Voyager web series, radio show, website, blog, and overall brand. Having grown the Healthy Voyager from a small blog and internet travel show in 2005 to a well-respected and followed healthy and green living brand, Carolyn continues to gain attention from the mainstream press, including *USA Today* and CNN, while winning over folks with her fun and entertaining ways to live a happier and greener life, regardless of dietary restrictions and budget. Carolyn contributes content to a variety of publications and media, such as the Huffington Post and Yahoo Shine, and has her sights set on reaching a wide variety of people in new and innovative ways. An entrepreneur, holistic nutritionist, chef, filmmaker, and screenwriter, Carolyn is also a traveling, singing, dancing, fun-loving, healthy, and green-living wife. The Healthy Voyager aims to help people live well, one veggie at a time! Visit her at www.HealthyVoyager.com.

INDEX